BRITAIN by BRITRAIL

"Provides highlights of attractions, suggested day tours, distance and travel times, information about connections (including sea and air), selected departure schedules, and details about different grades of passes."

—The Associated Press

"Makes it easy to plan an itinerary with frequent stopovers in all the major cities of Britain, along with many day and overnight side trips to less traveled and historic villages nestled in the mountains and countryside."

—*Small Press* magazine

Also by George and LaVerne Ferguson
Europe by Eurail

BRITAIN by BRITRAIL
HOW TO TOUR BRITAIN BY TRAIN

Seventeenth Edition

written by
George and LaVerne Ferguson

contributing writer
Sandra Lambert

edited by
Christina DiLorenzo

contributing editor
Matthew Palma

A Voyager Book

The Globe Pequot Press

OLD SAYBROOK, CONNECTICUT

Photographs on pages 18, 38, and 306 courtesy BritRail Travel International, Inc.

Cover photo copyright© Nawrocki Stock Photo
Background photo copyright© 1996 PhotoDisc, Inc.
Cover design by Schwartzman Design

ISSN: 1081-1117
ISBN: 1-56440-977-5

Manufactured in the United States of America
Seventeenth Edition/First Printing

THE FERGUSONS' TEAM

LaVerne Ferguson is President of Rail Pass Express, Inc., a Columbus, Ohio–based small business that distributes Eurail and BritRail passes throughout the world. LaVerne and husband George Ferguson have co-authored *Europe by Eurail* since 1977 and *Britain by BritRail* since 1980.

Born in Marion, Ohio, LaVerne first discovered her love for travel in a third-grade geography class. Throughout her childhood she collected brochures and information about various countries and cultures. LaVerne majored in world history and English at The Ohio State University and completed courses in library search and business communications. She became a technical secretary and later a technical writer for Battelle Memorial Institute, the world's largest sponsored research organization.

George Wright Ferguson was born in Philadelphia twenty minutes after his mother was taken from a Washington–New York express train. He grew up alongside the Baldwin Locomotive Works on the "Pennsy" main line, and trains have continued to play an important role in his life.

A graduate of Penn State, George served in Europe during WWII as a test pilot and engineering officer with the Eighth Air Force. His first European train ride was aboard a vintage 1918 "40-and'8" freight car (meaning the car could hold 40 soldiers and 8 horses) between Munich and Antwerp, a trip that lasted four days and four nights! After a stint as editor and later publisher of a farm equipment magazine, George was recalled to active duty with assignments in Korea, Japan, and Vietnam, and with the Pentagon in Washington, D.C. As a senior Air Force logistician, he was commended by Defense Secretary Robert McNamara for his study of the Air Force's worldwide-movement capabilities. George retired from the Air Force in 1967 with more than 5,000 flying hours in his log book.

George's international experiences continued with a position as an international coordinator for, coincidentally, the Battelle Memorial Institute. His work included assignments in Europe, Thailand, Iran, and South America.

George and LaVerne's mutual love for travel brought them together. Throughout the first ten years of guidebook production, their readers had been clamoring for a more convenient and more knowledgeable source for Eurail and BritRail passes. In response, George and LaVerne began what eventually came to be known as Rail Pass Express, Inc.—the largest single-office sales outlet for European rail passes in North America.

Then, the "fickle finger of fate" struck in February 1993. While on a four-day business trip from their home in Dover, Delaware, to their office in Columbus, Ohio, George suffered two thoracic aortic aneurysms that nearly took his life. In spite of this devastating setback, LaVerne kept Rail Pass Express on track. The results are impressive—in 1995, the Eurailpass

Executive Committee selected Rail Pass Express to receive the 1995 Eurail Award for sales volume and outstanding promotion of the European rail system; Rail Pass Express' World Wide Web site (http://www.eurail.com) was featured in the June, 1996, issue of *Entrepreneur* magazine at the Internet World Conference in San Francisco; also in June, 1996, LaVerne was selected to appear in the National Directory of *Who's Who in Executives and Professionals.*

Sandra Lambert, who authored the London section of *Britain by Britrail*, lives in Europe six months out of the year where she continues to write for American and European publications about travel, art, lifestyle, and culture. Her extensive academic background—having studied in Paris, London, New York, and Columbus—includes degrees in philosophy, theatre, journalism, and communications.

Sandra has written for newspapers and magazines; coauthored books; produced television specials, and hosted her own public broadcasting show. Throughout her career she has met presidents, authors, artists, and film and fashion celebrities. She has become accustomed to the understated excitement of European train travel, with its efficiency, elegance, and endless expectations for adventure.

George, LaVerne, and Sandra welcome your comments and suggestions. You can write to them at Rail Pass Express, Inc., 2737 Sawbury Blvd., Columbus OH 43235-4583 or reach them via e-mail at ferguson@eurail.com.

CONTENTS

1   IN THE BEGINNING

As Edna St. Vincent Millay put it, "My heart is warm with the friends I make,/And better friends I'll not be knowing;/Yet there isn't a train I wouldn't take/No matter where it's going."

Train travel is an anomaly for most Americans. Millions of Americans have either forgotten or have never had the opportunity to learn what travel by train can be like. Perhaps our rugged individualism and our need to escape the norm—not to mention our abundance of inexpensive gasoline—shape us for the network of roads and the importance of automobiles that define our outlook on travel.

Europeans need trains for transport; thus, they have created trains with the simplest and yet most extravagant accouterments of their cultures. In so doing, they tend to provide fast, economical, and often elegant methods of moving from one place to another.

"I love it personally," said Pat Titley, Director of Marketing Services for BritRail Travel International, Inc. Titley, when in Britain and away from her Manhattan office, finds travel on Britain's rail system extremely restful. "I actually read a book. And when I look out the window, I'm still amazed that so much of Britain is very gentle countryside."

Like Pat Titley and thousands of other discerning visitors, you are about to learn that the British rail system offers a truly delightful way of vacationing throughout the length and breadth of Europe's only English-speaking nation—Britain. Welcome to Britain by BritRail! You are about to embark on a unique and rewarding traveling experience.

In size, Britain is a rather compact nation. It's about two-thirds the size of California or approximately one-third larger than the New England area of Maine, Vermont, New Hampshire, Massachusetts, Rhode Island, and Connecticut—the North American area to which Britain has contributed much of her heritage since Colonial days.

London is a tourist magnet, but despite what other writers say, London is not Britain. Britain has some of the most beautiful countryside in the world. Its mountains are no match for the Alps; its seas are not azure blue like the Mediterranean. But what it might lack in spectacular scenery is offset by a magical quality of green so peaceful and picturesque that, in a mere glance, the visitor becomes aware that what he sees is history. A visit to Britain that does not include at least a few days in the countryside is unthinkable.

The difference in traveling along Britain's congested highways and on BritRail's InterCity trains must be experienced to be believed. By rail, it is a smooth, relaxing journey uninterrupted by traffic lights and traffic jams. Rent-a-car visitors are usually too involved with starboard steering and keeping a close watch on the car in front to appreciate much more about Britain than the fact that the road signs are in English.

In Britain, you'll find more than 15,000 trains traveling to more than 2,500 destinations daily. The service is so frequent that if you miss a train, chances are you won't have to wait more than one-half hour to an hour for another. The British frequently seize such an opportunity to nip into a nearby pub for a quick pint and a game of darts. So follow the adage, "When in Rome, do as the Romans do." It applies equally well in Britain, which inherited some of Rome's customs, too!

Aboard a British rail train, the driver (that's what the British call their train engineers) takes care of all the driving while you sip on a beverage, enjoy an uninterrupted view of the countryside, and stretch out in a comfortable seat. You can even respond to "nature's call" at your own option rather than sweating out making it to the closest petrol (gas) station—many are closed on weekends and holidays!

There are few places in Britain that cannot be reached by train. By employing the base cities of London, Edinburgh, or Glasgow, the splendor of Windsor Castle, the academic aura of Oxford and Cambridge, or the Old Course at St. Andrews are all but an easy, comfortable train ride away. Northern Ireland, by the way, is a part of Great Britain, but its railways are operated by a separate company that does not accept the BritRail Pass. It does, however, accept the BritRail Pass + Ireland, which combines England, Scotland, Wales, Northern Ireland, and the Republic of Ireland.

Britain by BritRail

Britain by BritRail is a train travel guidebook written to provide detailed train-related information to its readers in a direct, pragmatic manner. *Britain by BritRail* does not rate or recommend hotels. A quaint coaching inn or a hotel's convenient location to rail services may gain comment. The book's primary purpose insofar as accommodations are concerned, however, is to point out the most convenient tourist information center or hotel booking (reservations) facility.

Restaurants are treated in the same manner. We appreciate good food, along with the service that complements it. But with few exceptions, the choice of what to eat and where to find it remains the option of the reader perusing the wealth of excellent publications catering to this most worthy pursuit.

Britain by BritRail, like its sister publication, *Europe by Eurail*, is devoted to the visitor who goes to Britain expecting that its train services will provide the necessary transportation for a holiday that is different. We have gone ahead of you, probed what can be done, and solved the problems of doing it long before you will arrive. Every city and day excursion has been personally experienced by one or more of our researchers and we are pledged to constantly recheck, revise, and expand subsequent editions. This is accomplished by personal visits and through our British and European network of correspondents in the areas described.

Britain by BritRail presents a concept for comfortable, unhurried travel by train in Britain. By utilizing the economy of a BritRail Pass, along with the innovative, *fully* described base city–day excursion method, you can really see Britain at its best—by train.

Britain by BritRail is the perfect traveling companion for visitors using the BritRail Pass. This book helps to introduce and establish the reader in the base cities of London, Edinburgh, or Glasgow. Once you are ensconced in affordable, comfortable accommodations and your sightseeing and shopping are attended to in the base cities, *Britain by BritRail* then introduces its recommended day excursions to interesting places based, for the most part, on train schedules and geographic locations that assure your return each night to the same hotel room. With a BritRail Pass and a current copy of *Britain by BritRail*, you become your own tour guide and avoid the constant packing and unpacking that accompanies most bus tours attempting to cover the same territory. You call the shots, not the tour bus driver.

Britons and their Continental cousins have employed BritRail's services for "holiday-making" on the British Isles for decades. Train travel is too fast for any possible chance of boredom setting in, yet it is leisurely enough to enjoy fully the constantly changing scene of hills and hamlets, farms and forests, countrysides and cities—everything that forms Britain's fascinating landscape.

Should you pause to ponder why, for example, an English gentleman would leave his motorcar at home when he's "off on holidays," you will find the answer very quickly when your train parallels a major highway or flashes across a bridge through the center of a British city. The superhighways right down to the ancient, narrow streets are packed with vehicles—all proceeding at a much slower pace than you and your train.

In the chapters describing the base cities and day excursions, *Britain by BritRail* meets the traveler upon arrival at the base-city airport or train station and then methodically *leads* him to those essential facilities such as currency exchange, hotel accommodations, and tourist information sources. *Britain by BritRail* provides an overall picture and then gives *explicit* directions on how to get to the cities' tourist information offices to obtain the most current information available to visitors. Readers requiring advance information regarding the base cities of London, Edinburgh, or Glasgow should contact the closest British Tourist Authority office listed in the appendix of this edition. With the opening of the channel tunnel in 1994 and a nearby terminal at Cheriton, Folkestone has become a departure point for Le Shuttle services through

Eurotunnel. Le Shuttle conveys motor vehicles through the tunnel. Passengers remain in their vehicles aboard the Le Shuttle rail cars. Journey time is approximately thirty-five minutes in the tunnel. Special arrangements for rental cars have been made with Hertz and Le Shuttle to exchange left- or right-hand drive vehicles at the Hertz/Eurotunnel terminal in Calais. This information is useful. If you have purchased a BritRail Pass + Car Option.

To avoid reader frustration, *Britain by BritRail* compiles addresses of information sources and useful telephone numbers in the appendix. Station plans and maps of transportation lines can be located easily near the end of the book.

Train schedules between London and the base cities of Edinburgh and Glasgow in Scotland are listed in chapter 10, which describes London. This particular information should prove to be helpful when you are initially planning your BritRail trip.

Train schedules for the day-excursion trips out of the base cities are provided in the text describing each day excursion. Trains departing from the base cities are normally on morning schedules; trains returning from the day excursions usually run in the late afternoon and early evening. Each day-excursion section begins with the distance and average train time for the trip, because we realize that there may be some days when you prefer a short trip rather than a great adventure. If the twenty-four-hour times shown in the train schedules boggle your mind, consult the "time converter" clock on page 295 of this edition.

Please remember that the timetables and schedules appearing in this edition are provided *for planning purposes only.* Every care has been taken to make the timetables and schedules correct. The information is checked with authoritative sources up to press time. *Britain by BritRail* and/or its publisher cannot, however, be held responsible for the consequences of either changes or inadvertent inaccuracies. Current rail schedules are posted in all British rail stations, and timetables from the base cities to every day-excursion point are available for the asking in the base-city stations. Please consult them.

Travel Economy

"Know before you go," the slogan of the U.S. Customs Service pertaining to what you may return with, also applies to the financial aspects of vacation planning. The rise and fall of the dollar's purchasing power in Europe over the past few years has left a lot of us wondering whether or not we could afford a vacation on the other side of the Atlantic. Although the inflation rate in the United States has been reduced to what bankers term "acceptable," it is still difficult to determine what effect Europe's inflation will have on your dollars once you're there.

Advance planning and purchasing vacation needs in advance (particularly transportation) in American dollars are probably the most effective ways to

12

combat inflation and price fluctuations. Basically, the program calls for buying as much of your vacation needs as you can before you go and planning to limit your out-of-pocket costs paid in foreign currency to a minimum. In this way, you are well protected against fluctuating currency values.

The idea of doing things that were previously thought impossible—like putting $48 worth of gas in a Ford Escort—emphasizes train travel in Europe as the best means of effectively stabilizing your travel dollars. Prepayment plans, such as the BritRail Pass, are ideal. Not only do you purchase the pass with American dollars prior to departure, but the BritRail Pass also provides the most inexpensive way to travel in Britain—the quickest, too!

American travel agents still have a penchant for wanting to sell a "fly-drive" program to any client who wants to vacation in Britain. But, in general, car rentals have one basic fault—"the price you see" is never "the price you pay," which is *always* higher. As a rule of thumb, add to the quoted price another 20 percent for personal accident insurance, collision insurance, and taxes. After that, consider fuel costs. And don't forget about the 17.5 percent value-added tax (VAT). Then, ask your agent to provide you with an economical BritRail Pass. Or, you can order one by calling BritRail's sales agent, Rail Pass Express, Inc., at **(800) 722–7151** (Internet address: http://www.eurail.com).

Accommodations almost always account for the greatest share of a traveler's budget. Low-cost air fares and transportation bargains like the BritRail Pass can get the traveler *to* and *around* the British Isles, but the real bite out of the buck comes when the visitor opens his wallet to pay for a night's lodging. Attractively priced accommodations packages are being offered by some American tour operators. But too few suit the needs of those preferring individual itineraries, as is the case for travelers on a BritRail vacation. With advance planning and advance payment, however, savings can be realized by those who are willing to put forth the extra time and effort.

Well ahead of your intended departure date—preferably two months in advance, but no less than six weeks—write to one of the British Tourist Authority (BTA) offices listed on page 281 of this edition and request information regarding lodging (including the "bed-and-breakfast" places) in the areas you intend to visit during your BritRail journey. You may make reservations, or "bookings," as the British call them, in various ways. Hotel accommodations may be arranged by mail with central booking offices in London and Edinburgh but generally not elsewhere. The best assurance that you will have a room waiting upon arrival is to make an advance deposit directly to the hotel, then take care of the balance with the hotel's cashier when checking out. By the way, always ask the hotel to confirm the room rate when you check in. This will avoid delays and possible financial embarrassment when leaving.

One final bit of advice on reducing the cost of accommodations in Britain—use your BritRail Pass. Too many of us overlook the fact that the BritRail Pass can actually provide exceptional savings in housing costs by permitting you to stay *outside* the base city's center, where hotel rooms, pensions, bed-and-breakfast housing, and the like are far less expensive than their downtown counterparts.

London particularly lends itself to such a suburban arrangement because there are many areas outside the city's center that are readily accessible by rail. Anytime downtown accommodations become difficult to find or too demanding on the budget, tell the housing people you have a BritRail Pass and can easily stay in the suburbs.

Staying in London's northern or western suburbs has other advantages, too. From many of the suburban stations, you can board a fast InterCity train for a day excursion without ever going into a London terminus. You can return to the suburbs in the evening, too, without becoming involved in London's rush hours.

Watford Junction, sixteen miles from London's Euston Station, is one of the stations in London's suburbs that offers excellent InterCity connections to such day-excursion points as Birmingham, St. Albans, Perth, and Coventry as well as the base cities Glasgow and Edinburgh. Most InterCity departures from Euston Station on weekday mornings pick up at Watford Junction sixteen minutes later. On weekday evenings, most InterCity trains set down at Watford twenty minutes ahead of their arrival times in Euston Station.

Other rail points in London suburbs are Luton, for direct rail connections to Nottingham and Sheffield; Stevenage, along the main line to Edinburgh via York; and Slough or Reading, for connections to Bath as well as the Welsh cities of Cardiff and Swansea.

There are times when accommodations in the base cities are extremely limited. Edinburgh, during its annual festival every August to September, is an excellent example. Lodgings in the suburbs, à la BritRail Pass, can be more economical and just as convenient as those in the base cities.

If you have your heart set on lodgings in London when inquiring as to their availability, you will be asked the inevitable question, "Where do you want to be near to?" Naturally, when you're traveling by rail, your response will be, "Near the rail station." You are in for a surprise—at last count, London had fifteen primary rail stations. Because these terminals rim the vast, sprawling city, a better site-selection statement would be to ask for a hotel nearby one of the major lines of the Underground (subway).

2 PLANNING A BRITRAIL TRIP

Webster's Dictionary defines a plan as "a program of action." Plans vary in detail and complexity, according to the nature of the user. For example, one person may require a detailed, hour-by-hour, appointment-by-appointment schedule for a day's activities; another may merely plan to get up in the morning and see what happens after that. This example categorizes the two general types of rail travelers we have observed down through the years—one adventurous, the other conservative.

One of the first questions asked when planning a trip is "When can I go and how much time can I spend there?" In Britain, April through October are the most popular months for tourists and for many events, and, during the Christmas and New Year's holidays, London literally sparkles. When planning your trip, take British Bank Holidays into consideration since banks, postal services, and most shops and attractions are closed, and some transportation services are reduced. Bank Holidays include New Year's Day, Good Friday, Easter Sunday, Easter Monday, May Day, Late Spring Holiday, Late Summer Holiday, Christmas Eve, Christmas Day, and Boxing Day. (See the "Tips and Trivia" section in the Appendix of this edition for specific 1997 dates.)

Whether you admit it or not, everyone has a problem budgeting vacation time. It's human nature to try to see as much as possible in as little time as possible. This "sightseers' syndrome" could be dangerous to your vacation. Avoid it by planning an itinerary that allows ample "free time." Also, vary the day excursions by going on a short one following a particularly long outing away from the base city. Press too hard by trying to see and do too much on your vacation and you will return home as a living example of the old adage, "A person who looks like he needs a vacation usually has just returned from one."

How long should your BritRail tour be? There are many factors bearing on such a determination, the most important being the individual. How much annual vacation time do you have? How do you use it—all at one time or in two or more segments? The folks issuing BritRail Passes are ready to accommodate just about anyone's personal needs, with passes ranging from eight days to one month of travel and flexible passes ranging from four days of travel to fifteen days in one month (two months for youth). The passes permit travel on all scheduled British trains, including the InterCity 225 train shown on the opposite page.

Travel magazines and the travel sections of the Sunday newspapers are usually loaded with one-week trips to almost anywhere—mainland Europe and the British Isles included. Based on our own experience, we believe that going to Europe for any period of less than two weeks is a waste of time and money.

In support of the foregoing statement, we invite you to take a look at the

15

logistics involved in a European trip. It takes an entire day to reach Britain by air from North America and an entire day to return. Although the flying time aboard a jet airplane ranges from seven to eight hours, airport to airport, it will be day two before you arrive in Britain. (Most eastbound transatlantic flights depart at night during day one and arrive the following morning—day two.) During the flight, you will be exposed to a cocktail hour, a dinner hour, a break for an after-dinner drink, followed by a full-length, feature motion picture. In the morning, as the sun rises in the east over Britain, you'll be awakened an hour or so before landing to be served breakfast.

Add up the time consumed by all the scheduled events while en route, and you'll quickly conclude that your night spent in the sky over the Atlantic Ocean consisted of many things—except sleep. Even if you did manage to sleep during the entire trip instead of eating, drinking, and watching movies, your body and all its functions will be arriving in Britain a few hours after midnight by North American time. You will crave adjustment to a phenomenon known as "jet lag," which will be trying its best to interrupt your plans for a carefree vacation.

When you discount the two full days utilized for air travel, plus a minimum of one day to get your sleep-eat cycle functioning properly again, the number of days left in a one-week visit hardly seems worth making the trip. Most of the economical excursion fares for transatlantic air travel evolve around day fourteen, meaning that your minimum time spent in Britain after departing from North America must be fourteen days in order to qualify for the reduced fares. Consequently, in consideration of both time and money, we recommend your stay in Britain be a minimum of two full weeks.

Having determined the length of time you will have for your BritRail trip, the next step is to develop a clear idea of where you want to go in Britain, what you want to see, and what you want to do. This process of developing objectives should be completed well before your departure date. We disagree with those who believe that anticipation of travel is more rewarding than its realization. But we do agree that the planning phase can also form a fun part of your trip. Properly done, this "homework" will pay substantial dividends when travel actually begins.

To get things started, write to or telephone the British Tourist Authority and Rail Pass Express, Inc. for information. *Be specific*. In your request, indicate *when* you will be going, *where* you wish to go within Britain, and *what* in particular you would like to see. If you have any special interests or hobbies, be sure to mention them in your request. Spelling out your information needs will produce better responses.

Don't overlook your local library as a valuable information source. For example, you will find an excellent condensation of British history in the

Encyclopedia Britannica. Back issues of *National Geographic* magazine are excellent sources for first-person explorations of the British Isles. Seek out friends and neighbors who have been to Britain. No doubt you'll find their experiences flavored with their own likes and dislikes. Nevertheless, any and all information you can gather prior to your trip will eventually find its place in your memory bank. Surprisingly enough, you'll find yourself recalling many of these fragments of information during your own journey.

One of the newest and most comprehensive sources of information is the World Wide Web on the Internet. Travelers who have computers and access to Internet can do an incredible amount of research and planning in the comfort of their own homes or offices. The great "information highway" is at your disposal.

You may want to start with some basic web sites about Britain in general and then do subject-specific searches. For example, to obtain general information on Britain, start with the British Tourist Authority's (BTA) web site: **http://www.bta.org.uk.** If you want to know more about British rail travel, check out Rail Pass Express' award-winning web site at **http://www.eurail.com.** Other sources of information may be found in the appendix of this edition.

You are now ready for the decisive phase of your trip planning—constructing an itinerary. The moment of truth is at hand! Your only limitations during this portion of the planning phase are the lack of more than twenty-four hours in a day and the fact that the week contains only seven days.

First, draw a blank calendar-style form covering a period from at least one week prior to your departure to a few days following your return. Make extra copies of the form—you'll need them. (Perfection is a long time coming in this project!) Now begin to block your itinerary into the calendar form, being mindful that the itinerary can be changed, but the number of days in a week remains fixed at all times. Possibly by the third time through the exercise, you'll begin to "see the light at the end of the tunnel." It's human to try to cram too many activities into a day, but it's better to discover your planning errors before starting your trip rather than during the middle of it.

With your itinerary in a calendar format, now you can determine your housing requirements, seat and sleeper reservations, and the other facets of your forthcoming trip. The days blocked out in advance of your departure can show your "countdown" items, such as stopping the newspaper, having mail held at the post office, and so on. Make several copies of your completed itinerary and leave some behind for the folks with whom you want to stay in touch. Above all, take copies of your itinerary with you—you'll refer to them frequently. If there have been any break-ins in your neighborhood, you should take steps to assure that it doesn't happen to you while you are gone. Alert the neighbors to

Train travel is conducive to establishing new acquaintances or starting new friend-ships. When travelers (vacationers or business persons) are sitting next to you, they naturally will be inclined to strike up a conversation—if you are so inclined, too. Photo courtesy of BritRail Travel International Inc.

keep a watchful eye for suspicious people and their activities. Many professional thieves have been known to park in a driveway in broad daylight with a moving van. The police should be advised regarding your absence. Also check with the insurance agency that writes your homeowner policy. "Am I covered?"—as they ask in television commercials—is what you ask. You may need additional coverage during your absence. One final caution. Don't have your forthcoming vacation plans announced in the newspapers. Thieves read, too. Save it for your return.

One item that you can't leave home without is a passport. If you do not have one or if yours has expired, write immediately to one of the U.S. passport offices listed on page 300 for information and applications. Allow a minimum of one month to obtain your passport. There are ways to expedite the process, but be safe by planning ahead and making this the first order of business when you've decided to make your trip abroad. U.S. citizens are admitted to Britain with only a passport. A visa is not required.

What to Take?

Obviously, the practical answer to this question is "as little as possible." A tourist tends to pack everything one conceivably might use during a vacation, lug it everywhere, use it very little, and return home with longer arms. In these days of wash-and-wear fabrics (and deodorants), this is no longer necessary. A good rule of thumb is to take one medium-size suitcase and a shoulder bag. Hold to this rule and you will have a more comfortable trip. Regardless of how comfortable the weather at your destination is expected to be, pack a sweater. Brief cold spells in Britain are not uncommon. Stow a small pocket flashlight in your shoulder bag together with a collapsible umbrella in the "unlikely event" that you may need them.

If you must take expensive jewelry with you, take as well a copy of its insurance appraisal as proof of purchase to customs officials upon your return. Same for watches produced by foreign manufacturers. You may have bought that solid-gold Rolex in a St. Louis pawnshop for a song, but the customs inspector may have you singing a different tune if you can't come up with the paperwork!

If you wear prescription eye glasses or contact lenses, take a copy of the prescription with you. The same applies for prescription medications. Even if you only use over-the-counter drug products, we suggest taking an adequate supply of the item. Many such products are not available in Europe or are sold under a different label or packaging.

Samsonite, one of the major manufacturers of quality luggage, has published an interesting booklet on the subject of suitcases and travel. With the catchy title *Lightening the Travel Load—Travel Tips and Tricks*, it is crammed with helpful tips, everything from analyzing your luggage needs and the basic points of safeguarding it through packing for a trip. Helpful hints on carry-on luggage, how to tip, how to clear customs, and how to stay healthy while on your trip are also included. For a free copy, write to Samsonite Traveler Advisory Service, P.O. Box 39603, Denver, CO 80239. Be certain to include a self-addressed business envelope with postage affixed to cover up to two ounces first-class.

We also recommend the *Thomas Cook European Timetable* as part of your BritRail trip planning. It contains complete timetables covering every major rail route in Britain honoring the BritRail Pass.

In the United States and Canada, copies of the *Thomas Cook European Timetable* can be purchased from Rail Pass Express by calling (800) 722–7151 or online at http://www.eurail.com. In Britain, the timetable may be purchased at most Thomas Cook travel agencies and bureaux de change (money exchange offices) or by calling 01733–505821. If you find the timetable too bulky to take with you, keep in mind that rail schedules are available at all major rail stations.

How to Get There
Transatlantic air traffic is so frequent and varied today that no description of it—short of an entire book—could do it justice. Excursion fares are available in a multitudinous variety. Charter flights are available, too, and they are still mostly money savers. But some excursion rates are less expensive than charters. It is not uncommon on a regularly scheduled airliner winging its way to Europe to find that every passenger in your row of seats paid a different fare for the same flight on the same schedule with the same service!

We refer readers to their travel agents for airline information. But there has been an erosion of such information in travel agencies, brought about in general by the proliferation of air fares. The agencies face the almost impossible task of keeping tabs on the rapidly changing airline industry. Let's put it this way. If you've dealt with a reputable travel agency over the years, contact them the moment you've decided to BritRail through Britain, and ask them to come up with some air-excursion-fare options. At your leisure, call the various airlines' "800" telephone numbers and ask them for suggestions and fare information. We have listed the 800 numbers of a few airlines on page 307. Don't be disturbed if you receive a variety of responses. Sift them out until you find what you're looking for. Even if your travel agent didn't suggest the air fare you prefer and found through your own research, employ the agent's services in getting the tickets. You will pay the same price for the tickets whether you obtain them directly from the airline or from your travel agent.

Long-distance calls can be made in the United States without charge when calling businesses that have "800" service numbers. Obtaining the proper "800" number to call is easy: Dial (800) 555–1212 and tell the special operator the name of the airline information office with which you wish to speak.

Regarding charter flights, inquire about them but investigate them thoroughly before making any final decisions. Here again, get your travel agent involved, even if it's only to obtain the tickets. Even some of the most reputable air-charter carriers still operate on a "Go–No Go" basis. This means that if enough passengers sign up for the flight, it will go as scheduled; if there are not enough passengers booked, the flight will be scrubbed.

BritRail Passes

Visitors to Britain should consider purchasing a BritRail Pass if they plan to travel primarily by train. To help you decide whether or not to purchase a BritRail Pass, we have included a selection of British Rail one-way fares on page 304. The fares are listed in U.S. dollars. To obtain the rate for converting dollars into pounds, consult the financial section of your newspaper or the international department of your bank. Compare the individual fare costs with the BritRail pass costs shown on page 309 for your itinerary.

Keep in mind, when comparing the point-to-point rail fares to the cost of the pass, that convenience in travel has a value, too. Standing in line ("queuing") to purchase train tickets is an inconvenience that can be avoided. With a BritRail Pass, you need do this only once—when you validate your pass.

Even short-time visitors to the British Isles may find it advantageous to purchase a BritRail Pass in lieu of point-to-point tickets. For example, the cost of point-to-point tickets for a circuitous journey—like a quick dash out of London for a look around Edinburgh and Bath—exceeds the cost of an eight-day first-class adult BritRail Classic Pass; the economy of the pass becomes immediately apparent. Consider, too, that the London–Edinburgh–Bath–London circuit could be made comfortably in as little as three days, leaving five more days of unlimited rail travel available to the pass holder. Even if you could not extend your stay, you would still save money, in this case, by purchasing a BritRail Pass.

A BritRail Pass is a ticket for train travel in England, Scotland, and Wales. You don't have to purchase a rail pass to travel by train in Britain; having one, however, is very convenient and economical. For example, with a BritRail Pass, you do not have to purchase a ticket every time you want to make a trip somewhere by train. Just board any train that is going your way and travel whenever, wherever, and as often as you like throughout the period in which your BritRail Pass is valid.

BritRail Pass is not available in Britain and *must* be purchased in North America prior to departure. Order from BritRail's U.S. sales agent **Rail Pass Express (800–722–7151; http://www.eurail.com)** or from your local travel agent. A list of British and European rail passes and their corresponding prices

London's Waterloo International station (above) serves as departure and arrival point for the sleek Eurostar trains (below) journeying through the Chunnel to link London with Paris and Brussels.

is available in the appendix, beginning on page 309. Expand your horizons—don't leave home without one!

BritRail passes are available for first- or standard-class rail travel. First-class seats are wider; consequently, first-class coaches are more spacious since they accommodate fewer passengers. BritRail's standard class, however, is also comfortable. One thing is common to both classes—the view. Either in first or standard class, you can lounge in comfort while watching the country-side glide by.

When traveling in Britain on certain peak days, holidays, or summer Saturdays, seat reservations are recommended. You may make them at any rail station or at the rail counters in Heathrow and Gatwick airports. Although you can make seat reservations in the U.S. after you purchase your BritRail Pass, it is more economical to make your reservations in Britain.

There are two basic types of passes to choose from—BritRail Classic Pass and BritRail Flexipass.

BritRail Classic Pass: Unlimited consecutive-day rail travel in England, Scotland, and Wales. Choose to travel for 8, 15, or 22 days or 1 month. The BritRail Senior Classic Pass (available to adults sixty years and over) offers a 15 percent discount off the first-class BritRail Adult Classic Pass. BritRail Youth Classic passes are available for those ages sixteen through twenty-five; youth passes, however, are available in standard class only.

BritRail Flexipass: This pass provides exactly what its name implies—flexibility. Travel on any 4, 8, or 15 days within a one-month validity period in either first or standard class. Unlike the Classic Pass, your travel days need not be consecutive, thus enabling you to stay in your favorite location for several days until you choose to continue your journey. A BritRail Senior Flexipass (age sixty and over) offers first class rail travel at a 15 percent discount off the BritRail Adult Flexipass price. A Youth Flexipass (ages sixteen through twenty-five) is available in standard class only for any 4 or 8 days of travel in one month or travel any 15 days you choose within a two-month period.

BritRail Family Pass: With BritRail, kids count, too. With the purchase of one Adult or Senior pass, one accompanying child (age five through fifteen) gets a pass of the same type and duration Free. Additional children purchase the appropriate pass at a 50 percent discount off the price of a regular adult pass. Children under the age of five travel for free. The BritRail Family Pass program is available with BritRail Classic, BritRail Flexipass, BritRail Senior, BritRail Pass + Car, and BritRail Pass + Ireland.

BritRail Pass + Car: Although Britain's compactness makes it convenient to take the train and see the sights, there are but a few nooks and crannies that cannot be reached by train. Those who want to combine the thrill of driving on the left-hand side of the road with rail travel can opt for the BritRail Pass + Car. Use the fast, comfortable BritRail trains for the longer journeys and the freedom of a Hertz car to explore the beautiful British countryside. First, purchase your BritRail Pass + Car. The price includes a BritRail Flexipass for unlimited rail travel (choice of first or standard class) for any 3 or 6 days within a one-month period and car rental vouchers for any 3 or 7 days within the same one-month time frame. Then, *at least* seven days prior to departure, telephone Hertz toll free at (800) 654–3001 to reserve your first car rental date. Be certain to state that you have already purchased a BritRail Pass + Car. You should make these reservations as soon as possible, particularly if you want a car with an automatic transmission. For the remainder of your car-rental reservations, Hertz has rental offices and Freephones at rail stations throughout England, Scotland, and Wales.

Since your car-rental vouchers may be used only during the validity period of your BritRail Flexipass, the most economical way of utilizing them is to arrange for a car to meet your train at a day-excursion point, do your exploring, and return the car to the same station before returning to your base city by train. Prebooked requests for a car to meet your train will be honored seven days a week.

Each car-rental voucher includes a twenty-four-consecutive-hour rental with unlimited mileage, no drop-off charge, and government tax (VAT) of 17.5 percent. The renter is responsible for collision damage, personal accident insurance, and gas. Payment of these charges may be made by credit card or a deposit at the start of each rental period. Aside from gasoline, the other charges average about $11 (U.S.) per day. The BritRail Pass + Car Option rates are based on two adults per car.

BritRail Pass + Ireland: For unlimited rail travel in England, Scotland, Wales, Northern Ireland, and Ireland, this is the pass for you. The price also includes one round-trip ferry service on Stena Line (within the validity of your pass) between Holyhead and Dun Laoghaire, Fishguard, and Rosslare, or Stranraer and Belfast via ship, HSS (High Speed Sea Service) or Stena Lynx Catamaran. The BritRail Pass + Ireland is available for any 5 or 10 days of travel within a one-month period in either first or standard class (no senior or youth discounts; children under five travel free; one free child's pass, ages five through fifteen, with purchase of adult pass).

BritRail Southeast Pass: Casual, short-term, or business visitors to Britain may all benefit from this special flexible rail pass tucked in their pocket before leaving home. The Southeast Pass offers unlimited rail travel throughout a large area of southern England for any 3 or 4 days out of an 8-day period or for any 7 days within a 15-day period. Choose first- or standard-class rail travel; a free Guide Friday sightseeing tour is included; and special children's rates are applicable.

Freedom of Scotland Travelpass: The Travelpass offers unlimited rail travel in Scotland on BritRail's network, including travel to/from Berwick and Carlisle for 8, 15, or 22 consecutive days passes. A flexible pass for any 8 days of rail travel within a 15-day period is also available. They are available in standard class only and no discounts are available for children, youth, or seniors.

Other bargains include The Great British Heritage Pass, which provides entry to over 500 of Britain's public and privately owned historic sites; the London Visitor Travel Card for unlimited travel on London's red double-decker buses and the Underground (subway); and the BritRail + Eurostar pass to combine Britain with the Continent. Special rail tour packages are explained in Chapter 7 "Special Itineraries."

A catalog detailing BritRail's many economically priced programs may be obtained free of charge by calling Rail Pass Express at (800) 722–7151.

Trip Tips

Cash, Cards, and Credentials. Don't carry more cash than you can afford to lose; use ATMs (automated teller machine) or carry traveler's checks. You will, of course, need some cash on your flight to pay for tips, snacks, refreshments, and taxi fares at your arrival city. U.S. currency will do, but don't carry it all in one big roll—distribute it around in pockets, briefcase, money clip, and money belt. A money belt is an ideal way to carry the larger notes.

ATMs offer the best exchange rate on foreign currencies, but if you plan to use them, do your homework. Ask your bank for a list of ATM locations in Britain and whether or not your magnetic imprint needs to be modified to work in foreign ATMs. Be certain to know your PIN number and inquire if the bank will charge you per overseas cash withdrawal. Although U.S. banks have levied new surcharges for the luxury of using their machines, these charges do not extend to U.S.-issued cards at machines overseas. Remember, though, that a cash withdrawal is like a "temporary mini-loan", and there is an interest charge. You can avoid interest charges by using a debit card (cash withdrawals and purchases are deducted from your checking account).

If you do carry traveler's checks, cash them at the branch-bank facilities located in or near railway stations and airports. Banks and official currency-exchange services are government supervised and are required to pay the official exchange rates. Hotels and stores seldom give you the full exchange value and often add service fees.

Make a list of credit-card, traveler's check, and airline ticket numbers that you plan to take. Leave a copy at home and pack one in your suitcase or carry-on bag. Credit cards are handy for paying the larger expenses such as hotels and restaurants. The charge is converted into dollars at the applicable exchange rate on the date the charge is posted.

Make two copies of your passport. Leave one copy at home and take the other one with you. Carry a certified copy of your birth certificate and a few extra passport photos. Taking the time to do this will save you days of delay on your trip if your passport is lost or stolen. If your passport is lost or stolen, report it to the local police and contact the nearest U.S. Embassy or Consulate.

Cameras, Film. If you plan to take a foreign-made camera with you that you purchased in the United States, take the sales slip with you. Otherwise, go to a U.S. Customs Office before leaving the country and have your equipment registered. Carry a copy of the sales slip or the registration form with your passport and keep a spare copy tucked away in the camera case or shoulder bag.

Despite what airport officials tell you, their electronic luggage-checking devices can fog your film. The best way to avoid it is to not have film in your camera when you go through airport security, and place unboxed film in clear plastic bags. Ask that your cameras and film be inspected by hand. Above all, do not pack film in your check-through luggage. Although special lead-lined bags are available at most camera stores, luggage is subjected to a high level of radiation, and the film may still be damaged.

Color film in Britain includes processing and is usually more expensive than you can buy at home. Solution? Take all the film you'll need with you.

Do's & Don'ts Safety Tips. Picking pockets is an art that is practiced throughout Europe. Don't carry anything more valuable than a handkerchief in hip pockets. Money belts, holster wallets, or pouches that can be hidden are the safest way to carry cash and other valuables.

If you do not have a concealable money belt/pouch, women should place the straps of their purses across their chests and carry the purses in front—not on the side with the straps only on the shoulder. Motorcycle thieves can grab the purse from your shoulder very easily. Men should modify the inside pocket of a coat or jacket with a zipper. Or, sew a medium-size button both above and below the pocket opening. Loop a piece of shoestring or other strong string around the buttons when carrying valuables.

Don't leave cash, cameras, and other valuables in the hotel room or locked up in a suitcase. Take them with you or leave them in the hotel safe. We advocate leaving expensive jewelry at home, but if you must take it with you, leave it in the hotel safe when you're not wearing it.

Don't dangle your camera from around your neck or wrist; keep it in an inexpensive-looking camera bag.

Don't designate one individual to carry everyone's passport or other valuables, and don't carry all of your own valuables in one place. Split up documents and money in various locations.

Stay alert. Pickpocketing most commonly occurs in crowded public areas. Be leery of being bumped or someone causing a distracting incident.

Don't let the thought of someone picking your pocket alarm you. Just be aware of it and protect yourself against it. Actually, it's mild compared to what could happen to you on Main Street in your own home town in broad daylight.

3   EN ROUTE—THE FUN OF GOING

With all the luxuries of flight that modern aircraft offer, there is still something about flying that makes it a bit more demanding on your system than a similar amount of time spent at home or in the office. A transatlantic trip with a minimum of incidents and inconveniences is what we're after. Here are some suggestions that we have found helpful on our flights; perhaps they may help on yours.

In-Flight Comfort

If you plan to catch some shut-eye en route, ask for a seat alongside a bulkhead. Bulkheads don't mind being leaned on, but passengers do. If you need more legroom, sit in an emergency exit row, but be prepared to accept the responsibility for being physically capable of standing and opening the exit hatch if necessary. Also, be sure your seat reclines. On some planes, the row of seats forward of the emergency exits does not recline. Passengers in the forward section of the airplane generally experience less vibration.

Wear loose clothing. Unfasten your shoes, but don't take them off. Your feet will swell following several hours of immobility. The best remedy is to walk the length of the aisle in the airplane every hour or so. Try deep knee bends.

Flying dehydrates your body. Drink lots of water and watch what you mix with it—alcohol dehydrates, too. Special meals for special diets are no problem with the airlines, but requests should be made at the same time as reservations.

Tax-Free Purchases

Every international airport has a "tax-free" shopping service. The routine is generally the same. You select your purchases, pay for them and add them to your carry-on luggage, find safe storage for it during the flight, and then haul it off the airplane. Yet there are variations. For example, at JFK in New York, you select the items from a sample or catalog. The items are then delivered "for your convenience" to your departure gate for pick-up. The hazards of this system are many. If the delivery person gets things mixed-up and fails to make the right gate at the right time, you'll be off into the wild blue yonder sans purchases. Or if you are late passing the pick-up point, sometimes an unknown "benefactor" tries to help by taking your purchases on board the plane ahead of you. Finding this so-called "benefactor" can prove to be difficult. Solution? Buy your "booty" aboard the airplane while en route. Most international airlines carry aboard a good stock of "tax free" items, which you may purchase from the cabin crew. It's always best to check at the airline counter, however, to be certain that this "in flight" service will be available on your particular flight. "Tax-free," by the way, is a misused term. Most items, with exception of alcohol and tobacco, normally can be purchased cheaper in the arrival city.

Keep in mind that everything you purchase, "tax free" or otherwise, is subject to customs duty when returning home. Consequently, know your quotas and attempt to stay within them to avoid paying duty and the ensuing delays involved. Good luck with customs. Honesty is always the best policy!

Prior to Landing

Fill out all the customs forms your flight attendant gives to you and keep them with your passport and airline ticket. Keep this packet handy, but secure, until the credentials are required by the customs officials at the arriving airport.

Jet Lag and What to Do about It

Earlier, we mentioned jet lag. It can seriously affect your transatlantic trip unless you know how to deal with it. The following explanation of what jet lag is and some means to combat it should prove helpful to any traveler undergoing four or more hours of time change.

The human body has numerous rhythms; sleep is one of them. Even without sunlight, as in a cave, the body will still maintain a twenty-four-hour awake/asleep cycle. The heart rate falls to a very low ebb in the early hours of the morning, when you are usually asleep. Body temperature, which affects the mental processes, also drops during this time. Consequently, if an air traveler is transported rapidly to a time zone five or six hours ahead of that of the departure point, even though it may be eight or nine o'clock in the morning at the arrival point in local time, the traveler's body functions are at a low ebb. As a result, the traveler feels subpar, and this feeling can persist for as long as two or three days unless something is done to correct it.

To cope effectively with jet lag, start varying your normal sleep-eat-work pattern a week or so before your departure. If you are normally up by 7:00 A.M. and in bed around 11:00 P.M. or so, get up earlier and go to bed later for a few days. Then reverse the procedure by sleeping in a bit in the morning and going to bed ahead of your normal time. Vary your meal times, possibly putting off breakfast until lunch time. This will condition your body to begin accepting changes in routines. In turn, when the big transatlantic change comes, it won't be as much of a shock on your system.

To lessen the effects of jet lag en route, avoid excessive drinking and eating. After your arrival, exercise the first day by taking a vigorous walk, followed by a long nap. You should have set your watch to local time at your destination as you departed on your flight. By doing this, you subconsciously accelerate your adjustment to the new time zone. For example, how many times have you looked at your watch and then realized you were hungry? Get plenty of rest on the day of your arrival, and begin doing everything you normally do back home according to the new local time.

Some seasoned transatlantic travelers take even stronger precautions to avoid jet lag. They follow the rule of "no coffee, tea, food, wine, beer, or liquor" on the day of the flight to Europe, but they do advocate lots of fruit juices, vegetable juices, and water (no carbonated drinks). This method follows the theory that your body clock will then go on hold, waiting for you to restart it with breakfast the day you arrive in Europe. Resist the temptations of the airlines up to the point of breakfast and try to get some sleep. Some current studies have shown the hormone melatonin to be useful in combatting jet lag, but as with any other over-the-counter drug, you should first consult your physician. Respect jet lag by taking these precautions and you'll enjoy your vacation.

The Gatwick Express is the most efficient and inexpensive way to travel the 27-mile trip to and from London's Gatwick Airport into Victoria Station. Nonstop rail service runs every fifteen minutes during the day, hourly at night. Journey time is thirty minutes. Seventeen dollars, U.S. standard class; $23 U.S. first class. Ticket offices and machines at Victoria Station and Gatwick Airport are open 24 hours a day and accept credit cards and foreign currencies. Luggage check-in facilities and flight confirmation are available through airline ticket offices at Victoria Station.

4   ARRIVING IN BRITAIN

That big moment is about to happen. Years of dreaming, months of planning, and weeks of anticipation are about to become a reality. The NO SMOKING and FASTEN SEAT BELTS signs have been illuminated, and the cabin attendants advise that the aircraft will be landing in a few minutes. If this is your initial visit to Britain, you'll be straining to get your first glimpse of the land from your window; if you have been to Britain many times before, you'll be straining to get a glimpse of the land right along with the other passengers. There is always an unexplainable thrill about arriving in a foreign country. Enjoy this emotion; it's part of the reason for your journey—to experience the adventure of travel, to probe beyond the normal confines of your environment, to meet other people, to enjoy a bit more of the world than you did before the FASTEN SEAT BELTS sign came on.

The Airports

Within Britain, there are five international airports servicing traffic from the United States: Gatwick and Heathrow in the London area, Birmingham and Manchester in central England, and Glasgow in Scotland.

Gatwick–London: There are two terminals—the North Terminal and the South Terminal. Telephone: (0293) 535353. The Gatwick Express rail service departs the South Terminal for London's Victoria Station. Approximate journey time is thirty minutes.

Heathrow–London: There are four terminals—Terminals 1, 2, 3, and 4 with courtesy coaches operating between the terminals on a regular basis. Telephone: (081) 759 4321. Airbus A1 departs from outside each terminal for Victoria Station (sixty to seventy minutes journey time) and Airbus A2 goes to Euston Station in London (60 to 85 minutes journey time). For more detailed information on Gatwick and Heathrow airports, please consult chapter 10 (London).

Birmingham: Frequent train service from the airport to Birmingham New Street Station and direct train service to London (Euston Station, about one hour, fifty minutes), Brighton, Edinburgh, Glasgow, Leeds, Liverpool, Manchester, Newcastle, Oxford, Southampton, and York.

Manchester: There are three terminals: Terminal 1 Domestic, Terminal 1 International, and Terminal 2. Telephone: (061) 489 3000. The airport rail station is linked to Terminal 1 by a covered escalator and to Terminal 2 by a twenty-four-hour shuttle bus service. Up to six trains per hour from the airport station to Manchester Piccadilly Railway Station (twenty to twenty-five minutes).

Glasgow: One terminal, no rail connection at the airport, connect with

Paisley (2 miles from the airport). Telephone: (041) 887 1111. Scottish City Link 500 operates from Glasgow airport to the Buchanan Bus Station in the city center (about twenty-five minutes).

Clearing Customs

The customs-information cards given to you by the cabin attendants before landing will expedite your clearance through arrival formalities. Actually, you will go through two processes—customs and immigration—although they appear to be integrated. Immigration officials will want to examine your passport.

This is usually conducted at a barrier gate en route to the baggage-claim area in the airport. After collecting the checked baggage, you should proceed to the customs-inspection area, where you will find two color-coded lanes—green for "Nothing to Declare" and red for "To Declare." Everyone has some apprehension about passing through customs. For the most part, the apprehension is based on the question, "Am I doing it properly?" Doing it properly in Britain consists of going straight through the "Nothing to Declare" channel (unless you are asked to stop by an officer) and moving through into the airport's general-assembly area.

If the customs officials want to examine your luggage, they will indicate so as you approach them. Don't go through the "To Declare" lane unless you have brought amounts of tobacco or liquor with you that exceed the duty-free limits or have purchased a gift that you will be leaving with someone in Britain with a value exceeding £136.

The type and amount of duty-free goods that you may bring into Britain vary with your point of departure—a European Common Market country or otherwise. For transatlantic passengers, the limit is 200 cigarettes and a liter bottle of liquor or two bottles of sparkling wine and two bottles of still wine. You will have plenty of advance advice on duty-free imports posted in your departing airport and you can check with the cabin attendants on the airplane as well. Know before you go, and the clearing procedures in Britain will present no problem.

The phrase "know before you go" also applies to your return to North America. The U.S. Treasury Department publishes an informative booklet containing customs hints for returning residents. Write to the Department of the Treasury, Washington, DC 20229 for the *Know Before You Go* booklet. For U.S. Customs information while in London, telephone 499–1212 at the American Embassy.

When clearing through foreign customs, keep in mind that the average customs inspector is more interested in the luggage of a returning national than in yours. Always carry your customs declaration along with your passport and in full view as you unlock your luggage in case it has to be inspected.

British Currency

British currency is based on the pound sterling. The pound (£) is divided into one-hundred pence, just as the U.S. dollar is divided into one hundred cents. Paper notes are issued in values of £50, £20, £10, and £5. Scottish £1 notes are still in circulation in Scotland. Coins are issued in values of £1, 50p, 20p, 10p, 5p, 2p, and 1p..

British paper notes, like the majority of world currencies, vary in size according to their value, and a variety of them can wreak havoc to the orderliness of a North American's wallet. Certain notes, the £10 and £20 in particular, will require folding before they will fit into a wallet designed to hold dollars. Use discretion when engaged in this folding process, especially in public.

We proudly pointed out to one of our British friends how neatly organized our American wallets are because the U.S. dollar is the same size whether it's a $100 note or a $1 note. "Yes, that's quite neat," he stated, "but what do your blind people do?"

British Telephones

The modern, public, coin-box telephones in operation throughout Britain are simple—with a bit of explanation, that is. Basic differences still exist between British phones and ours, particularly in the signals they make. A ringing signal is two short rings, followed by a pause. The busy signal sounds the same—only busier. An all-circuits-busy signal is a rapid series of high-low tones, but when you have reached a telephone number not in use, a high-pitched continuous tone reminiscent of a World War II air-raid siren is heard. Coin operated phones are identified by a red stripe across the phone booth door. They operate much like ours, except when you hear a series of rapid pips, which is a signal that more coins must be deposited or your call will be terminated.

Phonecard payphones are identified by a green stripe across the door. They require the use of a prepaid Phonecard, which you can purchase in £2 (20 units), £4 (100 units), and £20 (200 units) denominations. The cards are sold at post offices and wherever the distinctive green British Telecom (BT) Phonecard sign is displayed. Instructions for the use of Phonecards are posted inside each booth, or you can ask an information office for the pamphlet, "How to Call Home from the UK."

British Traditions

Some visitors entering Britain for the first time may find some of the British traditions, customs, and way of life a little difficult to understand. Perhaps what follows may assist in the transition.

If a Scot from Edinburgh, a Welshman from Cardiff, and an Englishman from London were traveling together in North America, they would describe them-

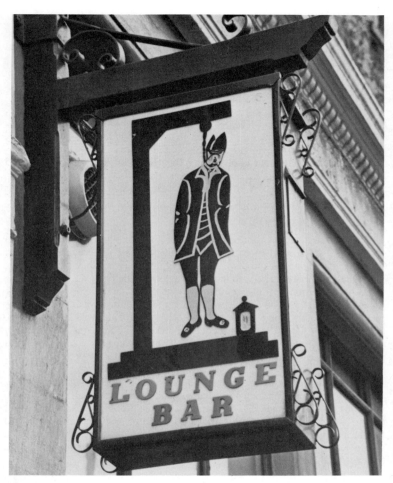

Local Hangout, The Gallows Pub in Edinburgh takes its name from the fact that it is located on the site of Gallows Hill, where executions by hanging were held in days not too dim in the city's past. British public houses frequently have taken their names from the activities previously conducted in the area, like Smugglers—or from folklore— George & Dragon. The Wicked Lady near St. Albans, however, has us puzzled.

selves as being "British." But among themselves, they would be Scot, Welsh, and English. These three nationalities, joined by the Ulstermen of Northern Ireland, make up what we refer to as the United Kingdom. Since the BritRail Pass is not accepted for rail travel in Northern Ireland, references in this book are to *Britain* rather than the *United Kingdom*, and the term *British* refers to the peoples of England, Scotland, and Wales.

Those who plan to add Northern Ireland and the Republic of Ireland to their rail itinerary should consider the BritRail + Ireland Pass (see Appendix for pass prices).

The British character will wear well on you after a few days. If you are taken by the strangeness of their manners, remember that the British are a well-disciplined people. If anything is at fault, more than likely it is the visitor, not the host. You might spill your tea the first time a waitress calls you "Dearie," but you'll learn very quickly that these figures of speech are actually a kind of politeness. You'll also learn very quickly that the British queue is the quintessence of "first-come, first-served."

On the surface, Britons may appear to lack a sense of humor. Once their facade is penetrated, however, you will find them capable of the highest mark of humor—they can laugh at themselves. This becomes most evident in their observations regarding their weather. "The way to ensure summer in England," snapped Horace Walpole, "is to have it framed and glazed in a comfortable room." Byron's observation was perhaps more terse: "The English winter—ending in July to recommence in August." Britain does have a tendency to be damp at times. You won't regret taking a small folding umbrella.

The Language Barrier

By now, you'll notice that there is one! It has often been said that the two great countries of America and Britain are divided only by a common language. Terminology, more so than pronunciation, appears to be the problem whenever an American and a Briton cannot communicate effectively. British/American Language Dictionary by Norman Moss (1991, Passport Books, Chicago, Illinois) would be most helpful during an initial visit to Britain.

Reading the daily newspapers and listening to the British Broadcasting Corporation (BBC) or watching the telly (television) are quick remedial methods for learning the language. These media communicate through a (more or less) middle-of-the-road lexicon. Regional and local dialects can be extremely difficult to comprehend on occasion. It has been said that if an Oxford graduate and a Cambridge graduate were locked together in the same room, neither would be able to converse with the other—even after being properly introduced.

One of the first things a visitor from "the Colonies" will notice is the manner in which directions are given. Americans geographically locate a point within a city by referring to the number of blocks distant from the point of inquiry, for example, "two blocks down the street." Britain's early road builders, however, never thought too much about a grid system and permitted their streets to wander along the easiest gradient. Consequently, directions given by a constable or a man on the street will usually be in terms of linear directions, that is, "straight-away for one-hundred yards," "a quarter-mile," "a mile or two," and so on. Visual objects are employed as well: "straight-away to the pub," "keep walking till you come to the third traffic light," and the like. Cabbies (taxi drivers) are particularly good sources for directional information and advice. Every cabby carries a street map in his taxi and will be glad to assist you.

Nuances in the American/British vocabulary can sometimes lead to trouble. In a public place, such as a train station, those in search of toilet facilities will do well to employ the term *lavatory* in their quest. The *WC* (water closet) seems to be losing its effectiveness in Britain, although it still brings direct results when used in Continental Europe. But if you want to be up on slang expressions, you might ask for the *loo*—that's where the "in crowd" goes to "spend a penny." Requesting directions for the *bathroom*, particularly in a train station, might lead you to the public showers. So take our advice and stay with lavatory.

Terminology in a train station should not present much of a problem. The baggage room is *left luggage*, and *lost property* translates easily into lost and found. Elevators are labeled *lifts,* but *subway* means a pedestrian, underground street crossing. The Underground, or *tube,* is the British version of our subway.

A *carriage* is a (rail) coach, and a *coach* is a long-distance bus. Should you hear the term *goods wagon* or *goods train,* that translates to a freight car or a freight train in American terminology. Aboard a train, the conductor usually is referred to as the *guard;* the engineer becomes the train *driver.*

The British measure their body weight in stones—a stone being a unit of fourteen pounds. A person weighing fourteen stone six pounds would gross out at 202 pounds avoirdupois. A popular measurement of elapsed time is *a fortnight,* meaning fourteen days or two weeks. Britain's conversion to a decimal currency system has not changed the slang for the pound sterling—it's still a "quid." You may hear a price quoted in *guineas,* a holdover from the old days meaning one pound and one shilling.

British Pubs

The pub is uniquely British and can be found only on the British Isles, because the ingredient that makes a true "public house" is not its construction, architecture, furniture, or the spirits it dispenses—it's its clientele. The "local," as most British pubs are lovingly referred to, is an organic part of the community. It ranks in importance along with the local postal office and the town hall—perhaps even higher. It is supported by "locals," who generally prefer to stand when they imbibe, for pub etiquette must be observed at all times. Pub etiquette also dictates that you pay for the "round" when served and if you accept a drink, you are expected to buy a round in return.

The term *public house* means just that. Everyone is welcome—even Americans and Australians. To accommodate the differences in drinking etiquettes of these visitors, most pubs have a second bar area, which is identified as a lounge or a saloon. There are more seats and usually the drinks cost a bit more.

When are the pubs open? Licensing hours now generally permit English pubs to remain open from 1100 to 2300 Monday through Saturday and Sundays from 1200 to 1500 and 1900 to 2230 in England and Wales; 1230 to 1430 and 1830 to 2300 in Scotland. You must be over eighteen to buy or consume alcoholic beverages in a pub. Children fourteen years and older may be admitted legally to a pub and may consume nonalcoholic drinks. Children of all ages are usually admitted to licensed restaurants; they are also admitted to "beer gardens" and family rooms, which many pubs have.

Closing time in a pub is quite an event and frequently can create confusion among the uninformed and the uninitiated. At the appointed hour, the owner or head barkeep announces, "Time, gentlemen!" in a loud, authoritative voice. At that instant, a bar towel is draped over the beer pumps, and everyone quickly attends to drinking up and hastily departing the premises. Without prior knowledge of this procedure, visitors have frequently mistaken closing time for a fire drill and have begun evacuating the building via the closest window!

A pub is usually rated by the congeniality of its owner, and unless "on holidays," he or she is usually found on the premises during operating hours. An entrepreneurial lot, many owners offer "pub grub" in their establishments. Visitors find it a good alternative to Wendy's or McDonald's for a snack or a lunch because a Frosty can never really compete with a good pint of ale or porter.

A pub's personality greets you at the door. You can tell in an instant whether or not it's your kind of place. If its ambience reaches out to you, enter. No doubt a local or two will note your entrance with a friendly nod as the barmaid beams at you and asks, "What'll you have, governor?" When advised, she'll then indicate with a slight directional nod of her head that it will be served in the lounge area. Pay when served. Tip the barmaid, but never tip the owner in the event he brings the drinks to the table to bid you welcome. He's the host; you are the guest. Later, you might join the locals at the bar; but remember, remain standing and pay for a round when it's your turn to buy. Who knows, the locals might suggest that you drop around again.

Food on the move includes a variety of service and menus. InterCity trains (above) feature three types of menus: Gold Star, Main Line, and Grill. Light refreshments may be purchased from the "roving" carts (below) aboard InterCity trains.

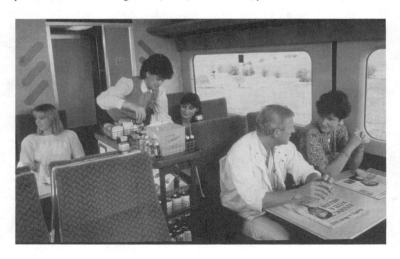

5   BRITISH TRAINS

Over the last decade, the services on the British rail passenger network have come a long way—with yet a long way to go. There is still a discernible difference between the operating speeds and the passenger comforts of the railroads of Continental Europe and those of the British, the latter being inferior; yet the gap is narrowing.

The front runner of the British rail stable is its High Speed Train (HST), the InterCity 125. Nicknamed the "Journey Shrinker," the world's fastest diesel train is shrinking journeys on many of the main routes out of London. From King's Cross Station, for example, the Flying Scotsman, an InterCity 125, covers the 393 miles between London and Edinburgh in four hours flat—an average of ninety-eight miles per hour, and that includes a station stop at York and Newcastle in England before crossing the Scottish border. Hourly service by 125s links the two capitals. InterCity 125 service also extends from London to Plymouth and Penzance. Leading the 125 fleet to England's west is the Golden Hind, appropriately named after Sir Francis Drake's famous sailing vessel.

InterCity 125 trains offer comfort as well as speed. They have a whole range of luxury features, including air conditioning, soundproofing, automatic interior doors, and a wide choice of meals, snacks, and drinks. The trains are powered by two 2,250-horsepower diesel-electric engines—one at each end of the train. The 125 coaches are identified by letter (A, B, C, etc.), and the stations they serve have their platform positions marked accordingly.

The light at the end of BritRail's tunnel grows brighter and brighter. By InterCity 125 service from London, you can now reach Cardiff, in Wales, in one hour fifty-seven minutes. Running times are being slashed on all major British rail lines. A train trip from London to Glasgow used to take six hours; now you're there in only five hours and five minutes!

Aside from the InterCity 125s and the equally fast and comfortable all-electric passenger trains on major routes (the London-Glasgow line is completely electrified), there is a paucity of modern commuter-type trains on many of its intermediate lines. For example, although train service south of London is completely electrified, for the most part it is served by four-car units, some of which have already passed their thirty-eighth "birthdays." These trains have seen yeoman duty through the years and show more than a fair amount of wear and tear.

Along with Beatlemania, graffiti arrived in Britain accompanied by modern packaging, which produces litter in abundance. The older trains, however, were designed in the days when cleaning labor was plentiful and cheap. Washing as many as eighty windows on a single coach wasn't a problem then, but it is now.

Moreover, air conditioning is nonexistent in the older trains, although that's no great problem because summers in the British Isles are generally milder than those in North America. But heating can be a problem. Not many years ago, train passengers set out on their journeys wrapped in heavy overcoats and shod with thick-soled shoes. Full heat in the coach brought complaints of stuffiness. Today's grumbles from thinly clad travelers are very much the opposite.

The "old units" are gradually being replaced by new suburban-type trains, and some of the vintage units are being refurbished with more comfortable seats, better lighting, heating, and soundproofing. Nevertheless, it will be a while before the "generation gap" in British rolling stock is overcome.

Possibly on a day excursion off the main lines, you may ride in a locomotive-hauled coach with an exit door for each compartment. We've counted as many as nine doors to a side on some coaches. These cars are relics from the days when station porters opened and closed the doors for passengers. Consequently, you won't find any door handles inside the compartment. To get out, lower the window and open the door from the outside.

Sleeping, restaurant, buffet and Pullman cars are operated by British Rail, along with the standard passenger carriages (coaches). British Pullman cars differ from the Pullmans of North America in that they do not convert at night to provide sleeping accommodations. Instead, British Pullmans are the elite of the line, the best in daytime comfort, and exclusively first-class. Even travelers holding first-class BritRail passes are required to pay a supplemental fare for occupancy, and seat reservations are obligatory. This luxury service operates on the London-to-Manchester/Liverpool route. Basically, it is designed to offer the businessman morning and afternoon services between England's capital and its leading commercial center. It is worth the experience, but we suggest that you dress appropriately for the occasion if you want to engage in tycoon-to-tycoon conversations with other passengers. In London, the Pullman trains depart from Euston Station. When accommodations are available, last-minute reservations and supplementary payment can be arranged with the conductor.

First-class sleeping cars have single-berth compartments; economy-class sleepers have two-berth compartments. Sleeping-car charges in Britain are economical—$57 per person for first class and $48 per person for economy class. The sleeping cars are equipped with fresh bedding, washing facilities with soap and towels, a shaver outlet, and bottled drinking water. Sleeping-car passengers are served with morning tea or coffee and biscuits free of charge, and they generally can remain in the sleeping cars at destination until 7:30 A.M. The charge is standard for all destinations regardless of the distance.

With such attractive prices, an overnight trip aboard a sleeper may outweigh the alternative of seeking a night's lodging in a city and an early morning departure in order to make your destination on time. Consider the sleeping cars for excursions to Plymouth, Penzance, and Inverness.

Sleeper services operate between London and the main centers in Scotland, the north of England, south Wales, and the west of England. "Nightcap" service is available, too, in case you're interested.

Most InterCity trains haul restaurant cars. If not, there usually is a buffet car from which you can obtain snacks and beverages. Aboard the InterCity fleet, restaurant cars offer a wide range of freshly prepared traditional dishes. Gold Star restaurant service is available on many 125s and on selected "business" trains—the Manchester/Liverpool Pullman, for example. Passengers holding first-class tickets who wish to take meals can reserve seats in the restaurant car or in adjacent coaches. Breakfast aboard British trains has always been a great attraction. It's hearty and generally very good.

Some buffet cars offer "grill" meals, which you may enjoy either there, or back at your seat. Seating in the buffet cars is not assignable, thereby providing a reasonable opportunity to be seated while you select from the bill of fare. One innovation found aboard many food-service rail cars is beer and lager on draft. This, according to many railroad buffs, is an outstanding stride forward in the annals of railroad engineering!

Admittedly, dining aboard a speeding train is an unusual gastronomic experience, but it can be on the expensive side. Although food catering aboard a British train is far more economical than similar services on the trains of the Continent, those seeking less expensive food may want to utilize the food facilities found at most rail stations in Britain. They range in service from complete restaurants servicing a variety of hot and cold dishes to a snack bar–type operation. Some have off-license provisions allowing you to purchase alcoholic beverages for consumption elsewhere, but all bars operating in the stations, unlike those on the trains, must observe the local licensing hours for drinks.

The most economical food you may enjoy on a train in Britain is, of course, that which you bring aboard yourself. Many of the station restaurants will prepare box lunches for you to take on your trip. Ask for the "buffet-pack" service. Your hotel or bed-and-breakfast probably can provide the same service. We suggest that you make your initial inquiry a day ahead of your first planned day excursion.

First Class, Standard Class?

On most British trains you have a choice of first- or standard-class travel. BritRail Passes and Flexipasses are sold for both classes. First-class seats are wider and more spacious. If that is the sort of accommodations you want, then it is worth paying the extra price. Standard class is, however, an excellent standard. All the facilities aboard the trains, such as restaurant and buffet services, are available for both first- and standard-class travelers.

The average British citizen usually travels by standard-class carriage (coach). In fact, it is so much the custom that if you want to purchase a first-class ticket, you must specifically state "first-class"; otherwise, you will automatically receive a standard-class ticket. This does not mean that you will find the standard-class carriages crowded, while the first-class sections remain vacant. First class offers extra comfort and is less crowded. First-class accommodations for weekend and holiday travel are particularly desirable. Seats may be reserved in both classes, which is a wise move if your journey is a "must" and the distance is great. "Riding the cases" (sitting on your suitcase for lack of a seat) is not a comfortable way to travel.

Seat reservations may be made in any major train terminal throughout Britain. In addition, Gatwick, Heathrow, and Stansted airports have rail ticket booths where you may make reservations immediately after your arrival. It is possible to obtain advance reservations prior to arriving in Britain, but it is far more economical to make them when you get there.

Travelers holding first-class BritRail passes may travel in either first- or standard-class carriages—which is a nice option for bachelors when the good looking "bird" you've been yearning to chat with boards the standard-class section. It's a disaster, however, if she moves to the first-class section while you're holding a standard-class ticket!

You will find some single-class trains operating on branch lines. This means that the first-class accommodations are not available aboard that particular train. It is a nice, polite British way of avoiding the somewhat unrefined term *second class only*.

Similar to those on the Continent, first-class British rail cars are marked distinctively by a yellow band running the length of each car above its doors and windows. On other-than-mainline service, where both first- and standard-class accommodations may be provided in the same car, a yellow band will be shown for only the first-class portion of the car. Restaurant cars, buffets, and cars containing other forms of food-catering facilities are identified by a red band above their doors and windows.

Except for those of the InterCity 125s and 225s, it is difficult to determine exactly where the first-class coaches will halt during an en route station stop. The non-English-speaking nations of Europe generally provide a diagram of each train's composition and where it will stop in the station. Not so in Britain. According to the equipment in use, the first-class section of a British train can be at the head, the rear, or the middle of the train. Through experience, we have devised a system that is relatively effective in determining where the yellow-striped cars will stop.

Position yourself midway on the platform and scan for the yellow band as the train enters the station. Should it pass you, take off to the head of the train;

if it doesn't, head in the other direction. Should the yellow-striped car stop directly in front you, fate has been kind to you this day, but you can bet it won't happen again soon.

There is an increase in the nonsmoking accommodations aboard British trains. The overall percentage of nonsmoking seats currently is about 75 percent, reflecting the noticeable change in the public attitude toward smoking. There is a stiff fine for violating the rule. So if you are a smoker, keep your eyes alert for the red nonsmoking signs and smoke only in the areas so designated.

Train Schedules

British timetables are generally divided into sections according to the pattern of services provided. A typical two-part division is "Mondays to Saturdays" and "Sundays." You may run across a mix, however, including "Mondays to Fridays," "Mondays to Saturdays," or "Saturdays and Sundays." All days stated are inclusive. In other words, "Mondays to Saturdays" includes all six days. (The schedules appearing in *Britain by BritRail* are stated as "Mondays *through* Saturdays.")

Always be certain that you look at the correct part of the schedule for the particular day of the week on which you wish to travel. Another caution: Services may be modified on days preceding and immediately following bank holidays. Best bet for a "must" trip, a late night return, or an early morning departure is to check your plans with the train personnel in the station travel centers. Extensive engineering work is often conducted on the British rail system on weekends, which frequently affects passengers' schedules. Telephones may also be employed for inquiries. Useful telephone numbers are given on the *Britain by BritRail* schedules for this purpose.

You should experience little difficulty in verifying the departure time of your selected train or locating the platform from which it departs once you've made it to the station—providing that in London you've gone to the proper station. Airport-style digital displays are the usual source for such information in most British stations. You will find them in the main station halls and also on the train platforms in many stations. Even the old-fashioned train bulletin boards, however, can still provide the needed information. Augmenting displayed train-departure information are the usual vocal announcements in the station halls and on the platforms. For the most part, they differ from those made by Amtrak because you can understand them. Perhaps it's the accent that makes it possible.

Ask the Guard

Every British passenger train travels with a conductor aboard. As previously explained, his official title is guard. This gentleman carries with him—in either his handbook or his head—a potpourri of valuable information. For example, if you are required to change trains in order to arrive at your final destination, ask the guard. The London day excursion to Lincoln is one in which you should change trains at Newark Northgate, approximately one and one-half hours after departing London. Will the train departing there for Lincoln Central be standing across the platform from the train you arrive on from London, or will a platform change be necessary? The guard has this information, and it's yours for the asking.

Perhaps en route you learn that the train you are traveling on will be passing a famous British landmark, say a castle. On which side of the train will it pass? If you are a castle buff, maybe you would like to come back on another day to visit the castle. Is there a local train station near the castle? Is there a local bus to take you there if the castle is beyond walking distance? Is there a pub or inn in the vicinity? Surprisingly, you'll probably get responses to all of the above plus a condensed history lesson on the castle and its surroundings—all from the guard.

The guard becomes invaluable when you decide to change your itinerary or vary the time to return to your hotel. With a quick reference to his handbook, he will be able to tell you the time of the next train or the last one you may take that evening. He is also an excellent source of the correct time, for his watch is always set to the second and checked with the British station's master clock. In many ways, the guard becomes your unofficial tour guide—or guardian angel, as the case may be.

6 TRAIN TRAVEL TIPS

"What affects men sharply about a foreign nation," wrote G. K. Chesterton, "is not so much finding or not finding familiar things, it is rather not finding them in the familiar place."

For many of us coming to Britain for the first time, we find a confusion of terminology and learn too late that what we sought was really available throughout our visit. Our problem was merely not knowing the proper place to look or the proper name to ask for. Perhaps some things might be set in better order for the pleasure of your BritRail adventures with the following train-travel tips.

Handicapped Travel

One important tip to mention first is that the British rail system is a leader in providing facilities in its stations and aboard its trains for the disabled and the handicapped. Through such efforts, rail travel is becoming more and more a chosen method of transportation and recreation for disabled persons. Many aids for the handicapped have been incorporated into rail station design. Trains are being designed with wider doors for wheelchair access; some even have a removable seat to make room for a wheelchair. Ramp access to toilets, buffets, and other facilities is being provided. Folding wheelchairs are also available at main stations so that occupants may be transferred to a regular seat once aboard the train. BritRail is most eager to provide as comfortable a journey as possible for the disabled passenger. To do this, prior advice of the intended travel plans would be most helpful to both the traveler and the authorities.

For those readers who want to learn more about this innovative approach to travel for the disabled and the handicapped, we suggest writing to the Royal Association for Disability and Rehabilitation, 25 Mortimer Street, London, W1N 8AB, England, for details. The association has published *A Guide to British Rail for the Physically Handicapped.*

In the United States, contact Mobility International USA, P.O. Box 10767, Eugene OR 97440 (503–343–1284) for information about services and referral to international affiliates. They also produce a book, *A World of Options for the 90s: A Guide to International Educational Exchange, Community Service and Travel for Persons with Disabilities.*

If you plan to travel in Britain with a handicapped person, write or call BritRail Travel International, 1500 Broadway, New York, NY 10036–4015 (telephone 212–575–2667) as soon as you establish your itinerary and begin making arrangements. The same applies to the airline you'll be using for your transatlantic flight. Provide them with all the details of your itinerary, the nature of the disability, and any other information that will help them to help you.

Specifically, special diets, medications, and toilet and medical-attention requirements should be made known. With these details attended to, you can look forward to a pleasant journey.

Baggage Carts

Many otherwise able train visitors to Britain impose a severe disadvantage upon themselves by arriving with more luggage than three men and a small boy could possibly carry. Train porters are nearly an extinct species, and their demise was expedited by the luggage trolley—Britain's version of our baggage cart—an elusive device that, whatever your position on the train platform, haunts the extreme opposite end. Our number-one tip to all train travelers is to "go lightly." At most, take one medium-sized suitcase augmented by a modest shoulder bag. There still will be times when you will wish you could discard your suitcase. If you have purchased a model with built-in wheels, however, it usually will follow at your heels like a well-trained dog as you apply minimum pulling power. Unlike a dog, the wheeled suitcase cannot climb stairs, so be prepared to lift it on and off the train.

Rather than relying upon the trolleys in the train stations, you might consider investing in your own baggage cart to take with you or purchasing a suitcase with built-in wheels. There are many types available. You will see more and more train travelers proceeding through rail stations in Europe with wheeled equipment.

When loading your luggage onto a baggage cart or station trolley, keep the load as narrow as possible. You must pass through ticket barriers going to and coming from the trains. The barriers are rather narrow. A Samsonite suitcase loaded sideways on a baggage cart or one of the station's trolleys will just clear, but a wardrobe case is trouble every time. The trolleys provided by the station should not be taken aboard the train, although we've seen it tried. Again, if you are taking your own cart with you, fold it before boarding. If you don't, you may spend an embarrassing ten minutes or so on the station platform extracting a hapless fellow traveler from it as your train eases out of the station without you.

Using the Lifts

The greatest problem in using the train station's luggage trolleys (or your own baggage cart) is traversing the station hall to the platform area, because practically every station has stairs. You can overcome this problem by using the station's lift (elevator). This polite announcement is found posted in most British Rail stations: "Lifts are available for passengers who have difficulty in using the stairs. Please contact station staff if assistance is required." In searching for a lift, don't always look for a modern, automatic-door elevator brightly lit with soft music playing. Sometimes you will find instead the old-fashioned, double-door, manually operated freight elevator, large enough to hold a Mack truck and usually illuminated with a single, bare light bulb—but it works. As the sign says, station staff will assist you. If you use the lifts frequently, however, you will develop the knack of handling them all by yourself. One word of caution: The lift will not operate until *both* barriers (usually a door and a gate) have been closed securely. Furthermore, the lift will be left inoperative if you fail to close the doors after you have used it. Be considerate of other passengers and the station staff by making certain that the lift is left operable for the next user.

As a matter of interest, if your rail journey takes you to Continental Europe, the use of rail-station lifts by passengers is usually forbidden.

Porter Services

Porter service is on the wane but still available in some train stations, particularly in the larger ones. The best way to locate a porter is to inquire at the "Left Luggage" (baggage storage) area or at the station's incoming taxi stand. If your luggage has been checked in at the station, there will be a handling charge, but the tip remains a personal item between you and the porter. We suggest £1.00 minimum as a reasonable gratuity. Most porters will take your bags to the train and place them aboard in the luggage racks over your seats. Porters are rather scarce on arrival platforms. If you must have assistance, approach the stationmaster's office or the train conductor prior to departure with the request that a porter be asked to meet your train upon arrival at your destination.

If you are transferring between base cities or changing hotels from one city to another, you can request the hall porter at the hotel you are leaving to arrange for the arriving hotel's hall porter to meet your train upon arrival. A small tip should arrange everything.

A Few More Train Tips

A few more train-travel tips to make your trip more enjoyable: "Mind the doors!" British rail cars of the vintage class appear to provide a door for each passenger. There is a great din of door slamming prior to departure and an equal amount of confusion each time the train makes a station stop. If you are waiting at an en route station for a train, stand well back from the platform edge. Passengers impatient to alight from the train are prone to open the doors before the train comes to a complete stop. In so doing, they're actually extending a bludgeon that could kill you, maim you for life, bruise you, or just scare the daylights out of you—the last being preferred over any of the others. There are posters positioned in the stations where these multi-door cars are in service, asking folks to "please don't open the carriage door until the train has

47

stopped" and "please don't stand close to the platform edge."

Show your BritRail Pass, or ticket, upon request, and in the case of the pass, have your passport handy should the conductor like to see it. Don't place your feet on the seats of the train unless you have removed your shoes or have provided a protective covering for the seat. Place your luggage in the overhead racks provided for that purpose—not on the seats so that other passengers won't be able to crowd you. Observe the smoking/nonsmoking areas and rules. There are rather stiff fines that can be imposed for those smokers who violate the nonsmoking areas.

Observe seat reservations. Seating that has been reserved is marked. Even though it is apparent that a seat is unoccupied, if there are other passengers seated opposite, ask if the seat is open. It will avoid embarrassment later if the person holding the reservation happens to return.

Regarding dining-car reservations, on long-distance trains it is best to arrange for them soon after boarding. Inquire from the guard (conductor, remember?). If he cannot make them for you, a member of the dining-car crew will do so. Generally, they pass through the train prior to the first serving for that purpose. Usually, there are two servings, so be prepared to select the one to your liking. You can also inquire regarding the menu at the same time. The second serving is scheduled so that the dining-car crew has time to tidy up before the train reaches its destination. Therefore, the first serving is preferred by many because it does not seem to be rushed.

If you plan an overnight journey on a sleeper, ask the attendant to explain the manner in which the equipment in your compartment operates. For example, the newer sleeping cars have electric shades. A push of the button and they open; another push of the same button and they close. If you did not know the button's function, you just might try pushing the button while the train is standing in a station and you are not dressed for the occasion! It's proper to tip the attendant for his services; the proper time to do so is when he serves breakfast.

SeaCat catamarans ply between England and France at a cruising speed of 35 knots. 240 feet in length and with a beam of 85 feet, the SeaCats carry 450 passengers and 80 vehicles. Known as a wave-piercing catamaran, the SeaCat hull passes through the waves rather than riding over them. (Courtesy of Hoverspeed.)

7   SPECIAL ITINERARIES

In addition to the day excursions offered by this edition of *Britain by BritRail,* there are some special itineraries that are made possible through the unique features of British rail services and its associated transportation facilities. Two of them, the Continental Quickie and the BritRail by Night excursions, are our own concoctions. Britainshrinkers have been offered by BritRail since 1973.

Continental Quickie

If you have never been to Continental Europe before, here's an opportunity to set foot on French soil, explore the seaport city of Boulogne, and yet return to London in time for a dinner appointment. Hoverspeed's service makes this day excursion possible by skimming across the English Channel in one of the company's super SeaCats between Folkestone and Boulogne in less than thirty-five minutes port to port! Train connections are made out of London's Victoria or Charing Cross Station to Folkestone Central Station.

Boulogne is the largest fishing port in France. It was from Boulogne that Caesar set out to conquer England. Boulogne is really two towns—the Basse Ville that lies along the waterfront is very modern, while the Haute Ville poised on the hillside is much older and has a fine medieval wall surrounding it. You may want to include a side trip to Calais on this excursion. Rail and bus services between the two cities are frequent and convenient. If interested, make inquiry with the Boulogne tourist information center at the hoverport when you arrive.

If you are planning a day trip to France during the valid period of your BritRail Pass, you will need to purchase a Port-to-Port round-trip ticket. Your BritRail Pass will get you to the port and return you to London once you are back on British soil.

Britainshrinkers and Eurostar Tours

Britainshrinkers is a program of fully escorted tours leaving London in the morning and returning in the evening. Britainshrinkers also offer two-, three-, and four-night tours, called "Overnighters," enabling you to venture into scenic Scotland. The Britainshrinkers and Overnighter programs differ from Britain by BritRail's day excursions and out-and-back excursions only in that Britainshrinkers and Overnighters are fully escorted.

Britainshrinkers Day Trip to Paris. Want to take in the Louvre or do a little shopping in Paris? Ride from London to Paris on the state-of-the-art super train—Eurostar—through the 31-mile long Channel tunnel on this fully escorted trip. First developed in 1995, these successful tours now offer several options: Tour P—standard class (no meals); Tour PF—first class (breakfast and dinner included); Tour PL—standard class (guided visit to the Louvre included); and Tour PFL—first-class (breakfast and dinner plus a guided visit to the Louvre included).

All of the tours include a guided panoramic tour of Paris, including the Champs-Elysees, Arc de Triomphe, and the Eiffel Tower. From May through September, the tours depart daily except Sunday. March through April, plus October, they depart on Monday, Wednesday, and Saturday. During January, February, November, and December, they depart on Wednesday and Saturday. Britainshrinkers and Eurostar Tours depart London's Waterloo International Terminal between 0630-1030 and return in late afternoon or evening.

A Capital Day Out: Brussels *and* Paris in a Day. No, we're not kidding. This fully escorted day excursion will take you from London to Brussels and Paris via the Eurostar train through the Channel tunnel and the new TGV "Thalys" train—the fastest train in Europe. Only three hours and fifteen minutes after departing London's Waterloo International Terminal, you'll arrive in Brussels and take a guided motorcoach tour of Brussels. Then return to the station for a two-hour journey aboard the high-tech TGV Thalys into Paris. After the guided sightseeing tour of Paris, return to London on board an evening Eurostar train. First class passengers receive breakfast and dinner on Eurostar and lunch on the Thalys train.

Other Britainshrinkers Tours include fully escorted tours to Salisbury/Stonehenge, Leeds Castle/Windsor Castle, Warwick/Stratford, Edinburgh, and York/Scotland for two, three, or four nights.

Britainshrinkers Tours are usually fully booked in advance, so you should make your tour reservations as early as you can prior to departure date. The tours are easy to take—just arrive at the London rail station indicated on your ticket. A guide in a red uniform will take your ticket at the Britainshrinkers check-in point, which is easily identified by its sign.

The BritRail Classic or Flexipass is accepted as supplemental payment for the rail portion of the Britainshrinkers tours—you could save up to 40 percent of the cost of each Britainshrinkers tour you take if you have a BritRail Classic Pass or BritRail Flexipass. For more information on Britainshrinkers Tours and other BritRail products, contact BritRail's U.S. sales agent, **Rail Pass Express, at (800) 722–7151** or on the internet at **http://www.eurail.com**.

BritRail by Night

Here's something that you can do with your eyes closed. BritRail's sleeper services are excellent and inexpensive—a great way to save both time and money.

British rail sleeper services operate between London and the main centers in Scotland, the north of England, south Wales, and the west of England. First-class sleepers accommodate one person; connecting bedrooms are available. Standard-class sleepers offer double accommodations—the two berths are stacked one over the other like bunk beds. Both services provide wall-to-wall carpeting, hot and cold running water, soap and towel, a comfortable mattress, and that all-important call button that will bring you a nightcap or your wake-up coffee.

The cost of sleeper accommodations based on single occupancy is $52 for first class; $43 for standard class. Usually, you can take occupancy thirty minutes before departure time and stay aboard until 0800, even if the train arrives at your destination several hours earlier.

The Caledonian sleepers depart London's Euston Station for Edinburgh, Glasgow, Aberdeen, Inverness, and Fort William. The Night Riviera sleeper departs London's Waterloo Station for Plymouth and Penzance. Sleeper service also is available from either Edinburgh or Glasgow to Inverness.

Overnight sleeper service opens a new door to the adventurous rail traveler. The sleeper charge compares favorably to economical hotel rates, so you can make the sleeper your "hotel on the move." By reserving sleeper accommodations for successive nights, an itinerary could be planned for a night on the train; a day at the destination; a night on the train returning to London; sightseeing, shopping, or a short day excursion out of London; and a night to another destination.

Expanding on the above, an adventurous traveler could depart London's Waterloo Station about midnight, arriving early morning in Penzance to begin an all-day sightseeing trek extending to Land's End. Back in Penzance, the adventurer could board the sleeper that evening for London, spending an entire day there before boarding another sleeper in Euston Station for Aberdeen, Britain's "oil city." After spending the day in Aberdeen, our traveler could reverse his travel and journey to either Edinburgh or Glasgow, where he could then board a sleeper bound for London—or board the Aberdeen sleeper direct to London. Another option is Inverness. After arriving in Edinburgh overnight from London, there's ample time in the day to entrain to Inverness, search for "Nessie" on Loch Ness, then return to Edinburgh on a late train out of Inverness in time to board the Edinburgh-to-London sleeper for the last of four nights' sleeper travel.

8   THE CHANNEL TUNNEL AND
CROSSING THE ENGLISH CHANNEL

The newest method of crossing the English Channel is to go under it via the tunnel (affectionately known as "The Chunnel") connecting England with France and the rest of Europe. Direct rail service from London to Paris or Brussels takes you from city center to city center in only three hours to Paris and three hours fifteen minutes to Brussels.

Another convenient way of crossing the English Channel between England and France is by P.&O. European Ferries, Stena Line ship or Stena Line Lynx (catamaran) services between Dover and Calais. Hoverspeed SeaCat operates between Folkestone and Boulogne.

The Chunnel and Eurostar Services

In 1888, Louis Figuier proclaimed that "linking France and England will meet one of the present day needs of civilization." On May 6, 1994, England's Queen Elizabeth II and France's President François Mitterrand brought Figuier's words to life and inaugurated a new era in European train travel—the linking of England and France via a tunnel that runs underground and under the English Channel. More than 17 million tons of earth were moved to build the two rail tunnels (one for northbound and one for southbound traffic) and one service tunnel.

Plagued by delays and billions of dollars in cost overruns, the Chunnel has proven to be one of the world's largest undertakings. The project cost more than $13 billion and took seven years to complete. Napoleon's engineer, Albert Mathieu, planned the first tunnel in 1802, incorporating an underground passage with ventilation chimneys above the waves. For obvious reasons the British were nervous. Later, in 1880, the first real attempt at a tunnel was undertaken by Colonel Beaumont, who bored 2,000 meters into the earth before abandoning the project. When work on another tunnel began in 1974, the Beaumont tunnel was found to be in good condition. Construction of the current tunnels, which are 38 kilometers in length undersea and have an average depth of 40 meters under the seabed, began in 1987.

Operated by the British, French (SNCF), and Belgian (SNCB) railways, the Eurotunnel provides three different types of service between England and the Continent. Eurostar provides passenger service, and Le Shuttle provides automobile, coach, and lorry service between Folkestone and Calais. International rail freight rounds out the list.

Eurostar service is offered from London's new Waterloo International Eurostar Terminal to Paris' Gare du Nord or Brussels Midi station, in either direction. Travel times from London to Paris are reduced from more than five hours to three hours; Brussels is only three hours and fifteen minutes away, thus making a European Capitals tour nothing more than a day excursion. BritRail pass holders receive a discount on Eurostar tickets.

Eurostar services are expanding to include Eurostar originations from Glasgow, Edinburgh, York, Manchester, Birmingham, and cities in between that link them to Paris and Brussels in either direction. These direct daytime Eurostar Regional Services reduce travel times from Edinburgh to Paris, for example, from more than twelve hours to just under nine hours. European Night Services are also being added for those wishing to arrive in Paris or Brussels in time for breakfast. Night services will include departures from London to Amsterdam, Dortmund and Frankfurt, Germany. Both seated and sleeper accommodations will be offered for overnight departures, featuring on-board catering and luggage storage compartments.

The Eurostar Trains

The sleek Eurostar trains *(Trans Mache Super Trains)* each carry 794 passengers (210 in first class and 584 in second class) and reach speeds of 200 miles per hour in England, with speeds through the Chunnel of 80 miles per hour. The train is based primarily on the TGV but was redesigned to accommodate the three different voltage types encountered enroute. The trains are accessible to handicapped passengers and provide sufficient storage for luggage.

Those taking advantage of a trip from Paris or Brussels to London on a Eurostar train are in for a treat. The trains offer the comfort and amenities comparable to few trains in the world. From departure you're in store for a smooth, quiet, ride, and even when you enter the tunnel the only noticeable change is the sudden darkness. Those concerned with changes in air pressure needn't worry. Air flow through the tunnel is regulated to minimize changes in pressure, and few, if any passengers notice discomfort.

Eurostar staff are multilingual and are available to provide assistance the minute you enter the terminal to the minute you exit the platform. You'll notice them right away, with their navy blue uniforms with accented yellow scarves or ties. If you have any questions, don't be shy—they're there to serve you, and serve you they do.

Passengers travelling first-class are treated to an on-board meal ranging from breakfast to dinner depending upon the time of day. Second-class passengers won't starve either, as a buffet car and roving refreshment cart services are available at nominal costs. Whichever service you choose, you're in for a moving experience!

The Eurostar passenger train departs from London's Waterloo International Eurostar Terminal and arrives at Paris' Gare du Nord in non-stop comfort. The jaunt, which used to take seven hours, now only takes three hours. Direct service is also available from London to Brussels in just over three hours.

Le Shuttle trains transport cars and trucks across the English Channel. The trip from the Folkestone, England, terminal to the Calais, France, terminal will take under an hour. Travelers drive their cars into the enclosed rail cars, where passengers ride in air-conditioned comfort.

Eurostar Passenger Timetable

Given the frequency of rail service and the speed of travel, it's easy to see how a "quick-trip" to Paris, Brussels, or any Continental destination can be accomplished. To purchase Eurostar tickets, telephone (800) 722–7151, fax (614) 764–0711 or visit **http://www.eurail.com/eurostar**.

London to Paris			Paris to London		
Depart	**Arrive**	**Notes**	**Depart**	**Arrive**	**Notes**
0453	0923	(6)(10)	0637	0846	(3)(8)
0453	0917	(7)(10)	0710	0909	(4)(8)
0619	1023	(2)(8)(10)	0716	0909	(3)
0723	1123	(2)(10)	0807	1030	(5)(8)(10)
0810	1223	(5)(10)	0813	1013	(2)(10)
0823	1223	(2)(10)	0910	1109	(2)(9)
0853	1253	(2)(9)	1019	1213	(2)
0957	1353	(11)	1019	1230	(5)
1010	1417	(5)	1143	1343	(2)(9)
1023	1417	(2)	1143	1347	(5)(9)
1157	1556	(8)	1304	1526	(2)(8)(10)
1253	1653	(10)	1304	1526	(5)(8)(10)
1357	1756		1416	1609	(11)
1510	1923	(5)(8)	1519	1713	
1523	1923	(2)(8)	1607	1813	(8)(10)
1623	2029	(9)(10)	1710	1913	(10)
1653	2056	(5)(10)	1818	2013	
1715	2117	(3)	1919	2113	(1)
1723	2117	(5)	1934	2139	(5)(9)(10)
1748	2153	(2)(8)	2007	2213	(9)(10)
1753	2153	(5)(8)	2049	2243	(5)
1853	2253	(2)(10)	2113	2316	(11)
1853	2247	(5)			
1923	2323	(5)(10)			

London to Brussels			Brussels to London		
Depart	**Arrive**	**Notes**	**Depart**	**Arrive**	**Notes**
0653	1110	(2)(9)(10)	0731	0943	(2)(9)
0827	1244	(2)(9)(10)	0827	1043	(9)(10)
0914	1344	(5)(9)(10)	1031	1247	(9)
1027	1438	(2)(9)	1231	1447	(9)
1214	1644	(5)(9)(10)	1528	1743	(9)(10)
1410	1834	(5)(9)	1722	1939	(9)(10)
1423	1834	(2)(9)	1827	2043	(2)(9)(10)
1719	2138	(3)	1927	2143	(5)(9)(10)
1723	2138	(4)(10)			
1827	2245	(9)(10)			
1927	2343	(5)(10)			

Reservations are mandatory.

Times listed are daily unless otherwise noted. *Note:* 1997 schedules not available at press time. Schedule reflects change in time zone between Britain and the Continent.

(1) No service on Saturday
(2) No service on Sunday
(3) No service on Saturday or Sunday
(4) Saturday service only
(5) Sunday service only
(6) Monday service only

(7) Tuesday to Friday service only
(8) Train stops at Calais-Frethun
(9) Train stops at Lille Europe
(10) Train stops at Ashford
(11) Friday service only

Stena Line

Stena Line services on the English Channel are one class only; both first-and second-class accommodations, however, are available on the boat trains between London and Dover. The BritRail Pass is accepted for the rail portion of the journey from London to the port. Separate tickets, however, must be purchased for the sea portion. These tickets are available at the ticket offices of London rail stations or at the Stena Line Travel Centre at the head of platform 2 in the Victoria Station. Seat reservations are advisable throughout the year for the boat trains departing from this station. The term *boat train* applies to those trains departing from Victoria Station for direct connection at Dover's Western Docks with Stena ferries crossing to the French port of Calais.

Hoverspeed's SeaCat

Boat trains go directly to the pier. Boat trains going to the port of Folkestone for Hoverspeed SeaCat services do not stop at Folkestone's Central Station. Regular train service is available to Dover, terminating at Dover Priory (Dover's main station), and to Folkestone, where trains call at Folkestone Central but not at Folkestone Harbor. Due to the myriad of sailings to the Continent, we suggest that you check with the Stena Line Travel Centre at the head of platform 2 in the Victoria Station for additional information, reservations, and current schedules.

Aboard a SeaCat, you get the sensation of traveling in a wide-body jet airplane. You can settle into an aircraft-style seat; or you can stroll around the cabin, which is four times wider than the largest jumbo jet; or you can watch the captain and the crew through windows just behind the bridge as they guide the ship across the busy English Channel at a cruising speed of 35 knots. Passengers are advised of the SeaCat's safety and emergency procedures by a video demonstration quite similar to the way that such briefings are now conducted on transatlantic aircraft. But that is where the comparison ends!

A SeaCat vessel is 242 feet in length with a beam of 85 feet. It can carry 450 passengers and 80 vehicles on a separate car deck. It is powered by four diesel engines housed in the vessel's side hulls that generate jets of water for steering and for propulsion at speeds of up to 42 knots, making it the world's fastest passenger ferry. Known as a wave-piercing catamaran, it has a narrow hull that is designed to pass through waves rather than ride over them. In 1990, the Hoverspeed *Great Britain* earned its place in history by making the quickest crossing of the Atlantic by a passenger ship since 1952. This record-breaking voyage took just 3 days, 7 hours, and 52 minutes at an average speed of 36.6 knots. It also holds the record for the fastest crossing of the English Channel by a passenger ship.

Because the cabin of the SeaCat is on flexible mounts and the engines are positioned down in the side hulls away from the passenger area, the levels of noise and vibration are greatly reduced. The stylish interior is more like an airliner than a ferry boat. You can stretch your legs by taking a stroll on deck and watch the waves whiz by, pick up a sandwich in the snack bar, or enjoy a drink in the panoramic stern bar. A duty-free shop is also available to help you stock up on bargains.

What we found most amazing about the SeaCat was its maneuverability, which is made possible by having steering and reversing controls on waterjets fitted on both outboard hulls of the craft. On the evening prior to our crossing to Boulogne, we observed our SeaCat arriving in the harbor in Folkestone, where it turned about on its own length and then docked *sideways!* This same maneuver was repeated as we landed in Boulogne the following day. Together with fast check-in, boarding, and disembarkment procedures, the SeaCat's maneuverability adds up to an enjoyable, high-speed crossing of the English Channel.

Even with the opening of the English Channel Tunnel, Britain's ferry operators are optimistic about what the future holds in store for them. We are of the opinion that with watercraft like the SeaCat and the Stena Lynx—and even bigger ones are on the drawing board—crossing the Channel by ship will always remain a delightful alternative.

Choosing a Channel Crossing

Since there are various ways of crossing the English Channel and the North Sea en route to Europe, which one should you select? The fastest route from London to Paris or Brussels is through the tunnel *under* the Channel, utilizing the Eurostar passenger services departing London's Waterloo International Eurostar Terminal.

For those who prefer to skim *over* the channel rather than *under* it, the fastest means of crossing the English Channel for direct rail connections between London and Paris is by Hoverspeed's Hovercraft or Stena Lynx catamaran. If time permits, however, you may want to select a Stena Line crossing by regular displacement vessel. The ultra-modern fleet of Stena Line ferries plies the waters between England and the French port of Calais in an elapsed time of one hour and thirty minutes, compared to the thirty-five minute crossing aboard a hovercraft. or the forty-five minute journey by Stena Lynx catamaran. The slower crossing provides more time for shopping in the ship's duty-free store, however, and time to enjoy a leisurely meal as well.

As previously described, London to Paris by Stena Line ferry takes you from London's Victoria Station to Dover by special boat train right to the dock. After the crossing, a French National Railroads' train will be waiting in Calais for you to continue your journey on to Paris. You will arrive in the Gare du Nord (North Station) of Paris approximately three hours after you reach the French port.

Other Crossings

Ramsgate–Oostende. Oostende Lines the Belgian marine services of Regie des Transports Maritime [R.T.M.], in conjunction with Sally Ferries, cross between Ramsgate and the Belgian port of Oostende with train service connecting with Brussels and Köln (Cologne). A Jetfoil service is also available on this route. A supplementary fare of approximately $12 U.S. is payable for travel by Jetfoil. The ferries and the Jetfoil are one class only; connecting rail services are both first and second class.

Train departures for the boat ferries and Jetfoil leave from London's Victoria Station. Jetfoil passengers must report to the Jetfoil Lounge at track 14 for a boarding card at least twenty minutes before train departure. This route is the most direct sea connection with Brussels. By rail and Jetfoil, the average time between London's Victoria Station and Brussels Midi (South) Station is five hours; travel by the rail and ship combination requires eight hours plus forty minutes.

Newhaven–Dieppe. If you are looking for an alternate route between Britain and France, Stena Line ship and Stena Lynx catamaran services are available from the English port of Newhaven, east of Brighton, to the maritime terminal of Dieppe in France. The sea route is seventy-one miles and the crossing takes four hours by ship and two hours fifteen minutes by catamaran. Night crossings are made throughout the year.

If the English Channel is not in a huffy mood, this can be a very pleasant crossing. Victoria Station is the point of departure from London. The boat train calls at Gatwick Airport en route to the Newhaven harbor. The French National Railroads' express-train service between Dieppe and Paris takes slightly more than two hours. St. Lazare is the rail terminal in Paris. The entire trip takes approximately nine hours.

Harwich–Hook of Holland. This is an excellent routing for travelers ranging between Britain and the Netherlands by sea. Ships are provided by Stena Line. It is the most direct sea link between London and Amsterdam. Convenient connections may also be made from the Hook of Holland (Hoek Van Holland) to Brussels, Belgium.

Both day and night crossings are available on this route. Sleeping accommodations aboard begin at modest prices. Reservations for the night crossings are obligatory and should be made well in advance of your journey. Departure out of London is from the Liverpool Street Station.

Many famous express trains utilize this North Sea crossing as well as regular through-train service to Belgium, Germany, Russia, and Switzerland. If you are looking for international intrigue, you'll be most likely to find it on the Harwich-Hook of Holland crossing. Running between the Liverpool Street Station and the Harwich harbor takes one hour and twenty minutes. Once aboard, the daytime crossing is completed in six hours and thirty minutes; passage at night requires up to eight hours and thirty minutes

Portsmouth–Cherbourg/Le Havre. Trains depart London's Waterloo Station and arrive in Portsmouth Harbor rail station in about one hour, thirty minutes. P.&O. European Ferries provide ship services. Arriving in Portsmouth, passengers are advised to use the bus service between the Portsmouth Continental Ferry Port and the Portsmouth Harbor rail station. The crossing from Portsmouth to Cherbourg takes four hours and forty-five minutes (eight hours, thirty minutes to nine hours forty-five minutes at night); the sailing to Le Havre requires five hours and forty-five minutes (seven to nine hours at night). Both routes to the French capital pass through Normandy, where the Allies stormed ashore on 6 June 1943 in the invasion of Hitler's "Fortress Europe."

Ramsgate–Dunkerque. After departing from Ramsgate Harbor at the most easterly point of Kent County in England, the ferries operated by the Sally Ferries provide two and one-half hours at sea (where the English Channel meets the North Sea) before docking at Dunkerque, the French port where German military forces held off the Allies throughout World War II until VE Day on 9 May 1945. After going ashore, you might want to roam the restored streets of Dunkerque before proceeding on to Paris, Brussels, or connections for other points.

Note: BritRail Passes are not accepted by Stena Line, Hoverspeed, or any of the privately owned shipping companies operating on either the English Channel or the North Sea. In addition, BritRail Passes cannot be utilized for rail travel in Continental Europe. Point-to-point tickets must be purchased for all sea voyages and continuing rail travel once you have departed Britain. If you hold a Eurailpass, you may have it validated at the rail station of the European port upon arrival and then continue your rail trip without the inconvenience of having to purchase point-to-point tickets. Holders of BritRail, Eurail, or Europass also receive discounted fares on Eurostar services.

9 CROSSING THE IRISH SEA

Many of the ferry crossings on the Continent of Europe involve loading the passenger-rail cars aboard the ferry. When this occurs, the passengers need not disembark. But at all ferry ports in Britain, passengers are required to leave the train and board the ferry. Then they board another train after landing. You will find that this change of transportation mode is no great hardship. In fact, it can be a very enjoyable experience by including drinks and dinner aboard the ferry, followed by a chat with fellow passengers. The salon of a ferry is a good place for meeting people. Everyone has a common interest in travel, and everyone is going to the same destination.

Crossing the Irish Sea is very much like crossing the English Channel by ferry, except you cannot forward your luggage on to the Republic of Ireland. What you take is what you carry. So again, adhere to our admonition to "go lightly" when it comes to luggage. Porter service is almost nonexistent at the marine terminals, except by prearrangement. It is best not to expect porter service. Furthermore, the trolleys (baggage carts) found in the majority of British rail stations are missing at the piers because their use is impractical on the sloping ramps and gangways used for access to the vessels.

When you visit Ireland, keep in mind that the Republic of Ireland and Northern Ireland are two separate political states. Northern Ireland is a part of the U.K., while the republic is independent. There are no customs to contend with when arriving in Northern Ireland from England, Scotland, or Wales. On the other hand, customs formalities entering the Republic of Ireland should present no problem for the bona fide traveler. The efficient "declare" or "nothing-to-declare" system is used by Irish Customs.

Duty-free shops are operated on all of the shipping lines crossing the Irish Sea between Britain and the Republic of Ireland. Crossing times are adequate enough to permit shopping at leisure. Except for tobacco and alcoholic beverages, however, there are few bargains. Check with the salespersons to be certain that you are not exceeding the import limits. Duty payments on excesses can be stiff. Tax-free shops are not available on routes to Northern Ireland.

BritRail + Ireland Pass covers the complete network of trains in England, Scotland, Wales, Northern Ireland, and Ireland (Republic of). The pass also includes a round trip on the Stena Line between Holyhead and Dun Laoghaire, Fishguard and Rosslare or Stranraer and Belfast via ship, HSS (High Speed Sea service), or Stena Lynx Catamaran. The new HSS ships cruise between Dun Laoghaire and Belfast at twice the speed of conventional ships. If you prefer a more leisurely cruise, choose Stena's comfortable conventional ship.

Choose five or ten days of travel to be completed within one month in first or standard class.

Sea Links to Ireland

Stranraer–Belfast. Stena Line's HSS (High Speed Sea Service) ferry or catamaran and Hoverspeed's SeaCat (catamaran) cross from England to Northern Ireland (Belfast) in only one hour, thirty minutes. The SeaCat departs from Stranraer West Pier and arrives at Belfast Donegall Quay. Conventional ship service takes three hours. Food and beverage services are available aboard. No customs formalities for entering Northern Ireland from Scotland. No tax-free shops aboard.

Train connections from London through Euston Station with overnight sleeper service are available between London and Stranraer. First- and second-class accommodations are available aboard ship. Access to England, Scotland, and Wales by rail is through Glasgow. Direct train service from the Glasgow Central Station to Stranraer Harbor takes two hours, six minutes. Note that BritRail Passes are not accepted on trains in Ireland unless you have purchased the BritRail Pass + Ireland option.

Holyhead–Dun Laoghaire. This crossing is from Holyhead in Wales to Dun Laoghaire (a suburb of Dublin) in Ireland. The elapsed time from port to port is three hours, thirty minutes. Stena Lynx catamaran service is also available, taking only one hour, thirty minutes. Food and beverage services are available aboard the ferries, and tax-free shops are open during the crossing. Customs formalities are observed upon disembarkation. Train connections from London's Euston Station to Holyhead provide through-coach and sleeper accommodations. The ferries offer first- and second-class accommodations.

Connections from the port at Dun Laoghaire into Dublin can be made by train, city bus, or taxi. All of these transportation modes are available at the pier. Eurailpass and BritRail Pass + Ireland option are accepted on the trains of the Republic of Ireland; the BritRail Classic and Flexipass, however are not.

Fishguard–Rosslare. This Stena Line ferry crossing is recommended for train travelers bound for Cork, Killarney, and the Shannon Airport. Conventional ship service takes about three hours, thirty minutes; Stena Lynx catamaran service takes only one hour, thirty minutes. Food, beverages, and tax-free shops are available during the voyage. Customs formalities are observed at disembarkation.

Train connections from London's Paddington Station to Fishguard take about four hours (daytime service only); train time from Rosslare Harbor into Dublin is three hours; to Limerick for connections to Shannon Airport, three hours, twenty-five minutes; and transportation time from Limerick to Shannon Airport is about forty-five minutes.

SAILING TO THE CONTINENT

One-way Fares (1996) in U.S. Dollars. 1997 rates not available at press time. Exact rates will be quoted at time of booking.

From London To:	Services Per Day	Approx. Journey Time (hrs)	One-Way Fares First	Standard
Amsterdam† (via Hook of Holland)	2	11-13	$139	$118
Boulogne* (catamaran)	2	3	87	72
Brussels* (via Oostende)	3	8	99	77
Brussels††* (by jetfoil)	3	5½	108	86
Calais* (ship)	2	4	84	69
Dieppe*	2	5½	71	60
Hook of Holland†	2	8-10	112	100
Oostende* (ship)	3	6	77	62
Oostende††* (jetfoil)	3	3½	86	71
Paris via Calais* (ship)	2	10	180	135
Paris via Dieppe*	2	9½	164	99
Paris* (by catamaran/hovercraft)	2	6½	183	140
Sea Crossing Only To:				
Boulogne/Calais* (catamaran)	31	50 min		39
Calais	18	1½-1¾		38
Oostende* (ship)	3	4		29
Oostende††* (jetfoil)	3	1½		38
Dieppe	2	4		30
Hook of Holland†	2	6-8		70

Notes: Round trip: Double one-way fares. All prices subject to change. Reservations required on all services during peak travel periods $5.00 per person each journey. Use of TGV in France (Calais to Paris) cuts one hour from the journey and adds $96 (first class) or $66 (second class).

*   One-class ship or catamaran or Jetfoil

** First-class train and ship

†   Sleeping berth and cabin reservations are essential on Harwich-Hook of Holland overnight service. Cancellation penalty 15%.

†† Via Oostende, both ship and Jetfoil service available; approximately $12 supplement for Jetfoil service. Reservations required.

SAILING TO IRELAND

From London To:	Services Per Day	Approx. Journey Time (hrs)	One-Way Fares First	Standard
DLE (via Holyhead)	2	10	$107	$83
Rosslare (via Fishguard)	2	9	107	83
Larne (via Glasgow/Stranraer)	1	11	155	117
Sea Crossings Only To:				
Holyhead-Dun Laoghaire	4	5	123	93
Fishguard-Rosslare	2	3½		34
Stranraer-Larne	9	2¼		40

Notes: Round-trip: Double one-way fare. Special fares available on some routes upon request. One class on ship. Reservations ($5.00 per person per journey) are required for all port-to-port-only journeys, and for through journeys during peak travel periods. Sleeping berths/cabins available on some overnight services.

Big Ben, London's most famous landmark, stands in the clock tower of the Houses of Parliament (officially known as the Palace of Westminster). Actually, it's the bell, not the clock, that is called Big Ben. The thirteen and one-half-ton bell's name honors Sir Ben Hall, Commissioner of Works in 1858.

10 LONDON

Exploring London is a bit like wandering through an old but still occupied English castle. Vestiges of the past mingle unpretentiously with the latest of modern innovations, and together they provide a provocative yet pleasant place.

London is perhaps the most sophisticated tourist city in the world. This is due no doubt to the calm, cordial demeanor of Londoners themselves, with their air of unruffled understatement often illustrated by the common use of the ambiguous word *quite*. It is a city as at ease with crowds; its cacophony of pageantry, its nuances, accents, and traditions separate Europe's largest metropolis into village-like neighborhoods.

Central London is just that, the most central part of the city located on the river Thames, about 40 miles from the estuary to the North Sea and bounded by the Underground Circle Line.

"The City" is the oldest section of Central London. It is marked by first-century Roman walls; the Tower Bridge and infamous Tower of London; St. Paul's Cathedral, the third largest in the world; and today's Old Bailey law corridor and the heart of the city's finance and trade.

The newer section, only about 1,000 years old, is "The City of Westminster," with famous sites such as the Palace of Westminster, Westminster Abbey, Buckingham Palace, and the Houses of Parliament. Central London also includes The Royal Parks, Piccadilly Circus, Trafalgar Square, Covent Garden, and Soho.

Throughout and surrounding Central London are thirty-two boroughs that comprise the city. (Thirty-three if you include "The City," which has been a completely separate entity since the eleventh century.) Chelsea is a former haven for punk rockers, "beatniks," and artists, and is full of expensive flats; the Southwest; The East End, is known for its ever-distinguishable Cockney accent and menacing memories of Jack-the-Ripper; Regent's Park, in the Northwest, houses an open-air amphitheater and London's famous zoo; you also can collect Sherlock Holmes memorabilia and attend Madame Tussaud's collection of celebrities in wax in Regent's Park.

These areas are depicted with postal designations that appear with their addresses (e.g., Buckingham Palace SW1) and on maps and signposts. These designations enable the tourist to more easily identify and distinguish between regions, especially since the streets follow no particular pattern.

First-time visitors to London should consider taking an introductory guided tour—a convenient way to become familiar with various sections of the city. London Coaches operates "The Original London Sightseeing Tour," which runs every fifteen minutes in summer and every thirty minutes in winter. It takes about one and one-half hours to complete and provides tourists with a glimpse of the city's major historic and contemporary attractions with commentary in several languages. The cost is about $15 (U.S.) for adults and $8 for children. Board the tour at Piccadilly Circus, Victoria, and Baker Street Underground Station locations.

Once familiar with basic sectors of the city, adventurous travelers may access the Underground, known colloquially as "the Tube." The Tube is a mammoth yet truly user-friendly underground train system comprised of ten basic lines that provide speedy travel from 0530-midnight Monday-Saturday and 0730-2330 on Sunday. Zones determine the fares, with a standard fare charged when traveling anywhere within a zone. Fares increase as you move from zone to zone. If you plan to travel the Tube more than once a day, take advantage of the variety of passes available for access on the trains and buses as well. Consult large maps posted in any station for the system you require, and feel free to consult ticket agents and line supervisors who are usually courteous and helpful, even allowing you through to the correct system when you have inadvertently entered the wrong zone.

River tours are a picturesque way to acquaint yourself with London. The tours provide views of historic and modern sites often not discernible within the confines of city streets. From the piers at Westminster, Charing Cross, and the Tower of London, various tours proceed eastward to destinations such as Greenwich, renowned as the timekeeper of the world and for its magnificent buildings. Sir Christopher Wren (architect of St. Paul's Cathedral) designed what is now the Greenwich Royal Naval College and Flamsteed, the original Royal Observatory.

Before you depart from the United States, contact the British Tourist Authority for free tour information and literature about London. The New York office of the BTA is located at 551 Fifth Avenue, New York NY 10176–0799; (212)–986–2200; world wide web http://www.bta.org.uk.

The British Travel Centre, located at 12 Lower Regent Street SW1, London, also provides a slew of information regarding travel, accommodations, events, and entertainment in London and throughout Great Britain, as well as a comprehensive booking service for theater tickets, sightseeing tours, and rail tickets within the same building.

The London Tourist Board has recently developed "VisitorCall," a telephone guide to London with the most up-to-date information about events and information about the city. When in London, simply dial 0839 123 plus the last three numbers as shown below:

400 – What's on this week
401 – What's on during the next three months

The bookings hotline can be accessed by dialing (0171) 824–8844. The Metropolitan Office Forecast for Greater London Weather may be reached at 0839–500–951.

Melding the old with the new attractions may be the best way to experience London on a short-term basis. On the traditional museum circuit, the British Museum and the National Gallery feature collections of archeology and prints and a Western art collection from the thirteenth to the twentieth centuries, respectively, and have free admission.

The famous Victoria and Albert Museum, informally called the "V & A", is considered the finest decorative arts museum in the world and includes the world's most exquisite collections of jewelry, furniture, and oriental carpets. The new Jewish Museum in the refurbished Raymond Burton House on Albert Street NW1 houses a unique collection of antiques illustrating Jewish history.

Shopping can be quite traditional—even stuffy—at Harrod's in Knightsbridge, where the royals shop. You will find exclusive leathergoods at Asprey's, and can seek out rare antiques at Sotheby's, on Bond Street. Oxford Street and Regent Street shopping is the most diverse, and the most crowded, in London, featuring famous London department stores Selfridges and Marks & Spencer and traditional British fare at Aquascutum, Austin Reed, and Burberry.

The Trocadero, near Piccadilly Circus, is a new two-acre enclosed entertainment, shopping, and restaurant complex. The Emaginator features two highly technical twenty-four seat cinemas that provide the exhilarating sensations of moving objects, such as a rocket race through space or a runaway truck. Planet Hollywood, also at the Trocadero, provides Hollywood memorabilia and an occasional appearance by celebrities along with a variety of the newest cuisine.

Though British taste is considered impeccable and immutable, their taste buds are moving along rather rapidly. Ten years ago, visitors to London might have listed English food as overcooked and boring, according to Lawrence Isaacson, Director of London's Tourist Board and one of the city's top restaurateurs. "Now we have more than 5,500 restaurants," which he explained includes pubs with food, "with fifty different cuisines."

"You could eat a different meal every day for thirty years," Isaacson said, adding "we're much more exciting than Paris." Isaacson attributes the dramatic change to the rise of economic standards. "We have more households with two wage earners and more people traveling abroad and experimenting with different foods. And there is an appreciable rise in fine, young British chefs," Isaacson explained, "with great expectations who are not departing for the Continent." The result has been adventurous foods in glamorous settings.

Isaacson's Soho Soho ground-floor café and upstairs formal dining room on Frith Street in Soho exemplifies the new food mood. The food here is freshly prepared, light fare—salad and omelets with cheeses—in a simple decor of clay tile floors and vivid art work. Such gourmet cafes and bistros set the trend for the new Soho and West Soho, with Carnaby Street at its center. Both areas are bedecked with fashionable boutiques, bookstores, craft shops, and expensive private clubs.

Nearby is the Piazza near the Covent Garden Underground Station. The Piazza replaced the Covent Garden flower and vegetable market, which was in age-old times the convent gardens of the Abbey at St. Peter at Westminster. The new Covent Garden is a boisterous compound of antiques, clothing, and craft stores, amid a plethora of indoor and outdoor cafes, pubs, eateries, and clubs.

The manicured gardens and pastoral grounds within London's vast Royal

London taxi stands briefly in front of Eros Fountain in the center of London's most celebrated traffic circle, Piccadilly Circus. The steps of the fountain were at one time the "marketplace" of London's flower sellers. Officially, the fountain is a memorial to the philanthropist Lord Shaftesbury.

Parks, once the hunting and recreational property of the Royal Family, now serve the people of London and their guests with something few mega-capitals have—quiet. The lake of St. James is so serene that it is a breeding ground for birds. Boats cruise the Serpentine River in huge Hyde Park, where there is room for riding trails and open-air concerts.

Summer Shakespeare festivals amid the roses of Queen Mary's Garden provide the solace of less-hurried times in Regent's Park, where lovers still glide through the canals in small, oar-operated boats.

London–At Your Service

Not unlike butlers on the BBC's (British Broadcasting Corporation) favorite situation comedies, service is an art—not an act—in Britain. You can expect helpful, courteous attention from professional tourist officials to be the norm.

The London Tourist Board provides visitors with detailed information about hotel accommodations, points of interest around the city, and their new twenty-four-hour information line on using London's extensive transport network of Underground, bus, and rail services.

London Tourist Board locations at your service:

Victoria Station: Located in the forecourt on the streetside outside platform 15. Operates 0800-1900 daily April-October; November-March, 0800-1800 Monday-Saturday and Sunday 0900-1600.

Liverpool Street Station: Located at the Underground Station Concourse. Open Monday-Friday 0800-1800; Saturday and Sunday 0845-1730.

Heathrow Airport: Located at the bottom of the passenger ramp in the concourse leading to the Underground station in Terminal 2. April-September, open Monday-Saturday 0800-1830 and Sunday 0800-1800; September-March 0800-1800 daily.

Selfridges Department Store: Located in the Oxford Street store's basement service arcade. Open during regular store hours.

The London Tourist Board also operates a telephone accommodations and tours reservations service for credit-card holders only Monday-Friday 0930-1730. Contact by telephone: 0171 824-8844.

Arriving and Departing by Air

London's Heathrow and Gatwick airports are America's primary gateways, with Stansted International Airport and London City and Luton airports primarily providing service within Continental Europe and Great Britain.

Heathrow Airport connects with Central London using the Underground (the "Tube") via the Piccadilly Line with access to all terminals. (Terminal 4 has a separate station. Tube service to Piccadilly Circus runs about every ten minutes from approximately 0545-0020 Monday through Saturday; Sundays 0700 to about 2325. The journey takes about forty-five minutes and costs about £3.20. The airport information number is 0181-759-4321; London Transport information, 0171–222–1234.

"Airbus" transportation to Heathrow is available aboard the A1 to and from Victoria Station and the A2 to and from Russell Square. Adult fare is £6 single, £10 return. Depending on the departure terminal, the Heathrow–Victoria Station journey time may be forty-five to ninety minutes. The A1-Victoria Station airbus departs every thirty minutes from about 0830-2045, with occasional late afternoon lapses.

The A1 airbus also makes stops at Hyde Park Corner Stop L, at Harrods, and three stops on the Cromwell Road—the Forum Hotel, the Swallow International, and near the junction of Earl's Court Road.

Depending on the departure terminal, the Heathrow–Russell Square run may take between an hour and an hour and a half. The A2-Russell Square airbus departs approximately every thirty minutes from 0540 to 2030. Stops are also made near the Underground stations of: Euston, Great Portland Street, Baker Street, Marble Arch, Lancaster Gate, Paddington, Queensway, Notting Hill Gate, and Holland Park. Some buses also call at King's Cross Station.

Golden Tours provides airport shuttle service from hotels direct to any Heathrow terminal at a cost of £10 per person. Book by calling 0171-233-9050. Heathrow Information Desk: 0181–759–4321

Gatwick Airport, about 27 miles south of London, provides easy-to-access, efficient, and swift train service into London aboard the Gatwick Express. The express train departs Gatwick's South Terminal rail station every fifteen minutes from 0530-2000 and then every thirty minutes until 2300.

Victoria Station Gatwick Express departures from London to the airport follow the same schedule with additional early departure times of 0430 and 0500. A single fare aboard the Gatwick Express is £8.90.

For train transportation to and from Gatwick during the remaining night hours, contact South Central trains, which run an hourly night service. Information on this or the Gatwick Express is available through British Rail in London at 0171–28–5100. Gatwick Express tickets may be purchased in advance in the U.S. by calling (800) 722–7151.

Flightline 777 coaches also provide transportation to and from London's Victoria Station and Gatwick Airport. Coaches run about every hour from 0725 to 1925. In addition, there are 0630, 2125, and 2325 departures from Victoria Station. The fare is £7.50 for a single, £11 return. To confirm times, phone 0181-668-7261 in London.

Golden Tours provides minibus service to and from your hotel to the Gatwick Express at Victoria Station, with porterage at both London and air-

London's Tower Bridge has remained in constant service since its construction between 1886 and 1894. The huge bascule sections of the drawbridge remain in operation, and the footbridge at the top is a major tourist attraction.

port stations and reserved seating aboard the train for £16 per person per trip. You can contact Golden Tours on 0171-233-9050.

Gatwick Airport Information Desk: 01293-535353.

Stansted Airport, 31 miles northeast of London, has fast and frequent links to London via British rail's Stansted Express service. Departures from the airport to London's Liverpool Street Station are daily every thirty minutes from 0600 to midnight. Liverpool Street Station departures to the airport are every thirty minutes Monday-Friday from 0530-2300, with the first Saturday departures at 0630 and the first Sunday ones at 0700. One-way fare is £9.80.

Stansted Information Desk: 01279-680-5100.

London's Rail Stations

London is a hub of rail travel for the Western world and a great introduction to the wonders of European train travel. With speed, little expense, and relative comfort, you have the opportunity to access some of the most stimulating sights of one of the world's most beautiful cities.

London's fifteen primary rail stations provide an abundance of travel opportunities within the city, to other cities, and to country and seasides. For the readers of *Britain by BritRail*, eight of these stations are well worth knowing:

Victoria Station is a sightseeing adventure in itself, with its arcade of shops, eateries, and currency exchange venues and as a hub of international travel from Gatwick and various airports. The south and southeast of England are most easily accessed from here. So is the Continent of Europe, where more than two million travelers are in transit through Victoria arranging sea-rail links to Belgium and France. The International Rail Centre is located to the left of platforms 3 and 4.

Euston Station is closely grouped with St. Pancras and King's Cross stations for rail services to England's Midlands, northern England, and Scotland. It serves as the terminal for Stena Line ship and ferry services to Belfast via Stranraer and to Dublin via Holyhead. It is also the London departure point for trains to Glasgow. The Travel Centre is open year-round Monday-Saturday 0700-2330 and Sunday 0800-2330. Waiting rooms, restaurants, and other conveniences are located on the far side of the station hall from the Travel Centre.

St. Pancras Station is the departure point for *Britain by BritRail's* day excursions to St. Albans, Nottingham, and Sheffield. The station is undergoing renovation to provide regional Eurostar passenger service from Glasgow, Edinburgh, Manchester, and Birmingham to Paris and Brussels via the Channel Tunnel. Directional signs for the Euston and King's Cross stations, as well as the London Underground, are prominent throughout the station.

Charing Cross Station is London's rail terminal for direct train service to

Folkestone, Canterbury, Hastings, Ramsgate, Dover, and other ports for Stena Sealink and Hoverspeed services.

King's Cross Station is the London terminal for InterCity 225 train service to Aberdeen and Edinburgh. The Travel Centre is open 0700-2300 daily. Full information, reservations, and advance ticketing services are available. Outside the station, to the left, a money exchange service is available.

Paddington Station serves the west with InterCity service through Plymouth to Penzance. It is also the London terminal for Stena Sealink services to Ireland via Fishguard and Rosslare. The Travel Centre is located in front of platforms 1 and 2 and operates 0800-2130 Monday-Saturday and 0900-2000 Sunday.

Liverpool Street Station, one of the oldest rail terminals in London, has undergone extensive renovation. The Underground (London Transport) Travel & Tourist Centre is in front of tracks 4 and 5 directly behind the stairs.

This station is the gateway for rail and ship traffic between the Netherlands, northern Germany, and Scandinavia. Trains departing Liverpool Street Station bound for that part of Europe proceed to Harwich, where passengers then embark from the Parkeston Quay by ship to Hook of Holland, a small peninsula jutting out into the North Sea. There, trains wait to take them to further destinations such as Amsterdam, Hamburg, Berlin, or the Scandinavian capital cities of Copenhagen, Oslo, and Stockholm. The ship crossing is made in eight hours and thirty minutes.

Waterloo Station is primarily for trains to the south of England, including the Isle of Wight. The Travel Centre is at the end of platforms 15 and 16. It is open 0800-2200 daily. The new **Waterloo International Eurostar Terminal** for service to Paris or Brussels via the Channel tunnel occupies tracks 20 through 24. Eurostar is the passenger service provided by the railways of Britain, Belgium, and France.

Ten to fifteen passenger trains make the daily runs through the "Chunnel," providing tourists and business travelers with quick, efficient travel to London, Paris, and Brussels. Maximum speed through the tunnel is 100 mph and 186 mph on the Continent. For more detailed Eurostar information, please see the introductory section of this edition.

Day Excursions from London

After you have seen London, it is time to see more of this wonderful country. You cannot get to know the country without experiencing the charms of its other cities and seeing first-hand the loveliness of the rural areas that separate them. There is no better way to do that than aboard a train, viewing the passing scene and conversing with the British themselves.

Like the road builders of Rome, Britain's rail builders laid their tracks leading to London—or, more properly, out of London. London serves as the center of a somewhat lopsided spider web with its radials running east and south to the sea on the short side of the web and the longer extensions running west to Wales and north into Scotland. Thirty-two day excursions from London await your pleasure.

Like a knight of old, perhaps you would prefer to sally forth on a short sortie or two before departing on a crusade. In that case, you will find the Greenwich, Windsor, and St. Albans day excursions to your liking. Ranging southeast out of London, Kent beckons with its towns of Canterbury, Dover, Folkestone, and Ramsgate. Southward, rail trails lead along the English Channel to the port/resort towns of Hastings, Brighton, Portsmouth, and Southampton and to the Isle of Wight.

Having whetted your appetite with the excursions above, you should be ready now to venture farther afield. Everything you plan to see has been there for quite some time—usually at least a century or two—so relax and enjoy your further travels throughout Britain.

West from London, excursions to Salisbury and Stonehenge, Bath, Gloucester, and Cardiff (Wales) await the train travelers. Ready to crusade? Go farther west to the pilgrims' Plymouth or the pirates' Penzance. You may want to make these "out-and-back" visits. If so, make arrangements with your hotel. If you plan to return, pack light and have the hall porter store your bulky luggage. In the heart of England you will find awaiting you excursions to Birmingham, Stratford-upon-Avon, Coventry, Nottingham, Sheffield, Lincoln, and York. From farther west beckons Chester.

Northeast of London is East Anglia, where historic King's Lynn, Bury St. Edmunds, and Ipswich abound in museums and memories of World War II. For academic flavor, visit Cambridge or Oxford, and school-tie types will appreciate Eton—a stone's throw away from Windsor.

LONDON–EDINBURGH TRAIN SERVICE
(First- and standard-class accommodations for all services listed)

DEPART FROM		ARRIVE IN EDINBURGH		
EUSTON	KING'S CROSS	MON–FRI	SAT	SUN
—	0610	1109	1109	—
—	0700	—	1137	—
—	0800	1216	1239	—
0825(R)	—	1428	—	—
—	0830	—	1259	—
—	0900	1342	1336	1445
—	0930	—	1413	—
—	1000	—	1431	1536
—	1030	—	—	1556
—	1030	1451	1451	—
—	1100	1532	1532	1639
—	1200	1625	1625	1724
—	1230	—	1710	1757
—	1300	1725	1739	1823
—	1330	—	—	1857
—	1330	1809	1805	—
—	1400	1823	1829	1924
—	1500	1905	1933	2022
—	1600	2025	2033	2103
—	1700	2114	2133	2157
—	1730	2216	—	—
—	1800	2223	2241	2312
2355(R)*	—	—	—	0635 + 1
2355(R)*	—	0635+1	—	—

Distance: 393 miles/632 km
References: Great Britain Passenger Railway Timetable, Table 26A
Thomas Cook Table 570

High-speed, food service available; reservations recommended for all above-listed trains
(R) Reservations required
* Sleeping cars only

Useful Phone Numbers

Tourist Information Centre	*Train Information*
All Scotland: 0131–332–2433	London: 0171–278–2477
Edinburgh: 0131–557–1700	Edinburgh: 0131–556–2451

LONDON–GLASGOW TRAIN SERVICE
(First- and standard-class accommodations for all services listed)

DEPART FROM		ARRIVE IN GLASGOW CENTRAL		
EUSTON	KING'S CROSS	MON–FRI	SAT	SUN
0620(R)(0610 SAT)	—	1212	1212	—
—	0700	—	1243	—
—	0800	1319	—	—
0840(0830 SAT)	—	1350	1350	—
—	0900	—	1443	—
0940(R)	—	—	—	1615
—	1000	1519	—	1644
1040(R)(1030 SAT)	—	1539	1539	—
—	1100	—	1643	—
—	1200	—	—	1832
1240(R)(1230 SAT)	—	1753	1753	—
—	1300	—	1843	—
—	1330	1919	—	—
—	1400	—	—	2032
1440(R)(1430 SAT)	—	1950	1950	—
—	1500	2015	2043	—
1530(R)	—	—	2114	—
1540(R)	—	2114	—	—
1640	—	—	—	2221
1725	—	2227	—	—
1715	—	—	2227	—
2355(R)*	—	0640 + 1	—	—

Distance: 402 miles/647 km
References: Great Britain Passenger Railway Timetable, Table 26A
            Thomas Cook Table 550

High-speed trains, food service available; reservations recommended for all above-listed trains
(R) Reservation required
* Sleeping cars only

Useful Phone Numbers

Tourist Information Centre	*Train Information*
All Scotland: 0131–332–2433	London: 0171–387–7070
Glasgow: 0141–227–4880	Glasgow: 0141–204–2844

The great Roman bath attracted visitors from all parts of the Roman Empire between the first and fifth centuries. It was constructed around a natural hot spring with waters rising from the ground at 116°. The abbey church tower of Bath looms in the background.

From London . . .

A DAY EXCURSION TO BATH
DISTANCE BY TRAIN: 107 miles (172 km)
AVERAGE TRAIN TIME: 1 hour, 20 minutes

Bath has been in the limelight of social attention during two eras of recorded history—once during the Roman occupation of Britain and again in the eighteenth century when Bath became the "in place" for royalty and other well-to-do's. Development of the only hot spring in Britain is attributed to the Romans soon after the Emperor Claudius invaded the land in A.D. 43.

To the Romans, the city's name was *Aquae Sulis*—literally translated, "the waters of Sul." By the end of the first century, the Romans had established a great bathing facility. The magnificent hot baths were said to have curative powers. Although modern scientists are doubtful of the waters' purported healing properties, there is no doubt that the only hot mineral springs in Britain played a major role in establishing Bath as the "hot spot" for socializing.

The baths made Aquae Sulis famous throughout the empire. Its fame lasted 400 years until the rising sea level and the fall of the Roman Empire brought the city's prosperity to an end. By the end of the seventh century, the city was described as "a ghostly ruin with crumbled masonry fallen into dark pools, overgrown and bird haunted, but still a wondrous sight."

The second revitalization of the city, a cultural one, began in 1705 with the arrival of thirty-one-year-old Richard Nash. Like the Romans, he, too, conquered, but not by force. Nash was Bath's first public relations expert. It was during his "reign" that Queen Anne visited Bath and it again became an elegant and stylish resort for the wealthy. When Nash died at the age of eighty-eight, he had created a kingdom of taste and etiquette over which he reigned as Beau Nash, King of Bath.

Although the hot springs were used again during the Middle Ages, the Roman ruins remained buried even during the times of Beau Nash, when the gilded bronze head of Minerva was uncovered by workmen while digging a sewer in 1727. Although the statues and columns of the present-day Roman bath were added by Victorian restorers, the original bath area still has the lead floor and limestone paving installed by the Romans.

The restoration of Bath's Roman past and the combining of the city's two eras of fame finally began in 1878 when the city engineer, while investigating a water leak, came upon the Roman reservoir and the huge complex of baths that it fed. In other words, someone finally called a plumber.

The Roman baths are one of Britain's major tourist attractions and draw visitors from all points of the globe to their waters. The baths rank a close second to England's number-one attraction, the Tower of London, and are well

BATH—*ROMAN ENGLAND*

A Day Excursion from London

DEPART FROM PADDINGTON STATION	ARRIVE IN BATH SPA STATION	NOTES
0815	0938	(2)
0915	1039	(2)
0930	1115	(3)
0945	1110	(1)
1015	1138	(2)
1030	1210	(3)

(Plus other frequent service)

DEPART FROM BATH SPA STATION	ARRIVE IN PADDINGTON STATION	NOTES
1427	1555	(2)
1512	1655	(3)
1527	1655	(2)
1607	1755	(3)
1627	1750	(2)
1657	1825	(2)(3)
1727	1855	(2)

(Plus other frequent service)

Distance: 107 miles/172 km
References: Great Britain Passenger Railway Timetable, Table 125
           Thomas Cook Table 530

(1) MON–FRI   (3) SUN
(2) MON–SAT

Train Information: 0345–484950
InterCity Services: 0171–262–6767
Bath Tourist Information Centre: 01225–462831

worth the short train ride to see them and the "glory that was Rome"—transposed to England.

The City of Bath abounds in sightseeing opportunities. We suggest that upon arrival in Bath you proceed immediately to the **Bath Tourist Information Centre** located in Abbey Church Yard and let it assist you in your visit. To reach the center on foot, proceed up Manvers Street directly in front of the Bath rail station until you cross North Parade Road. At this point, you will see the Bath Abbey tower to your left. Pass the Abbey on its right side and proceed through the Abbey Church Yard. At the columns, turn left and then take the first right into Bath Street. With the Roman Baths at your back, proceed down Bath Street. The Tourist Information Center will be on the right. Should you want to telephone ahead from the rail station, "ring up" on (01225) 462831. This will connect you with the Inquiries Office of the center.

The center has a wealth of information about the City of Bath and its surroundings. We recommend the pamphlet "39 Leisure Attractions In and Around Bath." This informative piece contains a city map and lists places of interest. Those interested in the story of fashion over the last 400 years will want to visit the Museum of Costume and Assembly Rooms (No. 27 on the pamphlet map), located on Bennett Street. Then, turn left on Bennett Street and proceed to nearby No. 1 Royal Crescent (No. 28 on the pamphlet map) to tour the beautifully restored eighteenth-century town house designed by John Wood.

The Tourist Information Centre sells a wide range of publications to help you get the most out of your stay. Bath has won many awards for its floral displays, and its natural beauty makes a walking tour through the city a real pleasure.

On the subject of tours, you should check to see if you may avail yourself of the Mayor's Corps of Honorary Guides. They conduct guided tours at various times throughout the summer season at no charge. These tours, which depart from the Abbey Church Yard, take approximately one and one-half hours. For advance information, ring up (01225) 477000 and ask to be put through to extension 7785. By the way, we'd appreciate having you mention *Britain by BritRail* when the Guides' office asks who recommended their services. We've been mutual admirers for years.

If you are on a tight schedule, the best sights in the city are cloistered about the Roman baths. The baths and the abbey practically adjoin each other. Upstairs from the baths, you may visit the Pump Room and sample its water. During your visit, take time to touch the worn paving. In that moment, you can recall the glory that was Rome.

Centenary Square. One of the world's great industrial cities, Birmingham has made spectacular strides in developing itself as a beautiful residential city and is no longer England's "ugly duckling." (Courtesy of Birmingham Marketing Partnership)

From London . . .

A DAY EXCURSION TO BIRMINGHAM
DISTANCE BY TRAIN: 119 miles (191 km)
AVERAGE TRAIN TIME: 1 hour, 30 minutes

Birmingham has more canals than Venice. This is rather unusual because Birmingham claims to be Britain's "city at the center." Although it is in the approximate geographic center of the British Isles, it was once the center of England's waterways, which carried most of the nation's industrial traffic. With the development of other forms of transportation, particularly rail, canal transportation dissipated. Most of the canals have been developed into recreation areas with walks, pubs, and restored buildings along their right-of-ways.

For decades, Birmingham has been recognized internationally as one of the world's great industrial cities. Along with the recognition came the image of a smoke-filled, grimy Victorian sprawl of a city. Since World War II, Birmingham has made spectacular progress in developing a beautiful residential city. The center of the city has been completely rebuilt. One of the most striking landmarks marking the city center is the Rotunda, a 250-foot tower. Beneath the tower is the "Bull Ring," the world's first under-one-roof-shopping complex. The multilevel, temperature-controlled Bull-Ring shopping center is linked by subways with major shopping streets of the city. It connects directly with the New Street railway station, where you will arrive from London on your day excursion. If you experience difficulty in gaining your bearings in the vast New Street Station, consult the travel center (train information) in the station's main hall on the extreme far right as you exit from the train platforms.

Something unusual in the development of a modern city is Birmingham's National Exhibition Center. For years the exhibition centers in Continental Europe lured the larger trade fairs. Now Britain has its own showcase at Bickenhill, only one hour and twenty minutes from London by InterCity trains. This modern exhibition-and-conference center is on a 310-acre site readily accessible by rail. Rail connections to the exhibition center may be made through the New Street Station on any trains departing in the direction of London. The stop, Birmingham International, is a short, seventeen-to-twenty-minute ride. Obtain full details from the tourist information center. With 1.2 million square feet of air-conditioned exhibition space in twelve halls, it is by far the largest complex in Britain, and it's still growing. With the opening in 1991 of the International Convention Centre in the city center, Birmingham can compete with any city in Continental Europe.

To reach the **Birmingham tourist information center** at 2 City Arcade, make your way to Corporation Street from the station, and behind the Superstore C&A, you will find the tourist information and ticket shop. The

BIRMINGHAM—*HEART OF ENGLAND*

A Day Excursion from London

DEPART FROM EUSTON STATION	ARRIVE IN BIRMINGHAM NEW STREET STATION	NOTES
0715	0857	(1)
0745	0923	(1)
0815	0957	(1)
0845	1023	(1)
0915	1057	(1)
0935	1123	(3)
0945	1212	(4)
1015	1157	(1)
1035	1223	(3)

(Plus other frequent service)

DEPART FROM BIRMINGHAM NEW STREET STATION	ARRIVE IN EUSTON STATION	NOTES
1345	1555	(4)
1445	1627	(1)
1515	1658	(1)
1545	1727	(1)
1615	1811	(3)
1645	1837	(3)(4)
1715	1902	(1)
1745	1927	(1)
1815	2001	(1)

(Plus other frequent service)

Distance: 119 miles/191 km
References: Great Britain Passenger Railway Timetable, Tables 65 and 68
  Thomas Cook Table 540

(1) MON–FRI (3) SAT
(2) MON–SAT (4) SUN

Train Information: 0121–200–2700
InterCity Services: 0171–387–7070

Birmingham Tourist Information Centre: 0121–643–2514

office is open 0930–1730 Monday through Saturday; closed on Sunday. (The telephone number is 0121–643–2514; fax 0121–616–1038.)

Check with the city tourist information center concerning a sightseeing tour. Despite a massive redevelopment program after World War II, the best of the old has been carefully preserved. The city has an interesting skyline. Historic buildings appear unexpectedly among new ones in a way that emphasizes the quality of both.

Also located in the Victoria Square vicinity and worthy of a visit for its classic elegance and Victorian style is the Town Hall. Opened in 1834, it was designed by Joseph Hansom, the inventor of the Hansom cab. It is the concert hall in which Mendelssohn conducted the first performance of *Elijah* in 1846. Many distinguished musicians have appeared there since, including Sir Edward Elgar.

Other historic buildings in the nearby suburbs include the Sarehole Mill (served by Hall Green Station), an eighteenth-century water mill restored to working order, and Blakesley Hall (Stechford Station), a seventeenth-century timber-framed yeoman's house furnished in period style and with an interesting garden. For rail buffs, a visit to the science museum is a must. It houses the world's oldest steam engine, which was built in 1784, and displays of early machinery, engines, and motorcars. Two and one-half miles north of the city center on Trinity Road is another seventeenth-century gem, Aston Hall (Wilton Station). The magnificent Jacobean mansion was begun in 1618 and took seventeen years to complete.

Birmingham's Civic Centre is a modern contribution to the city's skyline. It includes a repertory theatre and one of the largest and best stocked libraries in Europe, featuring a comprehensive Shakespeare collection. The city's Central Museum and Art Gallery houses paintings and sculpture by Van Gogh, Botticelli, and Gainsborough, and its pre-Raphaelite painting collection is the best.

After all the sightseeing, you may develop a thirst. You came to the right city. Birmingham has long been one of Britain's major brewing centers, and its beer is recommended highly by both locals and visitors. There are plenty of pubs in which you can conduct your own taste tests.

Birmingham is justly proud of its restaurants, which cater to every palate and purse. The city has stylish theater-restaurants with entertainment by international cabaret stars, as well as a wide selection of eateries providing French, Italian, Spanish, Greek, "Balti" cuisine from northern India, Chinese, and traditional English cuisine. There's no reason to leave Birmingham with an empty stomach or an unquenched thirst.

Birmingham has undergone many structural changes in recent years, and, undoubtedly, it is becoming one of Europe's outstanding cities.

Brighton's Royal Pavilion, onion-domed creation and seaside home of England's King George IV, still contains most of its original furnishings. The Banqueting Room is set out with period glass and gold plates in the festive style of an era past.

From London . . .

A DAY EXCURSION TO BRIGHTON
DISTANCE BY TRAIN: 51 miles (82 km)
AVERAGE TRAIN TIME: 55 minutes

Brighton is, and always has been, much more than a traditional seaside resort. Since the earliest days of travel, visitors have been attracted by the resort's unique sense of style and architectural splendor. These special qualities are as strong as ever. But they are only part of a continuing success story that secures Brighton's position as Britain's leading resort area.

Perhaps Brighton would have remained a tiny, humble fishing village originally known as Brighthelmstone if it were not for the efforts of Dr. Richard Russell and the Prince Regent (who later became King George IV). In 1750 Dr. Russell, a Brighton resident, published a book extolling the magical effects of sea air and saltwater. This started a fashionable trend that brought royalty and commoner alike to Brighton. The good doctor prescribed bathing in the sea and drinking a pint and a half of seawater daily as a cure for glandular diseases. Such a prescription, incredible as it seems, must have initiated a whole new series of maladies. Chronicles of that period, however, have failed to note them.

The gifted and wayward Prince Regent first visited Brighton in 1783. Enamored by it all (and well heeled with royal funds), he ordered his Royal Pavilion constructed there. Completed in 1822 from an architectural style taken somewhere east of Suez, it has been termed the most bizarre and exotic palace in all Europe. The Royal Pavilion's ostentatious onion-domed exterior, looking very much like a series of hot-air balloons about to ascend, is only surpassed by its even more amazing interior. It is fully furnished in its original style and open to the public daily. Queen Victoria, not at all amused by the pavilion's architecture, calculatedly was permitting it to fall to ruin when Brighton's citizenry saved it from demolition in 1850. The Royal Pavilion recently underwent a £10 million refurbishment to restore the seaside palace to its original condition.

The city maintains "The Lanes," where you take a step backwards into the old fishing-village days. The buildings in these narrow, twisting passages were fishermen's cottages in the seventeenth century. Today, they are quaint and fascinating antique, jewelry, and high fashion shops; pubs; and cafés.

Part of the changing scene in Brighton has been the introduction during the last twenty years of English-language schools, which attract international students from a score of foreign lands. This youthful input has made it one of the most vibrant resorts in Britain.

Brighton's train terminal was refurbished in 1986. A landmark, the wooden, manually operated dispatch board now rests in York's National Railway

BRIGHTON — *COLORFUL SEASIDE RESORT*

A Day Excursion from London

DEPART FROM VICTORIA STATION	ARRIVE IN BRIGHTON STATION	NOTES
0751	0852	(4)
0832	0947	(1)(3)
0908	0959	(1)
0932	1047	(1)(3)
1008	1059	(1)
1032	1147	(1)(3)
1108	1159	(4)
1132	1247	(3)(4)

(Plus other frequent service)

DEPART FROM BRIGHTON STATION	ARRIVE IN VICTORIA STATION	NOTES
1550	1643	(1)
1600	1716	(1)(3)
1652	1753	(3)
1700	1816	(1)(3)
1750	1841	(1)
1752	1853	(3)
1950	2041	(1)
2000	2116	(1)(3)
2200	2316	(1)(3)

(Plus other frequent service)

Distance: 51 miles/82 km
References: Table 186
                    Thomas Cook Table 502

(1) MON–SAT   (3) SUN
(2) SAT   (4) MON-FRI

Train Information: 01273–206755
InterCity Services: 0171–928–5100
Brighton Tourist Information: 01273–323755

Museum. Its digital replacement is at the head of the train platforms. The station's rail information center is located at the entrance.

Brighton's tourist information center is located in Bartholomew Square next to the Town Hall, about a ten-minute walk from the station. To reach it, walk directly out of the rail station and down Queens Road to the sea. Turn left at that point onto Kings Road. Where Kings Road becomes Grand Junction, turn left again and proceed to the Town Hall and the tourist information center. If you want to call ahead, the telephone number is (0273) 323755. The center is open every day (except Christmas) from 0900 to 1700, with extended evening hours in summer.

In English-style directions, had you denied yourself the turning at Grand Junction, you would have come quickly upon the gates of the Palace Pier, which extends out into the English Channel like a silent sentinel. Constructed in 1899, the pier has been restored and features free entrance, free deck chairs, and free entertainment. It opens daily at 0900. Have a look. It's free—and quite enjoyable.

If you would like to participate in a guided walking tour of Brighton's "Old Town," obtain details from the information center. From June through mid-September, the tours start at the tourist information center. Or you can pick up the Brighton "Mini Guide" at the information center. The "Visitor's Guide" features a town plan showing where to go and what to see.

Brighton's shopping center, including the Churchill Square Pedestrian Precinct, is one of the largest in southern England. The kids will love the Sea Life Centre and Peter Pan's playground. Because of the city's number and variety of shopping areas, Brighton is sometimes referred to as "London by the sea." Swank shops can be found in Brighton's east side and the adjoining Regent Arcade. For the more bizarre, shop the Upper Gardner Street junk market on Saturday mornings and the station car park's "carboot" (junk and antiques) sale on Sunday mornings.

Young and old alike should take a ride along the sea front on the Volks Railway, Britain's first public electric railway. Open daily between Easter and Labor Day, the railway travels along the beach on Madeira Drive to Black Rock. Lacking the speed of the InterCity 125s, the Volks Railway makes up for it with its nostalgia.

Brighton's marina is one of the largest in Europe. Whether you are a boating enthusiast or not, a visit there is well in order. A complete village is now the centerpiece of the marina with an eight-screen cinema, elegant shops, quayside restaurants, and, of course, traditional British pubs on the waterfront. The marina also stages many colorful events, such as boat shows and sailing regattas throughout July and August.

If you're caught up in Brighton's buoyancy, check with the tourist information center for hotel accommodations and catch a morning train back to London.

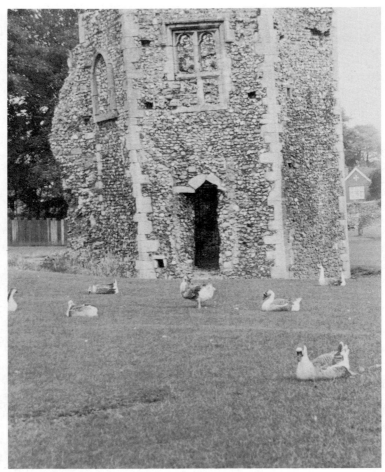

"Fowl play" in front of the dovecote. In 1327 the Abbey of St. Edmunds was badly damaged by townspeople protesting against monastic control. It is said that in 1214, English barons swore before the abbey's high altar to force King John to ratify the Magna Carta—which he did the following year at Runnymede.

From London . . .

A DAY EXCURSION TO BURY ST. EDMUNDS
DISTANCE BY TRAIN: 74 miles (119 km)
AVERAGE TRAIN TIME: 2 hours

For centuries, the East Anglian town of Bury St. Edmunds has been the scene of a fight for freedom of conscience, speech, worship, and the rights of the individual man.

In his *Pickwick Papers,* Charles Dickens described Bury St. Edmunds as " . . . a handsome little town of thriving and cleanly appearance." So it remains today. A monastery was built on the present site of Bury St. Edmunds in A.D. 633. In 903, thirty-four years after King Edmund of East Anglia was killed by the Danes at Hoxne, his body was brought to the town by Bishop Theodred. Thus, the town became known as Bury St. Edmunds. The abbey church was built soon afterwards to honor the memory of the king. For many, Bury St. Edmunds is regarded as one of the most famous towns in all England. It is said that in 1214, barons gathered at the high altar of the abbey to take a solemn oath to force King John to grant a charter of liberties, one of the events leading to the granting of the Magna Carta in 1215.

The town center is most notable for its pleasant Georgian atmosphere, recalling the days when the town was a leading social center within East Anglia. The great abbey was one of the largest in Europe at one time. It was sacked in 1327 by townspeople protesting against monastic control and again in 1381 during the Peasants' Revolt. In 1465, a severe fire damaged the church, which had to be extensively repaired. It was subsequently robbed of much of its stone for use in building materials in the town. A placard on the abbey gate indicates that the gate was destroyed and the abbey badly damaged by the townspeople in 1327 but was rebuilt in 1347.

Across from the abbey gate is the Angel Hotel, more than 500 years old, known for its association with Charles Dickens. His room, No. 15, is preserved exactly as it was more than a century ago. The hotel was originally one of three East Anglian inns on the site. A unique attraction of the Angel Hotel is its tavern room, dating back to 1433—fifty-nine years before Columbus discovered America.

During World War II, Bury St. Edmunds was ringed with American air bases. Today, the Third Air Force of the U.S. Air Force European Command operates RAF Mildenhall, west of Bury St. Edmunds. Visitors are welcome at the base but are advised to contact the base information office or its community relations advisor before proceeding there. The tourist information center can provide complete details.

The **tourist information office** is located at 6 Angel Hill, immediately

BURY ST. EDMUNDS—*MAGNA CARTA*

A Day Excursion from London

DEPART LIVERPOOL STREET STATION	ARRIVE IN IPSWICH	DEPART IPSWICH	ARRIVE BURY ST. EDMUNDS
0625(1)	0732	0806	0835
0830(1)	0935	0943	1014
0830(2)	0943	1025	1056
1030(1)	1135	1212	1249

DEPART BURY ST. EDMUNDS	ARRIVE IPSWICH	DEPART IPSWICH	ARRIVE LIVERPOOL STREET STATION
1405(2)	1437	1445	1554
1522(1)	1554	1630	1754
1722(1)	1759	1845	1954
1705(2)	1737	1745	1855
1846(1)	1925	1945	2054

Distance: 95 miles/153 km
References: Tables 12 and 15
             Thomas Cook Tables 580 and 583

Note: Via Ipswich. Service also available through Cambridge.

(1) MON–SAT
(2) SUN

Bury St. Edmunds Tourist Information Centre
01284–763233
Evenings and Weekends: 01284–764667

opposite the abbey-gate entrance to the ruins of St. Edmunds Abbey, a short distance from the train station. Station personnel will gladly provide directions. The information office is open during the summer months from 0930 to 1730 Monday through Friday, 1000–1500 Saturday, and 1000–1500 Sunday (June–September only). Winter hours are 1000–1600 Monday–Friday and 1000–1300 Saturday. The telephone number is 01284–764667.

Sightseeing in Bury St. Edmunds is, of course, highlighted by the abbey ruins and gardens. St. Mary's Church, which borders the southern boundary of the abbey grounds, is also a popular visiting spot. The Borough Council's Museum of Local History is housed in Moyses Hall. Constructed in the latter part of the twelfth century, it is a fine example of Norman domestic architecture. The Manor House Museum faces the abbey grounds. This restored Georgian mansion houses clocks, paintings, costumes, and objets d'art from the seventeenth to the twentieth century.

There are two distinct parts to the town. As was customary in most medieval towns with a monastic foundation, there was a physical division between the monastery and the townspeople—possibly the first example of separation of church and state. This division resulted in the business section and public buildings standing on a hill to the west of the abbey ruins today.

The Theatre Royal, one of the three surviving Georgian playhouses in Britain, was built in Bury St. Edmunds during 1819 by England's famous architect, William Wilkins. He also designed Downing College on the campus at Cambridge. The Theatre Royal's architecture displays in elegant fashion the style and form for which the Georgian architects were famous. This historical theater's repertoire features a broad scope of entertainment, plays, dance, opera, and every form of music ranging from classical to jazz and rock. In 1892, the Theatre Royal made international headlines by presenting the world premiere of *Charlie's Aunt,* a comedy that is still performed in every major language throughout the world.

Bypassed by time, Bury St. Edmunds is essentially a country town that was spared the industrial expansion of the Victorian Age. But the town stands tall in history. The principles of the Magna Carta, which had their foundation in Bury St. Edmunds and were developed over the centuries by English Common Law, have become the heritage not only of the British Isles but of countless millions throughout the world. As history records, the grant of the Magna Carta by King John is the basic source of the constitutional liberties of English-speaking peoples, forming a common bond of peace between them.

One of Bury St. Edmunds's local products is ale. Although the city boasts numerous pubs, we suggest that you sample a pint in the Nutshell, the smallest pub in England. Its single bar room measures twelve feet by seven feet.

King's College Chapel in Cambridge, universally known as one of the world's finest architectural structures, took seventy years to build.

The "backs," that portion of the River Cam passing the college buildings and gardens, is ideal for a placid boat tour of Cambridge.

From London . . .

A DAY EXCURSION TO CAMBRIDGE
DISTANCE BY TRAIN: 56 miles (90 km)
AVERAGE TRAIN TIME: 1 hour

Oxford graduates often refer to Cambridge as "the other place." Both universities hold one thing in common—organized along the classic federal structure, they house a number of largely autonomous colleges. Comparisons stop here. Cambridge is Britain's "university city." It is said that if you visit only one other English city besides London, it should be Cambridge.

Cambridge is situated on the River Cam around the original bridge over which all trade and communications passed between central England, East Anglia, and Continental Europe 1,000 years ago. It was a natural spot for travelers to pause to exchange news and opinions, thereby preparing the ground for a center of learning.

Several religious orders, including the Franciscans and Dominicans, established monasteries and affiliated schools in Cambridge early in the twelfth century. Students from the University of Oxford and the University of Paris left to study in Cambridge during the thirteenth century. The present-day colleges originated at that time, when students began residing in hostels and halls.

There are daily walking tours of the colleges with qualified guides who can tell you about the university and its colleges. Schedules and tickets for the tours may be obtained from the tourist information center. The main colleges are closed to visitors from mid-April until the end of June. A note of academic etiquette: College members are happy to welcome you to the grounds and their historic buildings, but they ask you to respect their need for quiet and privacy.

Arriving by rail from London, take the bus (No. 1) located immediately in front of the railway station to St. Andrew's Street and Downing. Cambridge is a complex blend of market town, regional center, university, and tourist attraction and defies neat analysis. Consequently, after getting off the bus in St. Andrew's Street, ask for directions to the **tourist information center** (tel. 322640) on Wheeler Street (behind the Guildhall) a few short blocks away.

The tourist information center is open Monday through Friday, 0900–1900, 0900–1700 Saturday, 1030–1530 Sunday (Easter–September); 0900–1730 (November–February). It opens at 0930 on Wednesdays. Telephone 01223–322640. Ask for the *Cambridge Mini-Guide* (nominal fee). It provides basic information about the colleges and museums and includes a street plan of the city. Other books and gifts are available for those wanting to know more about the history of Cambridge and places of interest outside the city.

If you plan to see Cambridge on your own, planning an itinerary may be difficult because there is so much to see. King's College Chapel is regarded

CAMBRIDGE—*UNIVERSITY CITY*

A Day Excursion from London

DEPART FROM KING'S CROSS STATION	ARRIVE IN CAMBRIDGE STATION	NOTES
0845	0937	(1)
0945	1037	(1)
0953	1111	(2)
1045	1137	(1)
1145	1237	(1)
1315	1407	(1)

(Plus other frequent service out of King's Cross and Liverpool Street stations)

DEPART FROM CAMBRIDGE STATION	ARRIVE IN KING'S CROSS STATION	NOTES
1554	1646	(1)
1619	1727	(2)
1654	1748	(1)
1707	1810	(2)
1754	1846	(1)
1807	1910	(2)
1824	1916	(1)
2032	2136	(1)

(Plus other frequent service into King's Cross and Liverpool Street stations)

Distance: 56 miles/90 km
References: Tables 20 and 25
              Thomas Cook Table 576

(1) MON–SAT   (2) SUN

Train Information: 01223–311999
InterCity Services: 0171–928–5100

Cambridge Tourist Information Centre: 01223–322640

universally as one of Cambridge's finest architectural structures. It was constructed in stages over a period of nearly seventy years and was completed in 1536. The chapel (nominal entrance fee) displays the carved coats of arms of Henry VIII. His initials, along with those of Anne Boleyn, can be seen on the screen. The chapel's stained-glass windows depict stories from the Old Testament and the New Testament. Rubens's *Adoration of the Magi* is the altarpiece.

Trinity College's great court is one of the largest collegiate quadrangles in England. It's so large that much of its detail goes unnoticed. It is said that taking advantage of this situation, Byron bathed nude in the fountain and shared his room with a pet bear, which he claimed he kept for the purpose of taking examinations. Sir Isaac Newton first measured the speed of sound in the great court by stamping his foot in the cloister along the north side.

The admission qualifications to the University of Cambridge are exceptionally demanding. Each year, approximately 8,000 students apply for admission. In the end, however, only about 20 percent are admitted.

The Cam River, the source of Cambridge's being and delightful throughout every season, deserves a portion of your visit. A tour of the city by boat along the "backs," as the placid stretch of the river is called, is an experience not to be missed. You can hire a punt, rowboat, or canoe to boat along the backs. If your selection is the punt—which is propelled with long wooden poles—be aware that these poles frequently stick in the mud and have been known to vault a punter into the river. A "chauffeur punt" service is also available.

Visitors have a wide choice of museums covering a wide range of interests. Allow yourself time to wander in at least one of them. The Fitzwilliam Museum on Trumpington Street features medieval and Renaissance objects of art, arms, and armor. The Folk Museum on Castle Street contains a vast array of domestic articles. Another point of interest is Kettles Yard Art Gallery at Castle Street on Northampton with its fine collection of modern paintings and sculpture.

Steeped in history, Cambridge has a reminder of a more recent historical event—Duxford Airfield, which is located eight miles south of the city. Now the site of the Imperial War Museum, Duxford was one of the many airfields from which Allied aircraft flew raids into Continental Europe during World War II. A visit to the museum is recommended. The American Military Cemetery, four miles from Cambridge, contains the graves of 3,811 American airmen who operated from bases in Britain. The cemetery and the museum may be reached by bus.

The Old Weaver's House in Canterbury owes its name to Flemish and Huguenot weavers who came to the city in the sixteenth century and set up looms in private houses along the River Stour. Now a small but attractive stream, the river played an important role in Canterbury's earlier times.

98

A DAY EXCURSION TO CANTERBURY
DISTANCE BY TRAIN: 62 Miles (99 km)
AVERAGE TRAIN TIME: 1 hour, 25 minutes

Canterbury, the Metropolitan City of the Anglican Communion, has a history going back to prehistoric times. It was a Roman settlement and the Saxon stronghold of the men of Kent. Here in 597 St. Augustine began the conversion of the English to Christianity, where Ethelbert, King of Kent was baptized.

Only ruins remain of the Benedictine St Augustine's Abbey, burial place of the Jutish Kings of Kent, but St Martin's Church, on the eastern outskirts of the city, is still in use. This church is stated to have been the place of worship of Queen Bertha, the Christian wife of King Ethelbert, before the arrival of St Augustine.

In 1170 the rivalry of church and state culminated in the murder in Canterbury Cathedral, by Henry II's Knights, of Archbishop Thomas Becket, whose shrine became a great center of pilgrimage, as described by Chaucer in his *Canterbury Tales*. After the Reformation pilgrimage ceased, but the prosperity of the city was strengthened by an influx of Huguenot refugees from the continent, who introduced weaving.

The Cathedral, with architecture ranging from the eleventh to the fifteenth century, is world famous. Modern pilgrims are attracted particularly to the Martyrdom, the Black Price's Tomb, the Warriors' Chapel, and the many examples of medieval stained glass. The Medieval city walls are built on Roman foundations and the fourteenth-century West Gate is one of the finest buildings of its kind in the country.

The poet and playwright Christopher Marlowe was born and reared in Canterbury and there are also literary associations with Defoe, Dickens, Joseph Conrad, and Somerset Maughan. The *Mayflower* was provisioned in Canterbury, before she set sail for Plymouth and her historic journey to America.

During World War II Canterbury suffered a severe bombing raid and in recent years parts of the city center have been rebuilt. Modern day Canterbury has a wide range of quality shops and comfortable hotels, many of these small family run buisnesses. The 1,000 seat Marlowe Theatre offers a program of first-class plays, opera, musicals, and one-night shows. Each autumn, Canterbury celebrates the International Arts Festival.

Canterbury has two railway stations—West Station and East Station. Trains departing London's Charing Cross and Waterloo stations arrive at Canterbury

CANTERBURY—*AND THE CATHEDRAL*

A Day Excursion from London

DEPART FROM VICTORIA STATION	ARRIVE IN CANTERBURY EAST STATION	NOTES
0735	0931	(4)
0833	0958	(2)
0835	1031	(4)
0935	1131	(4)
0941	1132	(2)
1035	1231	(4)
1041	1232	(2)

(Plus other frequent service)

DEPART FROM CANTERBURY EAST STATION	ARRIVE IN VICTORIA STATION	NOTES
1551	1748	(4)
1626	1757	(1)
1650	1845	(3)
1751	1948	(4)
1822	1947	(1)
1850	2045	(3)
2051	2248	(4)
2119	2315	(1)

(Plus other frequent service)

Distance: 62 miles/99 km
References: Table 212; Thomas Cook Table 500

(1) MON–FRI   (3) SAT
(2) MON–SAT   (4) SUN

Train Information: 01732–770111
InterCity Services: 0171–928–5100
Canterbury Tourist Information Centre
01227–766567

West. Those departing London's Victoria Station arrive at Canterbury East. For simplicity, day-excursion schedules are given for Victoria and Canterbury East stations only.

Arriving in Canterbury East Station, use the pedestrian bridge to reach the city walls. There's a taxi queue just outside the station entrance, or you can walk to the city center and the cathedral in about fifteen minutes. From the station entrance, you'll see a sign across the street that says, CITY CENTRE-MARLOWE THEATRE-CATHEDRAL. A blue sign showing a person walking indicates where to cross the highway. Proceed along the city's old Roman walls, which enclose Dane John Park. Climb the mound in the park for a view of the town and the cathedral. Farther along, you'll come to the city bus station. Descend from the wall at this point onto St. George's Street. Turn left and walk until the cathedral is in view on your right through the Christ Church Gate. Passing through the gate will bring you onto the cathedral grounds.

Not far from the Christ Church Gate is the Longmarket, a paved pedestrian area beginning at the intersection of Rose Lane and St. George's Street. Walking directly away from the Christ Church Gate on St. Margaret's Street will bring you to the Canterbury Visitor Information Centre at No. 34 (telephone 766567). The center is open Monday through Saturday year-round and on Sunday in the summer. City tours depart from this point.

From High Street, where it intersects St. Margaret's Street, walk down until you pass over a narrow bridge on the River Stour. On the far right of the bridge you will see the Old Weaver's House, built in 1500. Canterbury was the background for Dickens's novel *David Copperfield*, so your imagination can take over here for a few fleeting moments and transport you back into English history and literature. The structure houses a beautiful collection of English Church brass rubbings from the medieval and Tudor periods. Unfortunately, as of press time it is closed to the public temporarily due to a change of ownership.

Following World War II, Canterbury became an educational center of great importance. In 1962 Christ Church College was opened adjacent to St. Augustine's College. More recently, the University of Kent was established on a hill overlooking the cathedral and city from the west. Its buildings are designed in a modern idiom; in keeping with the theme of Canterbury, however, it was organized on the basis of colleges with emphasis on artistic and cultural development.

Canterbury, proud of its historical past, is nonetheless eager to respond to the demands of present "pilgrims"—visitors who come to see the cathedral and the other historical landmarks. The city of Canterbury has done an excellent job by exhibiting its history as a living part of a modern, living community.

Castle Clock Tower, an outstanding feature of Cardiff, was designed by Victorian architect William Burges. Commissioned by the Marquis of Bute in 1865 to restore Cardiff Castle, Burges replaced a turret of the castle with this magnificent clock tower as part of the restoration.

From London . . .

A DAY EXCURSION TO CARDIFF
DISTANCE BY TRAIN: 145 miles (234 km)
AVERAGE TRAIN TIME: 2 hours

A treat lies in store for those who take this delightful day excursion to the Welsh capital of Cardiff. You have the opportunity to travel on one of BritRail's "journey shrinkers"—the fabulous InterCity 125 trains. As an example, the 0900 InterCity out of London's Paddington Station will set you down in Cardiff Central Station exactly 121 minutes later, averaging an amazing speed of seventy-eight miles per hour along the 145 miles separating the two capital cities. As an added bonus, you can savor a delicious English breakfast while watching the western English countryside glide by.

Upon arrival in Cardiff's Central Station, we suggest that you first visit the tourist information center in the station to get your bearings, pick up some brochures, and then begin your sightseeing. The tourist center is on the ground floor in the main concourse near the main exit (telephone 01222-227281).

It's open during the summer on Monday and Wednesday-Saturday 0900-1830; Tuesday 1000-1830; and Sunday 1000-1800. Winter Hours are Monday and Wednesday-Saturday 0900-1730; Tuesday 1000-1730; and Sunday 1000-1600. If you visit Cardiff on a Sunday, you'll find the castle and the museums open as well as the larger shops and restaurants. We recommend purchasing the Jarrold Guide to the Welsh Capital City of Cardiff (£1.99) at the tourist center or at most of the bookstores. It contains a city map detailing a walking tour.

Cardiff was first developed by the Romans then by the Normans. Both left their marks in the form of formidable fortifications. The Romans found their way into south Wales, reaching the area that is now Cardiff about A.D. 76. At first they erected a wooden fort; but as Cardiff grew in importance as a Roman naval base, a stone fortress was erected, parts of which still exist today as a portion of Cardiff Castle. Following the conquest of England in 1066, the Normans arrived in Cardiff in 1091 and established a stronghold on the site of the old Roman fort.

Today's city is largely a creation of the nineteenth century—a city that has cast off its grim mantle of industrialism to reveal a sparkling center of shopping arcades, a glistening white array of impressive civic buildings, a most memorable museum (well worth the trip), and the restored Cardiff Castle.

Lofty Cardiff Castle is a lavishly restored medieval fortress with 2000-year-old Roman foundations and 10-foot thick Roman walls. The medieval stronghold was built by invading Normans, fell into ruin after the Civil War in the seventeenth century, and was saved by the first Marquis of Bute in the late

CARDIFF—*CAPITAL OF WALES*

A Day Excursion from London

DEPART FROM PADDINGTON STATION	ARRIVE IN CARDIFF CENTRAL STATION	NOTES
0700	0857	(1)
0800	0953, 1002 Sat	(2)
0830	1040	(1)
0900	1058, 1106 Sat, 1125 Sun	(3)
0945	1157	(4)
1000	1158, 1202 Sat, 1222 Sun	(3)
1100	1257, 1302 Sat, 1322 Sun	(3)

(Plus other frequent service)

DEPART FROM CARDIFF CENTRAL STATION	ARRIVE IN PADDINGTON STATION	NOTES
1500	1725	(5)
1525	1729, 1735 Sat	(2)
1535	1755	(5)
1625	1830, 1835 Sat, 1845 Sun	(3)
1725	1935, 1950 Sun	(3)
1725	1950	(3)
1755	2020	(5)
1825	2025, 2035 Sat, 2045 Sun	(3)
1925	2135, 2140 Sun	(3)
2025	2336	(5)
2125	2355, 2345 Sun	(6)

(Plus other frequent service)

Distance: 145 miles/233 km
References: Great Britain Passenger Railway Timetable 125
                   Thomas Cook Table 530

(1) MON–FRI   (4) SAT only   (6) MON–FRI & SUN
(2) MON–SAT   (5) SUN only
(3) DAILY

Train Information: 01222–228000
InterCity Services: 0171–262–6767
Cardiff Tourist Information: 01222–227281

1700s. The third marquis and the architect William Burges, known as the "eccentric genius," created the castle's extravagant rooms, reflecting an eclectic mix of influences from medieval England, Arabia, the Old Testament, and Islam—even fairy tales. Today, the castle interior provides the setting for medieval "Welsh Nights " and private or public receptions. The castle and its grounds provide a dramatic backdrop for a series of spectacular events throughout the summer, ranging from a hot-air balloon festival to massed military bands.

Cardiff's civic center lies beyond the castle, as does the National Museum of Wales. The civic center is one of the most impressive buildings in Europe. Separated by wide avenues and parks, the presence in the spring of cherry blossoms and tulip beds create a perfect setting for the white stone buildings. In the National Museum of Wales, you may view, among other art treasures, four tapestry cartoons by Ruben. Rodin's bronze statuary, The Kiss, is also housed there. The museum is unusual in that it contains a variety of exhibits—from priceless works of art to dinosaurs.

The Victorian shopping arcades blend well with the modern shopping areas. Cardiff claims to have had pedestrian shopping areas long before the phrase was invented. The two main shopping streets Queen Street and Mary Street form an L-shape that partially encloses Cardiff's largest shopping mall, St. David's Centre. For those with the "shop 'til you drop" syndrome, this is the place.

If time permits, take the fifteen-minute train ride from Cardiff's Queen Street Station to Caerphilly Castle, second in size only to Windsor Castle. Covering thirty acres and remarkably well preserved, it's crammed with interesting things, including a tower that even Oliver Cromwell's gunpowder couldn't topple—at least not completely. Trains depart Queen Street Station thrice hourly. When returning to Cardiff, you can ride through to the Central Station for connections with InterCity 125 trains back to London, unless, of course, you've fallen in love with Wales and decide to stay. Central Station is only three minutes beyond Queen Street Station.

To sample some traditional Welsh dishes served by waitresses in traditional costume, try the Blas ar Gymru (A Taste of Wales) Restaurant at 48 Crwys Road, about a twenty-minute walk from Cardiff Castle. Proceed north through the Civic Centre to Corbett Road, turn right and over the bridge into Cathays Terrace, right onto Woodville Road, and left onto Crwys Road. Reservations advised—telephone (01222) 383132.

The world-famous Rows, a double tier of shops with walkways at ground and first-floor levels, is Chester's most distinctive architectural feature. The Rows line streets originally laid down by Roman engineers almost 2,000 years ago. Extensive rebuilding followed the disastrous fire of 1278. The Rows also include a small museum and historic inn. (Courtesy City of Chester)

From London . . .

A DAY EXCURSION TO CHESTER
DISTANCE BY TRAIN: 178 miles (287 km)
AVERAGE TRAIN TIME: 2 hours, 30 minutes

"All's well" in Chester, but don't take our word for it. Check personally with Chester's town crier. He appears at noon (Tuesday through Saturday, April through October) in the center of the city to announce that fact. Chester is one of the few cities in England with its encircling walls completely intact. It is a splendid example of a fortified medieval town.

The center of Chester, known as the "Cross," takes its name from the stone "High Cross" standing in front of St. Peter's Church. From this point you may view Chester's distinctive landmarks, the Rows—two tiers of shops (one at ground level, the other immediately above), each with its own walkway. Developed in the thirteenth century, the Rows are unique and justly world famous. The upper levels are great for people watchers who like to linger undisturbed while observing the stream of passers-by in the streets below. The true origin of the Rows has never been satisfactorily explained, but they far exceed any modern day shopping center in utility and beauty. One opinion is that they served as a means of defense against the incursions of the Welsh raiders, who came to plunder their richer English neighbors.

The Romans gave Chester its street plan. Walk today along the four main streets within the city's walls and you will follow the lines laid down by Roman engineers almost 2,000 years ago. Part of the Roman wall survives and is incorporated in the massive tenth-century fortifications enclosing the city. You can find out more about the city's Roman heritage at the Dewa Roman Experience, just off Bridge Street (tel. 01244–343407). A walk on the walls provides an opportunity to enjoy the vista of the surrounding countryside.

Restoration has thrived on a large scale in Chester. Entire blocks were renovated in massive programs. The city's famous "black and white" Tudor buildings survived the ravages of time but did not escape alterations to their facades by Victorian architects. In all, however, Chester has managed to preserve its pleasant medieval appearance.

The railway station in Chester is about a fifteen-minute walk from the city's center. City Road, at the front of the station, will get you started in the right direction. Change at the pedestrian underpass onto Foregate Street, which turns into Eastgate Street and brings you to the center of the city's historic area. Or you can board a bus outside the station. The bus arrives at the town hall in approximately ten minutes for a charge of thirty-five pence. Taxi meters click off around £2.00.

Your first call should be at the **tourist information center** at the town hall

107

CHESTER—*MODERN "MEDIEVAL" CITY*

A Day Excursion from London

DEPART FROM EUSTON STATION	ARRIVE IN CHESTER STATION	NOTES
0840	1110	(2)
0820	1120	(3)
0950	1210	(1)

DEPART FROM CHESTER STATION	ARRIVE IN EUSTON STATION	NOTES
1521	1800	(2)
1526	1814	(3)
1607	1835	(1)
1731	2016	(3)

Distance: 178 miles/287 km
References: Table 65
                    Thomas Cook Table 555

(1) MON–FRI   (3) SUN
(2) SAT

Train Information: 01244–40170
InterCity Services: 0171–387–7070

Chester Tourist Information Centre: 01244–318356
01244–313126 (24 hours/day)

on Northgate Street across from the entrance to Abbey Square. It is open 0900–1730 Monday through Saturday and 1000–1600 Sunday from November through April; between May and October, weekday hours are 0900–1930 and Sunday, 1000–1600. It offers a wide range of facilities including a national room-finder service and ticket agency. Special guided walks are available: "Pastfinder" tours depart daily year-round at 1045; the "Ghosthunter Trail" departs at 1930 on Thursday, Friday, and Saturday from May through October; and the "Roman Soldier Patrol" sets forth at 1130 and 1430 on Thursday, Friday, and Saturday from June through September. Other tours may be made by special arrangement.

Opposite the town hall is Abbey Square, an island of quiet in the center of the city. By entering the square through its massive fourteenth-century gateway, you will find various buildings constructed anywhere from the sixteenth to the nineteenth century.

Chester also boasts a cathedral, which is within sight of the town hall. An abbey was founded on this site in the tenth century. It remained as a monastery until its dissolution in 1540, when the building was made a cathedral. The bell tower of the cathedral is a concrete structure that was finished in 1974, the first freestanding bell tower for a cathedral built since the fifteenth century.

If you're in Chester between June 30 and July 16, 1997, you're in for a prestigious event—the Chester Mystery Plays. Occurring only once every five years, this unique medieval tradition draws from stories of the Bible. The 1997 plays are in three parts: Heaven, Miracles, and Hell. Chester's Mystery Plays texts are the most complete, with the earliest surviving records dated 1546. For more detailed information, contact Mystery Plays Publicity Officer Eileen Jeffery at 01244–402463 (fax 01244–315789) or the **Chester tourist information center** at 01244–318356.

An interesting observation point that provides a splendid view of the city, the River Dee, and the locks of the Chester canal is located at the north end of the city walls. A spur wall connects there with the water tower, which was built to protect the port of Chester. Another vantage point is from Bonewaldesthorne's tower, about one-hundred feet from the water tower. If you participate in the Roman Soldier Wall Patrol tour, you will be able to enjoy this view.

Also in view at a bend in the River Dee is the Roodee, home of the Chester racecourse, the oldest in Britain. The main racing season is held in May and its richest prize, the Chester Cup, was first awarded 1824. As a matter of interest to sportive North Americans, the Roodee was, before horse racing, a football field. But due to the violent nature of the football matches, the city assembly members voted to terminate the sport in 1540.

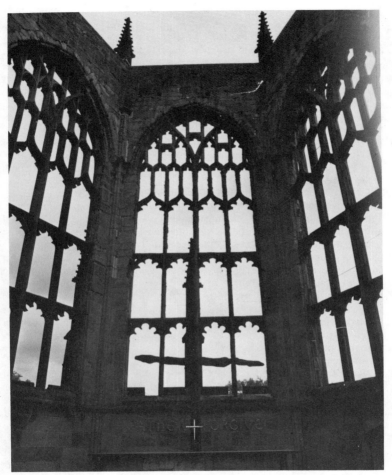

Stark ruins of Coventry's Cathedral of St. Michael stand alongside the city's fine new cathedral. Totally destroyed in a 1940 air raid, an altar of broken stones surmounted by a charred cross stands at the eastern end of the ruins, backed by the words, "Father, forgive."

From London ...

A DAY EXCURSION TO COVENTRY
DISTANCE BY TRAIN: 100 miles (161 km)
AVERAGE TRAIN TIME: 1 hour, 10 minutes

Explore the legend of Lady Godiva! Did she actually put everything on a horse—or has this tale, retold through the ages, changed with the telling? Was there a "Peeping Tom?" Was he late for the show? Coventry holds the answers.

Coventry is best described as a modern city with ancient roots. Among its tall office buildings, new streets and attractive shops, there is a scattering of old homes and churches, Coventry's remnants of its far-reaching past. The city was devastated in 1940 by Nazi bombers, but after careful and patient rebuilding, a bright new city emerged.

Coventry's new cathedral, consecrated in 1962, stands as visible proof that today's craftsmen can, in fact, create memorable works of supreme beauty, as did their medieval counterparts. In the new cathedral you will see outstanding examples of the finest modern works of art, including the Baptistery Window, the largest piece of modern stained glass in the world. The tapestry *Christ in Glory* hangs behind the altar. Weighing nearly a ton, it is the largest tapestry in the world; ten men worked for three years to complete it. The cathedral, open from 0900–1930 in summer, closes at 1730 in winter.

Alongside the new stands the old Cathedral of St. Michael, reduced to ruins by one dreadful air raid in November 1940. An altar of broken stones surmounted by a charred cross stands at the eastern end of the ruins, backed by the words, "Father, forgive." In the nineteenth century John Ruskin wrote, "The sand of Coventry binds itself into stone which can be built half-way to the sky." Attesting to this, the tower and spire of the old cathedral survived intact after the bombing. Built in the fifteenth century, it is the third highest spire in England. A visit to both cathedrals should not be missed.

Coventry's rail station lies outside its "ringway," a circular super highway surrounding the city. At the bus stop, you'll find a city map and information regarding Coventry's information center. Buses marked "Pool Meadow" (No. 17 or 27) will take you to the center of town in five minutes along a route that requires about twenty minutes to walk. Dismount at the shopping square by the Leofric Hotel. Lady Godiva's statue stands in a park immediately opposite the hotel, silhouetted against the spires of the cathedrals. Be certain to read the inscriptions on the east and west sides of the statue's pedestal. They were written by Alfred Tennyson, England's poet laureate.

The bus stop at the Leofric Hotel is Broadgate. The **tourist information center** is located at Bayley Lane and may be found via well-placed direction

111

COVENTRY—*LADY GODIVA LAND*

A Day Excursion from London

DEPART FROM EUSTON STATION	ARRIVE IN COVENTRY STATION	NOTES
0715	0826	(1)(4)
0745	0857	(1)(4)
0845	0957	(1)(4)
0915	1026	(1)(4)
0945	1056	(1)(4)
1015	1126	(1)(4)
1045	1156	(1)(4)

(Plus other frequent service)

DEPART FROM COVENTRY STATION	ARRIVE IN EUSTON STATION	NOTES
1507	1625	(1)(3)
1537	1655	(1)(3)
1622	1803	(2)
1707	1825	(1)(3)
1807	1925 (1938 SUN)	(1)(2)(3)
1937	2055	(1)(3)
2037	2200 (2220 SAT)	(1)
2107	2238	(2)

(Plus other frequent service)

Distance: 100 miles/161 km
References: Tables 65 and 68
              Thomas Cook Table 540

(1) MON–SAT   (3) Arrives 10 minutes later on Saturday
(2) SUN   (4) Departs 10 minutes earlier on Saturday

Train Information: 01203–555211
InterCity Services: 0171–387–7070

Coventry Tourist Information Centre: 01203–832303

signs. The center operates Monday through Friday, 0930–1700; Saturday and Sunday, 1000–1630. It remains open on bank holidays (except Christmas), 1000–1600. (Telephone 01203–832303/4).

Among many informative publications, be sure to acquire the *City of Coventry Mini Guide*. It contains a plan of the city's central area, along with a brief description of places of interest. It will lead you from Broadgate to a number of interesting places, including the two cathedrals. For the more ambitious visitor, a two-hour walking tour accompanied by a guide leaves the information center Saturdays at 1400. The tour passes Fords Hospital, a fine example of sixteenth-century almshouses, several sections of the remaining city wall, and Cook Street Gate, one of the twelve ancient gates erected in the fourteenth century. You will also be able to see some of Coventry's new buildings, including the Retail Market and the Belgrade Theatre. The price of the tour is £1.50 per person. When returning to the rail station, board the bus at the shelter directly in front of the Holy Trinity Church, opposite the hotel.

Lady Godiva was the wife of Leofric, the "grim" Lord of Coventry. Evidently, she bugged him about the heavy tax burdens he had levied on the townspeople. Legend says Leofric, weary of her nagging, agreed to decrease the tax rate if Her Ladyship would increase the town's morale by riding naked through its streets. Modern historians seriously doubt that Godiva made her gallop without benefit of even a riding crop. They believe her husband challenged her to ride *stripped of her finery and her jewels* and to ride humbly as one of his people and in full sight of them. Stripped of her rank—or just plain stripped—Her Ladyship *did* make the ride and taxes *were lowered*, but she commanded the people to remain indoors with windows barred. Legend says that one town resident called "Tom" unbarred his window to peep as she rode by. Before he could satisfy his gaze, he was struck blind, poor man!

In modern versions of the ride, Lady Godiva now rides her horse through Coventry wearing a body stocking—which is a considerable improvement of the event as conducted in Victorian days, when she was dressed up in petticoats.

Oddly enough, the Godiva story was told for some 500 years before the "Peeping Tom" version was added. In any case, a stunning bronze statue worthy of a *Playboy* centerfold perpetuates Her Ladyship's memory in Broadgate Park as Tom peeps out at her on the hour from the Broadgate clock. We can't help but wonder what effect Lady Godiva's ride would have on our modern-day Internal Revenue Service.

Famous white cliffs, probably Dover's best known landmark, attract thousands of sightseers. Dover Castle, standing guard atop the cliffs, boasts a fine keep, Hellfire Corner tunnels, a lighthouse of Roman origin, and a church dating back to Saxon times. Dover's importance as a port began during the Roman invasion of England. Today, Dover is still a principal British maritime port for passenger traffic to and from Europe.

114

From London . . .

A DAY EXCURSION TO DOVER
DISTANCE BY TRAIN: 77 miles (124 km)
AVERAGE TRAIN TIME: 1 hour, 30 minutes

For centuries Dover has been one of Britain's major channel ports. In theory, this is where England ends and the Continent begins. Here is where countless Englishmen have been parted from, or united with, their homeland. Here stand the white cliffs of Dover. Below, on the beaches, the legions of the Roman Empire stormed ashore in 55 B.C., only to be repelled and to land again, successfully, at Deal.

Atop the cliffs broods Dover Castle. Initially constructed in the 1180s by Henry II to repel invaders, it has been reinforced at every threat to England's shores, including Hitler's in 1940. From its ramparts, on a clear day you can look across the twenty-one miles of the English Channel and see France. Approaching from the sea, a dramatic panorama unfolds as the white cliffs slowly rise from out of the horizon.

You cannot deny it—Dover is dramatic. Brooding hangs over it on a rainy, windswept day; grandeur surrounds it on a clear one when, for example, Boulogne in distant France becomes discernible. The deafening ramjets of the World War II German V-2 "buzz bombs" have been replaced by the humming vacuums of the hovercraft. But the screams of the gulls and the relentless crashing of the sea continue on, unchanged by time. If you are one to "stand in history," Dover becomes a must visit during your stay in Great Britain. Few other places on earth swell the imagination as do the "white cliffs of Dover."

Train service from London to Dover follows two routes. Departures from Victoria Station split destinations at Faversham. Part of the train goes to Dover, the other part to Margate and Ramsgate. As a precaution against "splitting," our schedule is based on direct train service to Dover from London's Charing Cross Station. Readers can, however, avail themselves of either rail route. As a suggestion, depart Charing Cross and return via Faversham to Victoria Station. This way, you will be "joined" by the Ramsgate train instead of being "split" by it.

Leave the train at Dover Priory Station. It's a short walk from Dover Priory to Townwall Street, where you will find the **tourist information center** (telephone 01304–205108) next door to the County Hotel. It's all downhill from the station and in the direction of the sea, so you may walk easily and arrive at the center in about twelve minutes.

The information center is extensive, since Dover is a major debarkation point for visitors from the Continent. The center can provide information on all of Great Britain, as well as the local area. The center is open daily, 0900–1800.

DOVER—*ON THE WHITE CLIFFS*

A Day Excursion from London

DEPART FROM CHARING CROSS STATION	ARRIVE IN DOVER PRIORY STATION*	NOTES
0730	0917 (0928 SAT)	(1)
0830	1028	(1)
0855	1045	(2)
0930	1128	(1)
1100	1244	(2)
1130	1328	(1)

(Plus other frequent service)

DEPART FROM DOVER PRIORY STATION	ARRIVE IN CHARING CROSS STATION	NOTES
1548	1738	(1)
1621	1807	(2)
1651	1835	(1)
1849	2035	(1)
1921	2107	(2)
1949	2135	(1)
2107	2311	(2)

(Plus other frequent service)

Distance: 77 miles/124 km
References: Table 212
                  Thomas Cook Table 501

* Dover Priory is the last stop before the train arrives at the train-ferry docks for transport to Continental Europe.

(1) MON–SAT   (2) SUN

Train Information: 01732–770111
InterCity Services: 0171–928–5100
Dover Tourist Information Centre: 01304–205108

Ask for information on <u>Dover Castle</u> and how to reach it. No doubt you will also be interested in visiting the <u>Roman-painted house</u>, Britain's buried Pompeii. It was discovered by an archaeological unit in 1971. Roman legions took over the structure about A.D. 300 for shore-defense purposes. It gains its name from the brilliantly painted plaster of its walls, the oldest and best preserved painted walls in Britain. Incredible as it seems, the Romans even installed an elaborate under-the-floor heating system in the house. The house is a permanent museum, open every day, except Monday, from 1000 to 1700 (April through October). Admission is £.50 for adults and 50 pence for children.

Legend has it that if Romans are left alone long enough, they will build something. Apparently, this was the case in the second century, when the Roman legions constructed two lighthouse beacons on Dover's cliffs for the purpose of guiding their galleys into the sheltered anchorage below. The surviving lighthouse, reaching to a height of more than forty feet, is the tallest surviving Roman structure in Britain.

Dover can hardly be compared with the Continent's Riviera. Its beaches are small, tiny enclaves in the rugged face of the looming cliffs. And the height of the surf frequently becomes more than the average bather cares to contend with. Dover and its environs, however, lend themselves well to sunbathing, walking, and viewing. It is a point that more people pass through than pause to enjoy, but there is no other point in all of Britain more majestic than Dover. It is the very cornerstone of Britain.

During World War II, Dover was subjected to long-range artillery shelling from the Pas de Calais German gun emplacements. Dover's residents dug cellars deep into the cliffs as sanctuaries from the shelling. The surviving structures, most of which are small hotels, still maintain the shelters for use as wine cellars, bars, and boutiques. In addition, secret war tunnels, <u>Hellfire Corner</u>, a top-secret operations and command center used by the British to mastermind the evacuation from Dunkirk, has recently been declassified and opened to the public.

Have you ever been to France? If not, now's your chance! Take the train to Folkestone, a short distance to the west of Dover. From there you can whisk across the English Channel to Calais in about fifty catamaran minutes; to Boulogne, in fifty-five minutes. Day trips from Dover to the Continent are very popular. Stock up on wine and cheese, plus a yard or so of crusty French bread during your visit, and load up with duty-free tobacco and booze on the return journey. Plan ahead by asking any train information office for information on ferry, hovercraft, or catamaran services.

Small boat harbor provides protected haven for Folkestone's fleet of fishing and recreational craft. As a cross-channel port, Folkestone stands second only to Dover in cross-channel passenger vessels, which call at the city's harbor–train station pier and the Continent.

A DAY EXCURSION TO FOLKESTONE
DISTANCE BY TRAIN: 70 miles (113 km)
AVERAGE TRAIN TIME: 1 hour, 20 minutes

Folkestone is a "multiple treat" seaside resort. You may either stay within its confines for a delightful day of sightseeing and seafood, ply between Folkestone and Boulogne in France aboard Hoverspeed or elect to survey the thirteen-and-one-half miles of right of way on the world's smallest public railway—the Romney, Hythe and Dymchurch Light Railroad. Each of the three options should take a full day to enjoy, so perhaps you had better plan on making several trips out of London to Folkestone during your visit—or even stay over in Folkestone for a day or two.

With the opening of the channel tunnel in 1994 and a nearby terminal at Cheriton, Folkestone has become a departure point for Le Shuttle services through Eurotunnel. Le Shuttle conveys motor vehicles through the tunnel. Passengers remain in their vehicles aboard the Le Shuttle rail cars. Journey time is approximately 35 minutes in the tunnel. Special arrangements for rental cars have been made with Hertz and Le Shuttle to exchange left- or right-hand drive vehicles at the Hertz/Eurotunnel terminal in Calais. This information is useful if you have purchased a BritRail Pass + Car package.

With so many possibilities, we suggest that you make your way to **Folkestone's tourist information center** immediately on arrival. It can be reached by walking from the Folkestone Central Station down the pedestrian center to Old High Street. Sealink operates a free shuttle bus between Central Station and Harbor Station for the convenience of cross-channel passengers only. It leaves from the left of the Central Station entrance. A schedule is posted nearby explaining the shuttle-bus service, which operates 1000–2310 daily. The shuttle bus passes the information center but cannot stop until it reaches the Harbor Station, where passengers board the next outbound Hoverspeed vessel.

The scenery along the seawall of Folkestone's outer harbor is enjoyable, to say the least. From there, you will have a commanding view of the harbor. Hoverspeed's SeaCat catamaran service takes just fifty-five minutes. So if you are tempted to set foot on French soil, the Hoverspeed office will provide you with current fares and schedules if you choose to cross the Channel "topside" rather than go under it. You can obtain tickets at the pier office or at the tourist information office. Fares are listed on page 63.

Folkestone has a dual distinction. As a cross-channel port, it is second only to Dover in total passenger traffic. For beauty of location, it probably stands second to none. The Leas, Folkestone's famous cliff-top promenade, served as an inspiration for some of H. G. Wells's finest works. It surveys the town's

119

FOLKESTONE—*TRADITIONAL SEASIDE RESORT*

A Day Excursion from London

DEPART FROM CHARING CROSS STATION	ARRIVE IN FOLKESTONE CENTRAL STATION*	NOTES
0730	0904	(1)
0755 (0800 SAT)	0931	(2)
0830	1016	(2)
0855	1033	(3)
1000	1130	(2)

(Plus other frequent service)

DEPART FROM FOLKESTONE CENTRAL STATION	ARRIVE IN CHARING CROSS STATION	NOTES
1600	1738	(1)
1633	1807	(3)
1703	1835	(2)
1802	1936	(2)
1833	2007	(3)
1902	2035	(2)
2033	2207	(3)
2215	2358	(2)

(Plus other frequent service)

Note: Eurostar Passenger Services schedule not available at press time.

Distance: 70 miles/113 km
References: Table 207
Thomas Cook Table 501

* See page 302 for Folkestone station plan.

(1) MON–FRI   (3) SUN
(2) MON–SAT

Train Information: 01732–770111 (24-hour service)
InterCity Services: 0171–928–5100
Folkestone Tourist Information Centre: 01303–258594

beach from a vantage point more than 200 feet above. From there, one can view the landscape from Dover to Dungeness. Stretching behind the Leas are the spacious, well-planned business and residential quarters.

One side of the Leas promenade is lined with large hotels, the other with hanging gardens through which winding paths lead down to the beach. A route for the less hearty is the charming one-hundred-year-old "cliff lift," which plies between the Leas promenade and the picturesque harbor area.

Below the Leas, at harbor level, lie the city's marine gardens and the busy harbor pier, an endless source of interest to visitors. There are regular guided walks organized by the White Cliffs Countryside Project (tel: 01304–241806).

The harbor area has been redeveloped extensively. Only a few of the quaint, old, narrow streets remain. Nevertheless, the area has a marked nautical flavor that sets it apart from the rest of the town. With the increased interest in sail boating, more of these small craft may be seen in the harbor. If you happen to be in the harbor area at 1300 hours on a Thursday or a Sunday, you will see the Orient Express.

Sandgate, on the western outskirts of Folkestone, has become one of the major antiques centers of England. Numerous antiques and curio shops beckon to shoppers from Sandgate's narrow High Street. Also competing for shoppers' attention are several old-world inns and the Sandgate Castle.

Trains meeting the Hoverspeed's SeaCat catamarans at the Harbor Station proceed to London via Dover and *do not stop at Folkestone Central Station.* This, of course, makes possible a circuitous train trip back to London. But it could also lead to embarrassment if you boarded a London-bound train at the Folkestone Harbor Station but had friends or family waiting to join you at the Folkestone Central Station.

A bus from the city station will take you to the town of Hythe, west of Folkestone, in about twenty-two minutes. There, the young—and those not so young—may board the fascinating Romney, Hythe and Dymchurch Light Railroad for a delightful run by steam traction to New Romney, with stops in Dymchurch and St. Mary's Bay. Service is generally every hour, so you can stop en route at Dymchurch, England's "children's paradise," or at St. Mary's Bay, where boating and fishing are two highlights of that holiday center. The RH&D Railroad terminates its service at Dungeness, another five-and-a-half miles down the RH&D "road," where you'll find great contrast between its fishermen's shacks and its atomic plant.

Gloucester Cathedral, originally of Norman design (1089-1260), was remodeled (1331–1370) to house the tomb of King Edward II. The east window of the cathedral, one of the largest in England, was erected as a memorial to those who fought for England at Crécy in 1346.

From London . . .

A DAY EXCURSION TO GLOUCESTER
DISTANCE BY TRAIN: 114 miles (184 km)
AVERAGE TRAIN TIME: 1 hour, 50 minutes

Gloucester is steeped in history. First to arrive were the Romans, following their invasion of the British Isles. A legion fort was erected at the site of the present city center, and by A.D. 96–98, the Roman city of Glevum (now Gloucester) was established and flourishing. Little remains of the Roman presence in modern Gloucester. None of the Roman wall is now visible above ground, but its line is still followed by the principal streets of the city.

Although Gloucester is situated some distance from the open sea, by the construction of a ship canal in 1805, Queen Elizabeth I granted the city a charter and declared it a "port." Ocean-going ships of up to 5,000-ton capacity are able to dock at Sharpness, the terminal dock of the city's port system. The entire dock complex is being given a new "lease on life"; an ambitious redevelopment program is converting the site into a haven of recreation, education, and commerce.

The National Waterways Museum is the principal tourist attraction in the dock complex. Two hundred years of history, which shaped the fortunes of Britain, may be viewed there, housed in an imposing three-story building. The historic docks are also home to three other museums, an antiques center, shopping, restaurants, and pubs. Following this, you may ride in a horse-drawn wagon around the dockland area.

Gloucester's showplace is, of course, its cathedral. It consists of a Norman nucleus (1089–1260) with additions in every known style of Gothic architecture. Topped by a towering fifteenth-century pinnacle that rises 225 feet above ground level, Gloucester's cathedral is judged to be one of the six most beautiful buildings in Europe. If you have a limited amount of time to spend sightseeing in Gloucester, you will make the best use of it by concentrating on the cathedral and its surroundings.

The cathedral's origins began in 679, when the Saxons founded the monastery of St. Peter on the site. In the year 909, Alfred the Great's daughter gave relics to the priory, making it the Church of St. Oswald. The cathedral is the oldest building in Gloucester. It is a magnificent example of medieval architecture with its great Norman piers still in the cathedral nave. Since the fifteenth century, craftsmen have continued to work on the structure, gracing it with an elegant exterior of later architectural designs, but basically it remains a Norman edifice.

The city's **tourist information center** is located in St. Michael's Tower at the city's major intersection, "The Cross." Its hours of operation are 1000–1700 Monday through Saturday (telephone 01452–421188).

GLOUCESTER—*ON THE RIVER SEVERN*

A Day Excursion from London

DEPART PADDINGTON STATION	ARRIVE SWINDON STATION	DEPART SWINDON STATION	ARRIVE GLOUCESTER STATION	NOTES
0740	0833	0845	0932	(1)
0903	—	—	1047	(1)
0945	1047	1054	1141	(1)
0930	1043	1050	1138	(4)
1100	1156	1205	1252	(3)
1125	—	—	1308	(1)

DEPART GLOUCESTER STATION	ARRIVE SWINDON STATION	DEPART SWINDON STATION	ARRIVE PADDINGTON STATION	NOTES
1520	—	—	1720	(1)
1608	1656	1705	1810	(1)
1630	—	—	1830	(4)
1749	1836	1855	2000(A)	(2)
1900	1946	1954	2100	(1)
1918	—	—	2121	(4)

Distance: 114 miles/184 km
References: Table 125
                    Thomas Cook Table 529

(1) MON–FRI   (3) SAT   (A) 10 minutes later on Saturday
(2) MON–SAT   (4) SUN

Train Information: 01452–29501
InterCity Services: 0171–387–7070
Gloucester Tourist Information Centre: 01452–421188

Gloucester's Central Station is within walking distance of the city center or you may hail a taxi or ride a city bus.

To reach the tourist center on foot, walk toward the cathedral from the Central Station until you reach Northgate Street. Then turn left to where it intersects Eastgate Street at The Cross. Northgate and Eastgate streets take their names from the ancient city routes through the Roman wall.

Sightseeing in Gloucester has been made easy by the "Via Sacra," a walkway around the city center that follows the lines of the original city wall. It is described in several publications that are available in the information center. It can be recognized by the pattern of dark paving placed in the sidewalk to keep visitors from going too far astray. Ask for *The Gloucester Mini Guide*.

At the beginning of the walking tour, you can observe a considerable variety of early English architecture, ranging from fifteenth-century timber-frame structures to the Tudor facades of the present county offices. You will pass Blackfriars, the best preserved medieval Dominican friary in Britain. Although it is under restoration, a portion is open to the public. Greyfriars is also on the route. Unlike Blackfriars, however, most of it stands in ruins.

Stopping in the city museum and art gallery affords the opportunity to examine many archaeological items, including a part of the original Roman city wall. The museum is open 1000–1700 Monday through Saturday. It is also open 1000–1600 on Sunday from July through September.

Just beyond the city museum, for example, you will see the Eastgate Shopping Center, which provides traffic-free areas at ground level. The tour ends at the cathedral in St. Lucy's Garden, the approach to the college green.

Gloucester abounds with interesting eating establishments ranging from McDonald's to such ancient eateries as the New Inn on Northgate Street. But don't let the name fool you. The New Inn was built by St. Peter's Abbey to accommodate pilgrims in 1450. The inn courtyard was used for staging plays during the time of Queen Elizabeth I, and in the eighteenth century, the inn became renowned for its association with traveling menageries and exhibitions of "curiosities." It is said to be the finest medieval open-gallery inn in England, and the food served there today matches the excellence of its medieval decor.

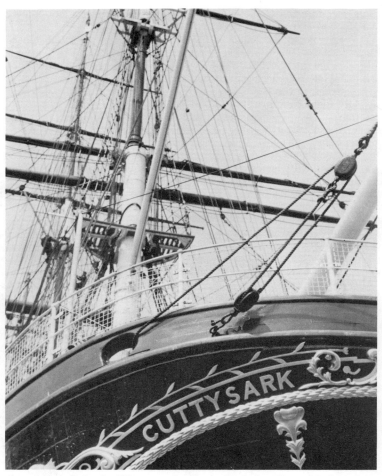

Cutty Sark, built for the China tea trade, rests in dry dock at Greenwich. One of the fastest of sailing ships, she once logged 363 nautical miles in twenty-four hours! Launched at Dumbarton, Scotland, November 1869, the dry-docked ship was opened to public view by Her Majesty Queen Elizabeth II in 1957 following refit.

From London . . .

A DAY EXCURSION TO GREENWICH
DISTANCE BY TRAIN: 7 miles (11 km)
AVERAGE TRAIN TIME: 15 minutes

Greenwich is the cradle of Britain's maritime history and the home of time. Henry VIII and Elizabeth I were born in the Royal Palace of Greenwich. It was here that Elizabeth greeted Sir Francis Drake upon his return from sailing around the world in 1580. In 1967, Queen Elizabeth II knighted Sir Francis Chichester for his solo circumnavigation of the world at a public ceremony at the Royal Naval College, which now stands on the site of the Royal Palace.

The clipper *Cutty Sark*, one of the fastest of sailing ships, lies in dry dock at Greenwich. The world's largest maritime museum, the National Maritime Museum of Greenwich, has in its fascinating collection the paddle tug *Reliant*, often described as "the world's largest ship in a bottle." At the Old Royal Observatory, visitors can stand astride the strip marking the Prime Meridian for Greenwich Mean Time (GMT), with one foot in an east longitude and the other one in west longitude. If time permits, you can walk *under* the Thames River to the Isle of Dogs and treat yourself to a panoramic view of Greenwich from that vantage point. Greenwich has much to offer.

Upon arrival in the Greenwich railway station, use the pedestrian subway (underpass) to the main station and the street. Turn left and walk along the road into the town. Follow the signs guiding you to the National Maritime Museum and the *Cutty Sark*. Where they split, continue to follow the CUTTY SARK signs until the ship's masts come into view. The local **Greenwich tourist information center** is just before the entrance of the *Cutty Sark* Gardens at 46 Greenwich Church Street. The center is open 1015–1645 daily throughout the year. Of the various publications available, we recommend the brochure, *Greenwich Visitors' Guide.*

The *Cutty Sark* was launched in 1869 and served in the China tea trade, as well as the Australian wool trade. Her curious name, which means "short chemise," originated in "Tam o'Shanter," a poem by Robert Burns in which the witch Nanny appeared in a *cutty sark*. The ship's figurehead represents the witch Nanny.

A short distance away stands the fifty-four-foot ketch, *Gypsy Moth*, which Sir Francis Chichester sailed solo around the world. Sir Francis sailed from Plymouth on 27 August 1966. He completed his circumnavigation of the world on 28 May 1967, when he sailed into Plymouth harbor to a tumultuous welcome. In his voyage, he covered a distance of 28,500 miles.

While at Greenwich, you can take the opportunity of viewing it from the Island Gardens on the Isle of Dogs, located on the opposite bank of the River

GREENWICH — *ON THE PRIME MERIDIAN*

A Day Excursion from London

DEPART FROM CHARING CROSS STATION	ARRIVE IN GREENWICH STATION	NOTES
0812	0826	(3)
0824	0840	(1)
0844	0900	(1)
0913	0927	(1)
0942	0956	(1)
0957	1011	(4)

Additional trains depart at twelve and forty-two minutes past the hour through 1542.

DEPART FROM GREENWICH STATION	ARRIVE IN CHARING CROSS STATION	NOTES
1531	1548	(2)
1607	1626	(1)
1731	1748	(3)
1829	1846	(4)

Additional trains depart at one and thirty-one minutes past the hour through 2331.

Plus frequent service serving Waterloo (East), as well as Cannon Street station.

Distance: 7 miles/11 km
References: Table 200

(1) MON–FRI	(3) SAT
(2) MON–SAT	(4) SUN

For a circuitous rail trip to or from Greenwich, inquire regarding The Docklands Light Railway (DLR) running between its London terminals, Tower Gateway or Bank, and the Island Gardens Station on the Isle of Dogs, with access to Greenwich via the foot tunnel under the Thames. Information is available by ringing up (0171) 918–4000. *BritRail Pass not accepted.* One-way fare, Tower Gateway to Island Gardens, adults £1.10; children under sixteen, 60 pence. The London Underground station, Tower Hill on the District Line, is within walking distance of the DLR's Tower Gate terminal.

Train Information: 0171–928–5100

Thames. To get there, take the Greenwich foot tunnel under the river. It takes only about four minutes to walk through the tunnel to the opposite bank. From this vantage point, it is possible to photograph the entire Greenwich complex. The domed entrance to the tunnel lies in front of the *Cutty Sark.*

A few yards beyond the *Cutty Sark's* stern is the entrance to the Royal Naval College. Built on the original site of the old Tudor Palace at Greenwich during the seventeenth-century reign of William and Mary, the present buildings were used as a hospital for disabled and aged naval pensioners. In 1873, it became the Royal Naval College to provide for the higher education of naval officers.

Visitors are admitted to the Royal Naval College's Painted Hall and Chapel daily except Thursday from 1430 to 1645. Admission is free (telephone 0181–858–2154). The Painted Hall is now used as the officers' mess of the college. After the Battle of Trafalgar, the body of Lord Nelson lay in state in the Upper Hall. The interior decorating, by Sir James Thornhill, took nineteen years to complete. (You'll find out why when you see it.) Benjamin West's painting of the shipwrecked *St. Paul* in the college chapel is one of the highlights of that beautiful structure.

There is an admission charge of £3.50 (child £2.50) for the *Cutty Sark*. To reach the National Maritime Museum, turn left on King William walk, leaving the Naval College. Walk past the Seamen's Hospital to Romney Road. Cross it and turn left. The museum entrance is a few yards beyond. An admission ticket of £5.50 (children £3.00) will admit entrance to the museum, The Queen's House, and the Old Royal Observatory. The National Maritime Museum tour leads you through its west wing where you can view the *Reliant* and the state barges once used on the River Thames. The museum houses an amazing display of old ship models and features naval history of the nineteenth and twentieth centuries. Also included are two galleries of Victorian paintings and Arctic exploration exhibits.

Adjacent to the National Maritime Museum stands The Queen's House, a royal villa from the time of Charles I. Reopened by Queen Elizabeth II in May 1990, the palace has been restored to its former glory with sumptuous furnishings and rich silk hangings reflective of its heyday when Henrietta Maria, wife of Charles I, was in residence there. It is the earliest example of English Palladian architecture.

In Greenwich Park, next to the museum, you may enter the Old Royal Observatory (telephone 0181–858–4422), an integral part of the museum. It is open daily 1000-1700. The Prime Meridian marking the line of zero degrees longitude on which GMT (Greenwich Mean Time) is calculated is located in the courtyard of the observatory's meridian building.

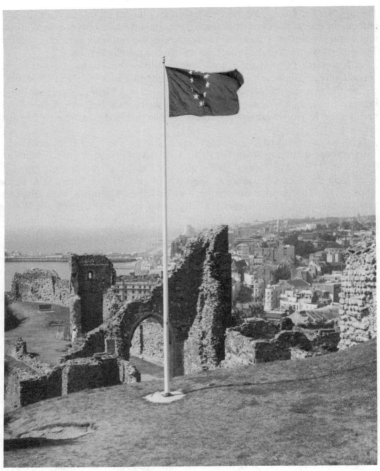

Hastings Castle beckons to visitors from atop the city's west hill, where it was built by William the Conqueror in 1067 following the Battle of Hastings the previous year. Among the castle ruins, you'll find an eleventh-century siege tent. Enter and you will be transported back to the most famous date in English history—1066! Below the fortress in the old city's narrow streets are many eighteenth-century houses. (Courtesy Tourism and Leisure Department, Hastings/Chris Parker)

A DAY EXCURSION TO HASTINGS ⚬
DISTANCE BY TRAIN: 63 miles (101 km)
AVERAGE TRAIN TIME: 1 hour, 30 minutes

Undoubtedly, 1066 is one of the most well-known dates in history. When dusk fell at the field of Senlac near Hastings on 14 October 1066, William the Conqueror, Duke of Normandy, had defeated the Saxon army of slain King Harold and had become the new king of England. Hastings holds the lore of the Battle of Hastings plus the lure of its ancient fishing village and Norman castle.

In addition to its rich historical heritage, Hastings has been an attractive seaside resort since the mid-eighteenth century, when London physicians began prescribing sea air and saltwater as a panacea for all their patients' ills. Three miles of promenades line its beaches, many of them two-tiered with sun-trapped shelters overlooking the English Channel. Sun is more sought after in Hastings than surf because the water is very cold. Examine any photo of an English seaside resort and you'll see that the majority of the bathers are on the beach, not in the sea!

There are four railway stations within the Borough of Hastings. Use the Hastings Central Station as a focal point. The **tourist information center** is at 4 Robertson Terrace (telephone 01424–781111). Leaving the Central Station, walk downhill to the seaside and orient yourself on Carlisle Parade. The information center is on the west end. The office operates Monday through Friday, 1000–1700; Saturday, 1000–1300. The sign on the center entrance reads TOURIST INFORMATION. During summer, the center is open longer hours during the week and on Sunday as well.

Contrary to popular belief, the Battle of Hastings was not fought in Hastings, nor was the Norman castle in Hastings involved. After landing, the Norman army marched northward about six miles, where they engaged the Saxons on the field of Senlac. The castle in Hastings, formerly a timber fort, was converted to stone in 1067, a year after the battle.

Harold's troops were not pushovers. Nineteen days prior to the Battle of Hastings, his men had put a Norse army to rout at Stamford Bridge near York. In the initial onslaught at Senlac, the Normans retreated with the Saxons in hot pursuit. In so doing, the Saxons had to break the tight formation of their Saxon wall of shields, and the Norman cavalry quickly took advantage of the hole opening up in the line and inflicted heavy losses upon the Saxons. This tactic was twice repeated and the conflict ended. Today's Super Bowl tactics may have developed in Hastings! To go sightseeing at the battleground, board any "Battle Abbey" bus.

During the Roman occupation, Hastings was one of the famous Cinque

HASTINGS—*FAMOUS BATTLE SITE*

A Day Excursion from London

DEPART FROM CHARING CROSS STATION	ARRIVE IN HASTINGS STATION	NOTES
0800	0941	(3)
0910	1038	(2)
0940	1117	(2)
1010	1146(5)	(4)
1140	1217	(2)
1210	1340(5)	(4)

DEPART FROM HASTINGS STATION	ARRIVE IN CHARING CROSS STATION	NOTES
1552	1721	(3)
1652	1822	(2)
1711	1857	(4)
1740	1921	(2)
1841	2021	(2)
1941	2121 (2101 SUN)	(2)
2111	2257	(4)

Distance: 63 miles/101 km
References: Table 207
            Thomas Cook Table 501

(1) MON–FRI	(3) SAT	(5) Trains arrive 5 minutes later on Sunday
(2) MON–SAT	(4) SUN	

Train Information: 01732–770111
InterCity Services: 0171–928–5100
Hastings Tourist Information Centre: 01424–718888

(five) Ports where the caesars moored their galleys. Later in history, however, the harbor was silted up by a series of violent storms, culminating with the great tempest in 1287. As a result, Hastings was reduced to the status of a small fishing community during the following four centuries.

The tourist information center has an excellent brochure entitled "Hastings 1066 Country." With it in hand, you can easily visit the Norman castle via the West Hill lift. After visiting the castle, venture a few more paces to St. Clement's Caves for the "Smugglers' Adventure." The Smugglers' Adventure is set in a labyrinth of caverns and secret passageways beneath West Hill, where the smugglers are brought to life.

After drinking in the panoramic sights from atop the hill, you can drift back toward the sea and Hastings' "Old Town." On Hill Street, observe the two cannonballs on either side of St. Clements Church belfry. The right one was shot into the tower by the French; the one on the left was added by the locals to balance things off.

The French artillery attack in 1337 also leveled the All Saints Church in the Old Town. Undaunted by the French shelling, the locals got busy and re-erected the church in 1436. The interior of the church contains a well-preserved fifteenth-century mural depicting the Last Judgment, with the devil casting souls into hell. The mural was intended to portray a lesson in morality for illiterate people of the Middle Ages. Today, television is utilized for the same purpose.

You'll pass many interesting points on your walk. Stop for a closer examination of the Old Town Hall on High Street. It is now a museum. Drop by the Stables Theatre opposite the Old Town Hall. It originally served as the stables for the Old Hastings House, which was spared demolition by being converted into a cultural center. Your next stop should be the Shovells, circa 1450, reputedly the oldest house in town. If you're desperate for a libation, you might try the Stag Inn opposite the Shovells, where remains of mummified cats and rats decorate the bar. Nearing the end of the Old Town walk, you will pass an unusual wedge-shaped house called the "piece of cheese," no doubt the funniest house in town. If you have time, head out on Rock-A-Nore Road to Hastings Sea Life Centre and take an incredible 3-D voyage from outer space to the depths of the earth's seas.

Don't miss the 243-foot embroidery in Hastings' town hall on Queens Road. It depicts eighty-one of the greatest events of British history since 1066, including the Battle of Hastings, the Boston Tea Party, and the first television broadcast.

The city of Hastings celebrates the famous battle every year by staging a program of events and attractions over a full week, encompassing the fourteenth day of October, to commemorate the battle day in 1066.

Station Hotel is a relatively new addition to Ipswich, considering the city was chartered in A.D. 1200. The hotel stands opposite the town's rail station, and its memorabilia of railroading provide a pleasant decor for luncheon, dinner, or a pint of ale while waiting for your train.

From London . . .

A DAY EXCURSION TO IPSWICH
DISTANCE BY TRAIN: 69 miles (111 km)
AVERAGE TRAIN TIME: 1 hour, 10 minutes

The architecture of Ipswich reflects its history. By-passed by the Romans, this town does not display the former grandeur of Rome. A seafaring community long before King John granted the town's first charter in 1200, Ipswich has always been engaged in commerce and has risen or declined along with the fortunes of its citizens' enterprises. The lack of Georgian buildings in Ipswich is evidence of the town's decline during that period, caused by the loss of its famous Suffolk cloth trade. A revitalization of its harbor by the mid-nineteenth century brought new prosperity to Ipswich and accounts for the number of splendid public buildings erected then, as well as the Victorian architecture of its homes.

Ipswich has withstood the onslaughts of the Vikings and other seaborne raiders down through the ages. Starting with World War I, the town's docks became the targets of a new type of raider coming from the sky rather than from the sea. From 1915 to the end of the conflict, there were a number of zeppelin attacks, but damage was light. During the years 1943–45, Ipswich was rimmed by no fewer than sixty-five air bases of the U.S. Eighth Air Force, from which were launched a staggering 3,000-plus bomber raids against the Third Reich.

Today, with a population of 120,000, Ipswich has a developing port and is an important industrial and commercial center with fine shopping, sports, and entertainment facilities. Ipswich considers its Tudor Christchurch Mansion, set in sixty-five acres of parkland, only a five-minute walk from the center of town, to be its finest attraction. The information office will gladly point out the way to you.

The **tourist information center** is easy to reach. It is located in St. Stephen's Church on St. Stephen's Lane (telephone 01473–258070). Departing the rail station proceed straight ahead down Princes Street to Friars Street and turn right. Friars Street curves and turns into Falcon Street. St. Stephen's Church will be on your left. If the weather is inclement, catch the "City Centre" bus or hail a taxi immediately in front of the station. Obtain a map at the information center before going off to explore the endless streets and enticing alleyways leading off Ipswich's Cornhill. Office hours are 0900–1700 Monday through Saturday, closed Sunday.

The town's Leisure Services Department has devised an excellent series of brochures *(Ipswich Historic Churches Trail, Wet Dock Maritime Trail,* and *Ipswich Street Map)* available for a nominal charge. The trails are signposted

135

IPSWICH—*CHARTERED IN A.D. 1200*

A Day Excursion from London

DEPART FROM LIVERPOOL STREET STATION	ARRIVE IN IPSWICH STATION	NOTES
0800	0900 (0913 SAT)	(1)
0830	0935 (0943 SUN)	(1)(2)
0930	1035	(1)
1000	1112	(1)
1030	1135 (1140 SUN)	(1)(2)
1130	1236	(1)

DEPART FROM IPSWICH STATION	ARRIVE IN LIVERPOOL STREET STATION	NOTES
1445	1553 (1555 SUN)	(1)(2)
1545	1653	(1)
1645	1758 (1755 SUN)	(1)(2)
1745	1854	(1)
1845	1953	(1)
1945	2053	(1)
2120	2233	(2)

Distance: 69 miles/111 km
References: Table 11
             Thomas Cook Table 580

(1) MON–SAT   (2) SUN

Train Information: 01473–690744
InterCity Services: 0171–928–5100
Ipswich Tourist Information Centre: 01473–258070

by black-and-white signs that are numbered to correspond with the descriptions in the brochure. No doubt the trail was laid out for British walkers, for it is much too ambitious a course for the average Yank to complete within the prescribed period of one hour—at least it was for us! The route is circular, so you can join (or leave) at any point.

Places along the Trails that may be of interest to you include the junction of Butter Market, St. Stephens Lane, and Dial Lane. As you can probably guess, the Butter Market was once a marketplace for many products, one of which was butter. The Ancient House in the Butter Market will remind you of the Market's age (more than 500 years old), for its windows represent the known world during its time—and Australia is missing because it had not yet been discovered. A seventeenth-century merchant, Robert Sparrow, added the exquisite, ornate plasterwork to the exterior.

Dial Lane is a traffic-free pedestrian area that gets its name from a clock that was once on the St. Lawrence Church. Although most of the church dates back to the fifteenth and early sixteenth centuries, its tower was rebuilt in 1882 to reflect its original design.

By passing the church and turning left into St. Lawrence Street and then right into Tavern Street, you'll come upon the Great White Horse Hotel. It is the only surviving inn that can be traced in the city records before 1571. Its Georgian brick facade, completed in 1818, covers a basically timber-frame structure from the sixteenth century. A young London news reporter, sent to Ipswich to cover an election, stayed in the Great White Horse and later wrote his recollections in a comic novel that changed the course of his life. The reporter was Charles Dickens; the novel, *The Pickwick Papers*.

Near the end of your walking tour, take time to pause at the junction of Tavern Street and Dial Lane. The view down Dial Lane to the Ancient House is one of the most photographed areas in Ipswich. The Tudor-style buildings reflect the detail and attention of the city's craftsmen. From this point, a left turn will take you to the Cornhill, the end of your Tourist Town Trail walk.

As you stand at Cornhill, it may be sobering to consider that only 400 years ago, nine people were burned at the stake on this hill for heresy. Before becoming too sober, however, we suggest you visit one of the bars in the Great White Horse Hotel. Distinguished visitors of the past, who, besides Charles Dickens, included such notables as King George II, Louis XVIII, and Lord Nelson, have quaffed many a draft there. A toast to these gentlemen would seem only proper. So have a go at it, mate, if you can get there before they call "time!"

Thatched roofs of Shanklin's old village area attract visitors to the resort town where poet John Keats once resided.

Hovercraft skims between the mainland and the Isle of Wight, augmenting catamaran service between Portsmouth and Ryde for residents and holiday makers on England's vacation isle.

From London . . .

A DAY EXCURSION TO THE ISLE OF WIGHT
DISTANCE BY TRAIN: 88 miles (142 km)
AVERAGE TRAIN TIME: 2 hours, 40 minutes

"Britain's miniature" is a term often employed to describe the Isle of Wight. Shaped like a diamond, the island is a veritable jewel of every feature of the mainland condensed into a mere 147 square miles. It is dotted with historic spots, sandy beaches, thatched villages, rolling countryside—and discotheques, too, if that's your pleasure. There is fun for everyone on the Isle of Wight, and getting there can be fun, too.

The majority of trains departing Waterloo Station in London for Portsmouth Harbor are InterCity trains. As they glide through the scenery of southern England bound for the coast, you'll be treated to a delightful kaleidoscope of England's landscape from the wide-vision train windows. Stay aboard when the train halts briefly in the Portsmouth and Southsea Station. Your destination is the Portsmouth Harbor Station, five minutes farther on.

Board the Portsmouth-Ryde catamaran at the end of the harbor station. Your BritRail Pass does not cover the passage. The fare is about £5.40 one way. The crossing takes only about fifteen minutes.

Docking at the Ryde pier head, you have three options of sightseeing on the island by train. The trains, by the way, run right onto the pier and look every bit like those of the Bakerloo Underground Line in London. All the coaches are one class, but try to select one with ventilators at the top of the windows. It can get a bit stuffy aboard the train in summer. The three options? They are Ryde, Sandown, or Shanklin. All three lie along the nine miles of track extending from the Ryde pier head to the terminal in Shanklin.

Ryde is the Isle of Wight's gateway. Set picturesquely on a hillside, it becomes a wonderful grandstand from which to watch the great ships of the world sailing by. The pier at Ryde is more than 2,300 feet long, so board the train after disembarking from the passenger ferry and ride the train to its first stop, Ryde Esplanade, where you will find the **Tourist Information Centre** ready to assist you during summer season (telephone 01983-862942; accommodations 867979). The pier has a pedestrian walk, if you elect to make your way to the shore in a more leisurely manner. Ryde has six miles of sandy beach backed by pleasant, wooded gardens. The town is also noted for its Regency and Victorian buildings and for its Royal Victoria Arcade shopping center.

Sandown is the next railway stop after passing the Brading Station. It has all the facilities for a summer holiday, including a new pier complex that offers a modern theater, licensed bars, cafés, and a restaurant. The theater

ISLE OF WIGHT — *THE HOLIDAY ISLAND*

A Day Excursion from London*

DEPART FROM WATERLOO STATION	ARRIVE IN SHANKLIN STATION	NOTES
0723	1006	(1)(4)
0800	1047	(2)(5)
0820	1106	(1)(5)
0900	1147	(2)(5)
0920	1206	(3)(5)(6)

DEPART FROM SHANKLIN STATION	ARRIVE IN WATERLOO STATION	NOTES
1536	1825 (A)	(2)(4)
1616	1911	(3)(5)
1636	1925 (A)	(2)(5)
1736	2023 (A)	(2)(5)
1834	2138	(1)(5)
1936	2247	(3)(5)

Distance: 88 miles/142 km
References: Table 167
               Thomas Cook Table 504
   (Above service through September 25. Inquire in station for off-season schedules.)

* Via ferry service between Portsmouth-Ryde to Shanklin on the Isle of Wight. One-class service between Portsmouth Harbor and Shanklin. Buffet and bar service is available en route. BritRail Pass *not* accepted on ferry crossing. Purchase tickets at pier.

(1) MON–FRI	(4) Trip requires 3 train changes. Transfer in Portsmouth and Southsea, Portsmouth Harbour, and Ryde Pier Head.
(2) MON–SAT	(5) Trip requires 2 train changes. Transfer in Portsmouth Harbor and Ryde Pier Head.
(3) SUN	(6) Train departs Waterloo 26 minutes earlier Sundays 28 January to 24 March
	(A) Arrives at 23 minutes past the hour on Saturdays

Catamaran service between Portsmouth/Southsea and Ryde runs frequently throughout the day. Purchase tickets at pier.

Shanklin Tourist Information Centre
01983–862942

offers a musical review, which opens in May and runs through the beginning of October. The sheltered Sandown Bay has more than five miles of attractive, sandy beaches, where you may find such diversions as miniature golf and a canoe lake. Motor-launch trips are popular. Check at the pier or the tourist information center on High Street for details.

Sandown and Shanklin are considered the twin resorts on the Isle of Wight. Because the distance between the two rail stations is exactly two miles, you should select one or the other for your day excursion. There is much to see and do in either resort.

Shanklin frequently holds the British annual sunshine record. It is built on a cliff with a sheltered mile-long beach lying below. It is the end of the line for rail travel. It is easy, however, to transfer to the buses operated by the island's bus company, Southern Vectis, for farther points such as Ventnor, Newport, and Cowes. Check with the Southern Vectis Travel Office on Regent Street, two blocks from Shanklin's train station.

Our personal selection of the Isle's options would be Shanklin. It is certainly one of the prettiest towns in Britain. Shanklin's Old Village on Ventnor Road is world-famous for its quiet beauty. From there, you may descend to Shanklin's beach esplanade via a walk through Shanklin's Chine, a cleft in the town's cliff with overhanging trees, plants, ferns, and a cascading stream. Passage through the Chine costs £1.80 for adults; for children, 50 pence. Check first with the town's information center at 67 High Street for all details.

One of the most gifted and appealing of England's nineteenth-century poets, John Keats, found Shanklin's climate congenial to his health and the town's scenic beauty so inspiring that he resided there for a long period of time. Keats Green, a spacious promenade on the cliff top of Shanklin, commemorates his loving association with the town.

Queen Victoria spent her holidays on the Isle of Wight and died there in Osborne House in 1901. This house, built by order of the queen in 1845, is maintained in good order with the queen's furniture still in place. In a shed on the Osborne House property, you can see the gardening tools of the royal children from more than a century ago. Each tool and wheelbarrow is marked with the small owners' initials. The Queen and Prince Albert used Osborne as a country residence, and it is said that the prince had a considerable influence on the design of the residence. The main rooms and many of the private apartments are open to the public between Easter Monday and the end of October. Situated at East Cowes, which is the northern one of the island's twin peaks, you can reach the Osborne House by bus from Ryde Esplanade Station.

Checker-work front graces the fifteenth-century Trinity Guildhall, located between the Victorian town hall and the sixteenth-century Old Gaol House, in King's Lynn. It houses an eighteenth-century card room and assembly rooms.

From London . . .

A DAY EXCURSION TO KING'S LYNN
DISTANCE BY TRAIN: 97 miles (156 km)
AVERAGE TRAIN TIME: 2 hours, 5 minutes

King's Lynn, once "Bishops' Lynn" and renamed when Henry VIII took over the bishop's manor, is one of the most historic towns in England. The old section of town still seems medieval, complete with narrow streets, guildhalls, and riverside quays, where the gulls reel and scream overhead. The town's former prosperity has left it with a rich heritage of architecture. Set along the east bank of the wide and muddy Ouse River, King's Lynn is the northern terminal of the London-Cambridge-Ely rail line.

King's Lynn came into being during the eleventh century on the middle of three islands, where four streams ran into the Ouse River. Water highways became vital to the commerce of the town. With these waterway connections to the English Midlands, the town of Lynn became an important trading port, bustling with the romance of foreign cargoes, sailing ships, and foreign accents. By the thirteenth century, the town found prosperity in the wool trade between England and the Continent. This aura of a wealthy medieval town still prevails. Today, the town is a thriving, modern port, an essential link between Britain and the rest of the Common Market.

Streets and alleyways in King's Lynn twist and wind about on a grand scale, so a town map will be an invaluable aid. We suggest you make your way immediately from the train station to the **King's Lynn Heritage Centre and Tourist Information Centre**. To do so, walk directly away from the front of the train station (which faces the west) down Waterloo Street. The street undergoes a name change at every intersection—Market, Paradise, New Conduit, Purfleet—but if one continues walking toward the west, one will come to King Street. Turn left onto King Street, which immediately becomes Queen Street. But don't despair—the Tourist Information Centre is a mere 200 yards away on the lefthand side in the Old Gaol House in Saturday Market Place.

You will be tempted to wander about in Queen Street with its lovely merchants' houses, each with a character all its own. Proceed to the information center and equip yourself with a copy of the *King's Lynn Town Walk* booklet. With it, you'll know where you are. The Information Centre operates on a variety of schedules. We suggest that you telephone ahead: (01553) 763044. Walking from the train station to the town hall takes about ten minutes.

The previously mentioned town-walk booklet is a masterpiece of simplicity. It is packed with facts about the town and its buildings. The trail follows a circular route, so you may start and finish wherever it is most convenient for

KING'S LYNN—*RICH IN ARCHITECTURE*

A Day Excursion from London

DEPART FROM KING'S CROSS STATION	ARRIVE IN KING'S LYNN STATION	NOTES
0652	0853	(1)
0743	0935	(2)
0845	1021	(1)
0913(5)	1116	(4)
0945	1126	(2)

DEPART FROM KING'S LYNN STATION	ARRIVE IN KING'S CROSS STATION	NOTES
1605	1748	(2)
1718	1910	(4)
1805	1946	(3)
1910	2046	(1)
1918	2110	(4)
1942	2136	(2)
2042	2238	(2)

Distance: 97 miles/156 km
References: Table 22
                Thomas Cook Table 575

(1) MON–FRI   (4) SUN
(2) MON–SAT   (5) Departs from Liverpool Street station
(3) SAT

Train Information: 01553–772021
InterCity Services: 0171–928–5100

King's Lynn Tourist Information Centre: 01553–763044

you. We suggest starting at the town hall. Rebuilt in 1421 after a fire, it houses the "Tales of the Old Gaol House" Exhibition, as well as King Lynn's regalia, including the magnificent King John Cup and the Red Register, purported to be one of the oldest books in the world.

A focal point in King's Lynn is the Tuesday Market Place, into which King Street leads. True to tradition, a country market is conducted there every Tuesday in the shadow of the Duke's Head Hotel, a most impressive seventeenth-century structure. The market is everything that one would expect it to be—stalls packed with the agricultural and manufacturing products of the area, augmented by absolutely free entertainment as the hucksters bid for attention.

If you miss the Tuesday market, there's another one on Saturday at a location appropriately named the Saturday Market Place. It is just opposite the town hall. A newer shopping center has been established in the center of town, on the site of the old cattle market, which was moved to one of the industrial estates outside of the town.

Visit St. George's Guild Hall at 27 King Street. It's the largest surviving medieval guild hall. When not in use as a theater, it is open Monday through Friday, 1000–1700, and 1000–1230 on Saturday. Built about 1410, it has been used as a theater, a court house, and an armory, and it is now a cultural center housing a theater and an art gallery.

King John, who ruled England between 1199 and 1216, granted the town its charter in 1204. The king came to Lynn in October 1215 in pursuit of rebellious barons. One story relates that after he was wined and dined by the burghers of Lynn, the king and his entourage set off in hot pursuit of the baronial rebels. Heading west out of King's Lynn towards Newark, the king and his entourage crossed the Norfolk tidal flats, where the River Ouse empties into The Wash, a shallow bay known for the treachery of its tides.

During the crossing, a high tide from The Wash wiped out the king's baggage train. King John reached the safety of higher shores, but he lost the crown jewels and everything else that went with such a collection in those days. King John was so distraught that he contracted dysentery (a bad "burger" perhaps?) and died a few days later. No one questioned the burghers as to exactly what they fed the king before he left Lynn. We have our suspicions, however, because reportedly all of the burghers felt fine the following morning.

The lost treasure has never been found. Somewhere near King's Lynn, buried under centuries of silt, lies King John's treasure. None of it has been recovered, and no one knows where to look for it. If you have any ideas, perhaps Robert Stack from television's *Unsolved Mysteries* show would be interested.

Magnificent Lincoln Cathedral has withstood fire, earthquakes—even Cromwell's artillery. Each of its three towers had a lofty spire, but because one fell during a storm in 1547, the other two were removed in 1807.

From London . . .

A DAY EXCURSION TO LINCOLN
DISTANCE BY TRAIN: 135 miles (217 km)
AVERAGE TRAIN TIME: 2 hours, 10 minutes

Lincoln's landmark is its cathedral. It stands on a ridge overlooking the city. Dominating the skyline, the cathedral appears as though it might be half church, half stronghold. There are actually two Lincolns—one, the cathedral and castle standing politely on the hilltop; the other, the city below girding the River Witham and buzzing with commerce. We suggest you scale the heights first and later return to the lower level by a dizzy descent down Steep Hill.

On arrival in Lincoln's Central Station, go to the city bus station, which is in front and to the right of the main station entrance (use the designated pedestrian walkways, because the vehicular traffic can be heavy at times). From the bus station, take city bus 1, 8, or 9 up the hill to the cathedral and ask the driver to let you off at the corner of Eastgate and Nettleham Road (next to Forte Posthouse). The **tourist information center** is at No. 9 Castle Hill.

On the other hand, if you abound with energy, bear to the left when leaving the station and walk a short distance on St. Mary Street to where it intersects with High Street. Turn right at this point, and, keeping the cathedral in sight, start walking in its direction up High Street. Disregard the fact that the street changes names several times. When you reach an area where a ski lift or a cable car would be most welcome, you'll be on Steep Hill—and it's appropriately named. Now gain the high ground (and your breath), and you will find yourself in Castle Square. With a right turn at the Exchequer Gate, you may enter the cathedral grounds.

Walking up the Lincoln hill from the railway station to the cathedral can give one a sense of accomplishment. It can also be hazardous to your health. Use discretion—take the bus or a taxi if there's any doubt in your mind about the climb.

Walking up Steep Hill, you will pass the Norman House said to be the house of Aaron the Jew, a money lender from the twelfth century who reportedly became the richest man in England at that time. Halfway up Steep Hill, and turning off at Danesgate, your visit will be well rewarded by an inspection of the Usher Gallery. You can view an assortment of personal property belonging to England's poet laureate, Alfred, Lord Tennyson, born in Somersby, a Lincolnshire village, in 1809. The gallery also houses an extensive collection of paintings by Peter de Wint (1784–1849). Should you arrive at Castle Square in need of lunch or a libation, seek out the Wig & Mitre, a licensed restaurant with a Dickensian atmosphere.

The tourist center atop Lincoln's ridge is between the castle and the cathe-

LINCOLN—*HILLTOP CATHEDRAL*

A Day Excursion from London

DEPART KING'S CROSS STATION	ARRIVE LINCOLN CENTRAL STATION	NOTES
0700	0907	(1)(5)
0820	1031	(1)(5)
0910	1210	(2)(6)
1030	1316	(1)(6)
1130	1409	(6)
1310	1659	(2)(5)

DEPART LINCOLN CENTRAL STATION	ARRIVE KING'S CROSS STATION	NOTES
1500	1730	(4)(5)
1608	1839	(2)(6)
1656	2003	(3)(5)
1705	1907	(1)(5)
1918	2141	(4)(5)
2033	2254	(2)(5)
2104	2331	(4)(5)

Distance: 135 miles/217 km
References: Table 30
              Thomas Cook Tables 569, 570 and 568

Note: Some trains are standard class only.

(1) MON–FRI	(4) SUN
(2) MON–SAT	(5) Change trains in Newark Northgate
(3) SAT	(6) Change trains in Peterborough

Train Information: 01302–340222
InterCity Services: 0171–387–7070

Lincoln Tourist Information Centre
01522–529828

dral. This office is open 0900–1730, except Friday, when it closes a half hour earlier. On Saturday and Sunday, it is open 1000–1700 in the summer and winter (telephone 01522–529828). There is a wealth of information available in both offices. The *Official Guide, City of Lincoln,* is published by the Lincoln City Council and is worth its purchase price. There is an abundance of other saleable and free literature available as well.

The cathedral is the main point of interest in Lincoln. When you view its exterior and examine the spacious areas under its roof, it becomes rather difficult to comprehend that it was built by medieval craftsmen in only twenty years. The Normans began construction of the cathedral in 1072. In 1141 the roof was destroyed by a fire, and in 1185, the main structure crumbled into ruins as a result of an earthquake. But it survived.

Reconstruction, which began in 1186, returned the cathedral to its original conforms, and, through the ensuing centuries, it was altered frequently. The central tower was completed around 1311. In more modern times, Lincoln's greatest attraction has withstood Cromwell's artillery and Hitler's bombs. If you have but a short period of time to visit in Lincoln, the cathedral *must* take priority over all else. In the summer, the cathedral is open 0715–2000 weekdays and 0715–1800 Sunday. In the winter, it closes at 1800 weekdays and at 1700 on Sunday. A contribution of £2.50 for adults and £1.00 for children is appreciated.

Lincoln Castle was built by William the Conqueror in 1068. It became the Normans' military stronghold in the area. Its construction is unusual in that it has two mounds: one crowned by the twelfth century Tower of Lucy, the other with Norman structures on which in the nineteenth century an observatory tower was constructed. From either of these points of vantage, there are beautiful views of the cathedral and the surrounding countryside.

Today the Lincoln Castle is a huge, walled enclosure of lawns and trees. The crown courts and the old county jail are located in the castle yard. On permanent exhibition is one of only four surviving originals of King John's Magna Carta. The castle is open Monday-Saturday 0930-1730, Sunday 1130-1730; winter closing time is 1600. Admission £2.00 adults, £1.20 for seniors, students and children.

If you wish to visit the "other Lincoln," start by descending (or plunging down) Steep Hill with its bow-fronted shops until you again reach High Street. You will find interest in the twelfth-century High Bridge, which crosses the River Witham. It is the oldest one in Britain to still carry a building on its structure, in this case, a sixteenth-century timber-framed house. The route leading from the cathedral down Steep Hill is studded with other interesting structures such as numerous public houses and restaurants. Modern Lincoln blends easily with its historical counterparts.

Ye Olde Trip to Jerusalem, one of Britain's oldest inns, crouches on the hillside below Nottingham Castle. It was so named because many crusaders stayed at the inn before setting off for the crusades. Its chimney, which runs about sixty feet through solid rock, is swept once every thirty years.

From London . . .

A DAY EXCURSION TO NOTTINGHAM
DISTANCE BY TRAIN: 127 miles (204 km)
AVERAGE TRAIN TIME: 2 hours

Nottingham is famous for many things, among them the legend of Robin Hood. Many tales of Robin and his band of merry men have been passed down through the ages by ballad and legend, though only scattered fragments remain of his origin. It appears that one Robert Fitzooth, reputed to be the Earl of Huntingdon, was born in 1160 during the reign of Henry II. Of noble birth, he squandered his inheritance at an early age; so either by necessity or by choice, he sought refuge in the forest. Here he was joined by men in similar circumstances, such as Little John, Will Scarlet, Friar Tuck, and—to add the love-interest angle to the legend—Maid Marian.

Robin Hood reigned in the forest, defying the powers of government, protecting the poor, and giving to the needy. The king's deer provided food and the king's forest provided fuel. Other necessities were obtained through barter. Taking the king's property was, of course, illegal and it drove the Sheriff of Nottingham "bananas," to the point where he offered a substantial reward for Robin's capture—dead or alive. Robin Hood eluded capture and supposedly lived to be eighty-seven years old. Records show his death occurred on 18 November 1247. This man, who lived in an age of feudal tyranny, endeared himself to countless generations and became the legendary hero of Nottingham. A fine statue to his memory stands in the courtyard of Nottingham Castle. Perhaps in the future there will be one of Kevin Costner, too.

Nottingham is also famous for its lace. For centuries it has been the center for lace making in England. The ale that Robin Hood quaffed so copiously is still a local specialty. Why not quaff some yourself in England's oldest inn, Ye Olde Trip to Jerusalem? It has been in Nottingham since 1189 waiting for you. A portion of the inn was dug into the almost vertical rock formation supporting Nottingham Castle above. Legend has it that Robin Hood scaled this rock in his invasions of Nottingham Castle.

The castle was built as a fortress in 1068 by William the Conqueror. It was destroyed during the English civil war, rebuilt, and again destroyed by an angry mob in 1831. Following its second restoration, the castle was transformed into a museum and art gallery late in the nineteenth century. There are a series of underground passages beneath the castle. Naturally, there are many tales of intrigue relating to their purpose. The castle is open to the public daily; the underground passages can be seen only on conducted tours.

The train trip from London's St. Pancras Station passes through England's Midlands en route to Nottingham, passing St. Albans, where Britain's first

151

NOTTINGHAM—*TALES OF ROBIN HOOD*

A Day Excursion from London

DEPART FROM ST. PANCRAS STATION	ARRIVE IN NOTTINGHAM STATION	NOTES
0700	0853	(1)
0730	0927	(3)
0800	0953	(1)
0900	1049	(1)
0915	1104	(3)
1030	1301	(4)
1100	1255	(1)
1215	1402	(3)

DEPART FROM NOTTINGHAM STATION	ARRIVE IN ST. PANCRAS STATION	NOTES
1433	1626	(1)
1533	1725	(1)
1552	1742	(3)
1636	1826	(4)
1733	1928	(1)
1759	1959	(4)
1903	2102	(2)

Distance: 127 miles/204 km
References: Table 53
Thomas Cook Table 560

(1) MON–FRI (3) SAT
(2) MON–SAT (4) SUN

Train Information: 01332–32051
InterCity Services: 0171–387–7070

Nottingham Tourist Information Centre
01602–470661

Christian martyr was executed, and Bedford, where John Bunyan wrote *Pilgrim's Progress*. For variety, you might want to return to London via Peterborough, transferring there to a train for King's Cross Station. Consult the train information office in Nottingham's station. It is located to your right as you exit from the trains. It is open Monday through Saturday, 0800–1830, and Sunday, 1000–1900.

The **tourist information office** in Nottingham is located at 1–4 Smithy Row at the Old Market Square, telephone 0115–947–0661. The office is within walking distance of the train station. But if your time is limited, you can hail a cab at the station and save some time as well as your shoe leather. Otherwise, take Carrington Street on your right leaving the station to where it intersects Canal Street. A left turn at this point, followed by a right turn onto Maid Marian Way, will have you pointed in the right direction. When you reach Friar Lane, turn right again and walk to where Friar Lane meets Wheeler Gate and South Parade. The Old Market Square will be on your left. You can't miss it—but if you do, just inquire at one of the taxi queues in that area.

Nottingham's tourist information center lies astride the city's two huge shopping centers—the Victoria and the Broad Marsh. Both are somewhat mind-boggling in size, and they are linked together by wide pedestrian avenues as well as a bus service running between the two establishments every eight minutes throughout the day, Monday through Saturday (price 35p).

If your time in Nottingham is limited, no doubt you should first see the historic castle area and return another day to see modern, downtown Nottingham. To visit the castle, turn right as you exit the rail station onto Carrington Street. It intersects Canal Street. Turn left onto Canal Street, and three blocks farther along in the same direction, you will come to Castle Road running up the hill to your right. Following it a short distance brings you to Ye Olde Trip to Jerusalem pub, where we suggest you rest before continuing up Castle Road to the Nottingham Castle entrance, just off Castle Place. The pub's "grub" isn't bad—in fact, it's downright good—so you might want to arrive there about lunchtime. Books about Nottingham and the lore of Robin Hood are on sale in the Ye Olde Trip to Jerusalem pub and in Nottingham Castle.

Meanwhile, back at the Old Market Square, the tourist information center is open Monday through Friday, 0830–1700; Saturday, 0900–1700; and Sunday, 1000–1600 during the summer. It has a wide selection of literature, souvenirs, and details of walking tours of Nottingham that take you, among other places, along one of the city's main thoroughfares, Maid Marian Way.

Tom Tower of Christ Church dominates St. Aldate's in Oxford. The tower houses the Great Tom Bell, which traditionally tolls at five minutes past nine to signify the closing of the gates to its original 101 scholars. The student body now numbers about 16,000.

From London . . .

A DAY EXCURSION TO OXFORD
DISTANCE BY TRAIN: 63 miles (102 km)
AVERAGE TRAIN TIME: 1 hour

The first glimpse of Oxford as you approach it by train from London confirms its title, "the city of dreaming spires." Towers, domes, and pinnacles soar on its skyline as an impressive preview of one of the great architectural centers of the world. For here in this small and compact city center are some 900 "listed" buildings, illustrating practically every style of architecture from the 11th century Saxon church of St. Michael at the Northgate to the present day.

Oxford is the oldest university in Great Britain. It had its beginnings in the twelfth century. Between the thirteenth and fifteenth centuries, it became an established national institution. It has a history of 800 years of continual existence. Oxford's student body has doubled in the past thirty years to about 16,000 students, of which the majority are undergraduates. There is no separate campus; most of its buildings lie within the center of the city. Basically, the university is a federation of independent colleges. Visitors coming to Oxford during the summer miss the normal sight of students passing between classes and the student sporting activities, but the buildings alone are worth the trip.

Apparently, there is no single explanation as to exactly how and when the university actually began. One theory claims that it was founded by English students who were expelled from the University of Paris in 1167. Others claim it came about from a gathering of various groups of students from monastic institutions in and around the growing city. From whatever origins, by the end of the twelfth century, Oxford was the established home of the first center of learning in England.

Less than half of the students come to Oxford University from exclusive schools such as Eton, founded by Henry VI in 1440. Students are only required to meet their tutor once or twice a week, either alone or perhaps with one other student. This seemingly free and easy system, which builds on individuality and confidence, is the hallmark of an Oxford education. All students live in the college for their first year and one subsequent year prior to graduation. Students are usually housed in single rooms, the restrictions on coming and going or on having guests are few.

A renaissance of reconstruction and rebuilding in Oxford during the eighteenth century destroyed much of the old street system and the houses inhabited by many religious groups. From this, the city that emerged was more spacious than before. Notwithstanding this urban renewal program, Oxford still has a certain organized clutter about it that becomes readily discernible as you move from the rail station to the city center.

155

OXFORD—*ANCIENT CITY CAMPUS*

A Day Excursion from London

DEPART FROM PADDINGTON STATION	ARRIVE IN OXFORD STATION	NOTES
0818	0924	(1)
0848	0953	(2)
0858	1003	(3)
0918	1020	(2)
1005	1110	(1)
1040	1143	(3)
1048	1153	(1)

DEPART FROM OXFORD STATION	ARRIVE IN PADDINGTON STATION	NOTES
1515	1620	(2)
1615	1720	(2)
1640	1745	(3)
1731	1851	(3)
1815	1920	(2)
1915	2020	(2)
2015	2120	(2)
2130	2242	(1)

Distance: 63 miles/102 km
References: Table 116
                    Thomas Cook Table 539

(1) MON–FRI   (3) SUN
(2) MON–SAT

Train Information: 01865–722333
InterCity Services: 0171–928–5100

Oxford Tourist Information Centre
01865–726871

In addition to being a seat of learning, Oxford—unlike Cambridge—has a strong industrial background. It was here that William Morris founded his automobile empire, now Rover car assembly. The commercial and academic worlds have combined to create other flourishing industries such as publishing, research and development, and tourism. Oxford is also famous as the home of several distinguished hospitals.

Today the use of cars is discouraged in the city center, with visitors making the most instead of Oxford's excellent train services, supplemented by an extremely efficient Park–and–Ride system for motorists. The city fathers also urge everyone to return to the traditional Oxford method of propulsion—the bicycle. By the way, be on the lookout for bicycles propelled by students pedaling themselves from their college to lectures or laboratories.

The **Oxford Tourist Information Centre** is on Gloucester Green, just a short walk from the rail station. The center is open during the summer months, Monday through Saturday, 0930–1700; Sunday and summer bank holidays, from 1000–1300 and 1330–1530 (telephone 01865–726871). To reach the Tourist Information Center follow the black and gold pedestrian signs via either Hythe Bridge Street or Park End Street.

You can also buy your ticket here for the Official Walking Tours which leave the Information Centre daily throughout the year from 1100–1400. The tours, which last two hours, will take you around the most interesting parts of the city and into those colleges open to the guides on that day. From this beginning, build your own plan of activities, perhaps to include the Oxford Story Exhibition of University History, a tour and tasting at Morrell's Brewery, punting and cruising on the Thames and Cherwell, an open bus tour or a visit to the ancient Bodleian Library or one of the university's five excellent museums, all of which are free.

Penzance pirate is portrayed on the roof of the Admiral Benbow Inn on Chapel Street in Penzance. The interior of this 400-year-old tavern is decorated with genuine ship figureheads. Its nautical theme and low-beamed ceilings add to the inn's charm.

From London . . .

AN "OUT-AND-BACK" EXCURSION TO PENZANCE
DISTANCE BY TRAIN: 305 miles (491 km)
AVERAGE TRAIN TIME: 5 hours

Penzance lends itself more to an "out-and-back" excursion than to a day excursion—although with British InterCity 125 trains, it is now possible to visit England's westernmost town in the course of a day and still be back in London that evening. An excellent way to visit Penzance is to board the sleeper that departs from London's Waterloo Station just before midnight. You can board about an hour before departure time, have the attendant make a nightcap for you, and be well into dreamland by the time the train rolls out of London's suburbs. At 0815 you arrive in Penzance Station after being awakened by the attendant bringing your morning tea or coffee and biscuits. After a full day's sightseeing in Penzance, you can board either the sleeper for your return to London or the InterCity 125 at 1630 and return to London by 2215 the same evening.

Penzance also offers a diversion. When you feel it's time to move on from London to the north and Edinburgh, check out of your London accommodations and take the sleeper to Penzance. Go sightseeing in Penzance, then arrive back in London as described above at 2215 and transfer leisurely to London's Euston Station to board the Night Scotsman at 2355. You'll arrive in Edinburgh the next morning at 0645. Passengers may remain aboard until 0800.

Sleeper reservations should be made well in advance—don't wait until the last minute or you may be disappointed, especially during holidays and peak summer travel periods. Don't forget to check the second-class-sleeper availability if first class is filled. Sometimes if you show up on the departure platform about half an hour before the train leaves, you can pick up a berth cancellation, but don't count on it.

When you arrive in Penzance, you are literally at "the end of the line" insofar as rail travel is concerned. Geographically speaking, you are also at the western end of England. A mere ten miles more would bring you to Land's End, where a road sign pointing to the west cryptically states, AMERICA 4,000 MILES. It is difficult to find a grander coastline. This is Land's End Peninsula—the sightseeing opportunities are endless. The **tourist information center** in Penzance is located on Station Road, immediately outside of the rail station (telephone 01736–62207). Upon arrival in the center, the first item of information you should collect is a Penzance & District map. This graphic presentation of the peninsula will help you put the area into the proper perspective for your visit.

Publications that are available in the information center will prove to be

159

PENZANCE—*WESTERN END OF THE LINE*

An "Out-and-Back" Excursion from London

DEPART FROM PADDINGTON STATION	ARRIVE IN PENZANCE STATION	NOTES
0740	1320	(1)
0750	1357	(3)
1015	1540	(4)
1045	1540	(1)
1325	1920	(3)(5)
1235	1755	(1)
1735	2230	(1)

DEPART FROM PENZANCE STATION	ARRIVE IN PADDINGTON STATION	NOTES
0845	1350	(1)
0846	1410	(3)
0937	1500	(3)
0940	1455	(2)
1437	2010	(4)
1443	1945	(1)
1629	2215	(1)

Distance: 305 miles/491 km
References: Table 135
            Thomas Cook Table 515

(1) MON–FRI   (4) SUN
(2) MON–SAT   (5) Summer only
(3) SAT

Note: Sleepers depart London Waterloo Station Monday through Friday and Sunday at 2350 and arrive at 0820. Sleepers depart Penzance Monday through Friday at 2200 arriving at London Waterloo at 0451; departing 2115 on Sunday arriving at London Waterloo at 0505.

Train Information: 01736–65831
InterCity Services: 0171–262–6767

Penzance Tourist Information Centre: 01736–62207

Please send me **FREE** rail pass information.

Mr/Mrs _____

Address _____

City _____ State _____ Zip _____

E-mail address _____

We'd like to know more about our readers. Information is for internal use only.

1. Departure date for Britain _____

2. Length of trip _____

3. Estimated cost of your trip to Britain _____

4. Number of people in your party _____

5. Is this your first trip to Britain: 01 ❏ Yes   02 ❏ No

       If no, how many times _____

6. This trip is for: 01 ❏ Pleasure 02 ❏ Business 03 ❏ Both 04 ❏ Study Abroad

7. Have you purchased your airline ticket: 01 ❏ Yes   02 ❏ No

       If yes, with which carrier ❏ 03 _____

8. Countries you expect to visit:

_____

9. What is your age:

       01 ❏ Under 18   03 ❏ 26-35   05 ❏ 46-54

       02 ❏ 18-25   04 ❏ 36-45   06 ❏ 55+

10. How did you hear about *Britain By Britrail:*

       01 ❏ Bookstore display   04 ❏ Recommended by friend

       02 ❏ TV/Radio   05 ❏ http://www.eurail.com

       03 ❏ Newspaper/Magazine   06 ❏ America OnLine Promotion

       07 ❏ Other _____

11. Would you buy another *Britain By Britrail:*   01 ❏ Yes   02 ❏ No

12. What features of the book did you like best: _____

13. Please use the remaining space to make any comments concerning the book:

_____

_____

Thank you for your time.

'97 - '98 Edition

Rail Pass Express, Inc.
2737 Sawbury Blvd.
Columbus, Ohio 43235-4583

extremely helpful to you as a visitor to Penzance.

When you leave the tourist information office fully armed with the publications needed to explore this most interesting area, we are certain that you will be immediately attracted to the harbor area lying to the left just beyond the rail terminal. We suggest that you make it your first "port of call," since it can readily put you in the proper adventurous mood to see the rest of the area.

At harbor side you will want to inspect the old warehouse and granary overlooking Battery Rocks. It has been converted to a craft center and art gallery. Next door is the Dolphin Inn, formerly a smugglers' hideaway and said to be haunted by an old sea captain's ghost. From there, a walk up Chapel Street away from the harbor brings you to a part of Old Penzance filled with Georgian town houses, fishermen's cottages, and the Museum of Nautical Art. This unusual museum, which takes the form of an eighteenth-century battleship with gun decks and life-size figures manning muzzle-loading guns, is filled with displays of actual navigational gear from former times. The museum is well worth a visit. It is a delight to young and old alike.

For a unique treat, visit the Trinity House National Lighthouse Centre, which holds probably the largest and finest collection of lighthouse equipment in the world. It's located on Wharf Road (telephone 01736–60077) and is open daily 1100–1700 Easter to October. Admission is £2.50 for adults, £1.50 for senior citizens; children admitted free when accompanied by two adults. Within the center, you can relax in the audiovisual theater and enjoy your trip back in time to the first lighthouses—those lonely citadels which guarded the treacherous waters around England's shores.

Termed the "Capital of the Cornish Riviera," Penzance occupies an unusually well-sheltered position on England's western coast. Because the town faces due south and is protected from all other points of the compass by a ring of hills, its climate is ideal year-round. Winter is mild and virtually without frost, followed by an early spring and a temperate summer. Botanically, Penzance is noted for its early flowers and produce.

You need not confine yourself to the limits of Penzance, although you'll find it almost impossible to get away from its magnetic attractions. Local bus service can take you to Land's End, and, as we have indicated on the schedule, rail connections can be made to other equally interesting points on the peninsula such as Falmouth, Newquay, and St. Ives. The tourist information center can give you the background on these interesting places, and you can ask the British Rail Travel Centre in the train station to work out the needed schedules.

Sir Francis Drake statue gazes seaward from atop Plymouth's Hoe, claimed to be the finest natural promenade in Europe. It was from this spot that Drake spied the Spanish Armada. Not overly impressed, he decided to continue his game of bowls—later defeating the Spanish in running naval engagements.

From London . . .

A DAY EXCURSION TO PLYMOUTH
DISTANCE BY TRAIN: 226 miles (363 km)
AVERAGE TRAIN TIME: 3 hours

Plymouth has one of the finest natural harbors in Europe. From Plymouth Hoe (a Saxon word meaning "high place"), there are magnificent views over Plymouth Sound and the harbor. Stand on this huge brow of a hill, which is claimed to be one of the world's finest natural promenades, and you stand in the midst of history. It was here that Sir Francis Drake continued his game of bowls before setting out to deal with the Spanish Armada in 1588. Earlier, in 1577, he set sail from the same harbor in the *Golden Hind* on a three-year voyage around the world. Here, too, in 1620 the Pilgrims embarked on the *Mayflower* for the New World. Too few remember that the first airplane to cross the Atlantic Ocean, the U.S. Navy seaplane NC4, touched down in Plymouth Sound. This spot is indeed steeped in historical heritage—much of it related to America. Stand here proudly!

Check in with the **Plymouth tourist information office** at 9 The Barbican, Plymouth's Elizabethan quarter (telephone 01752–264849). You can reach it on foot from the train station in about fifteen minutes through short underground passages and a pedestrianized area. There are streams, fountains, and gardens which form part of an outstanding display. You can also take bus No. 25. Board any bus stopping at the shelter to the right of the station entrance. Pay your fare and ask to be "deposited" at the Barbican. Folks who are in a real hurry can hail a taxi for the trip. There is a taxi queue just outside of the rail station; the bus stop is a few steps beyond.

The Plymouth Tourist Information Centre is open Monday through Friday, 0900–1700; Saturday, 0900–1700; and Sundays and bank holidays, 1000–1600. Train information is best obtained in the station's travel center, on the extreme right as you pass the ticket barrier. The travel center is open Monday through Friday, 0830–1745, 0830–1730 on Saturdays, and 1000–1730 Sundays.

While at the tourist information office, you should ask for a copy of the pamphlet, "The Attractions of Plymouth." It contains an easy-to-read map of the attractions within and near Plymouth that are of interest to visitors. For an introduction to Plymouth, we suggest visiting the city's latest attraction, Plymouth Dome. Situated on Plymouth's famous Hoe, the Dome is one of the most up-to-date centers of its kind in Britain. Here you can take a journey through time, use high-resolution cameras to zoom the shoreline, and do many other exciting things. We can guarantee that you won't run out of things to do while in Plymouth.

163

PLYMOUTH—*PILGRIM'S PROGRESS PORT*

A Day Excursion from London

DEPART FROM PADDINGTON STATION	ARRIVE IN PLYMOUTH STATION	NOTES
0735	1047	(3)
0740	1121	(1)
0915	1318	(4)
0935	1310	(1)
1015	1402	(4)
1045	1340	(1)

DEPART FROM PLYMOUTH STATION	ARRIVE IN PADDINGTON STATION	NOTES
1520	1831	(3)
1530	1845	(1)
1630	1945 (2023 SUN)	(1)(4)
1830	2205 (2225 SAT)	(2)
1908	2255	(4)

Distance: 226 miles/363 km
References: Table 135
  Thomas Cook Table 510

(1) MON–FRI
(2) MON–SAT
(3) SAT
(4) SUN

Train Information: 01752–221300
InterCity Services: 0171–262–6767

Plymouth Tourist Information Centre: 01752–264849

The Plymouth of today is a city of two distinct parts—the original Elizabethan section called the "Barbican" and the modern city center that has risen from the devastation and debris of the last world war. If your time in Plymouth is limited, we suggest you concentrate on visiting the Barbican area of the city.

The harbor area, where the old town of Plymouth nestled, derived its title, Barbican, from the fact that at the entrance to the harbor stood an outpost of the ancient Plymouth Castle. According to castle phraseology, such outer fortifications were called *barbicans*. The Barbican was spared much of the damage that Plymouth suffered during the bombardments of World War II. Consequently, there are still many old buildings and narrow streets in this area that recapture the Elizabethan atmosphere.

One Barbican landmark of particular interest to Americans is a memorial stone that marks the place on the harbor pier from which the *Mayflower* sailed. The Barbican's historic Elizabethan buildings include the Black Friars Distillery, home of Plymouth Gin since 1793. The distillery is still operating in buildings formerly used as a monastery and dating back to 1425. Visitors are welcome. The Merchants House on St. Andrews Street is the largest and finest structure remaining from the sixteenth and seventeenth centuries. Restored recently, it features displays of Plymouth's history with the theme, "Tinker, Tailor, Soldier, Sailor . . ." It is open daily, except Mondays, and there is an admission charge.

Towering over the Barbican, the Royal Citadel, built in the 1660s by Charles II, was erected as a warning to the citizens of Plymouth. Many of the fortress cannons still point toward the town and not out to sea, as one would normally expect them to do. They are open to the public daily between May 1 and September 30.

If you have ever sung a chorus or two of "The Eddystone Light," you are a likely customer for the engrossing book *The Four Eddystone Lighthouses* by Robert Sanderson. Additional information on the lighthouses may also be found in the booklet *Smeaton's Tower and the Plymouth Breakwater.* The first Eddystone lighthouse was blown down in a storm. The second lighthouse withstood the elements but was destroyed by fire. Smeaton's Tower stood on the Eddystone Reef from 1759 to 1884 and subsequently was reerected on Plymouth Hoe. The tower is open to the public daily, from the end of April to the end of October, from 1030 to 1700.

If your urge "to go down to the sea in ships" overwhelms you, take a boat trip on Plymouth Sound. The information center has the details, including how to view the nearby Royal Naval Base at Devonport. If your call to the sea is more limited, browsing in the Barbican area will suffice if you throw an occasional glance seaward to impress the locals.

HMS *Victory*, Lord Nelson's flagship at Trafalgar in 1805, has been described as "the proudest sight in Britain." She lies, meticulously preserved, at the Portsmouth Naval Base. One of the ship's cannon partially shields the *Victory*'s starboard sheet anchor.

From London . . .

A DAY EXCURSION TO PORTSMOUTH
DISTANCE BY TRAIN: 74 miles (119 km)
AVERAGE TRAIN TIME: 1 hour, 30 minutes

A visit to Portsmouth requires priorities—priorities involving the choice of what to see there. The city abounds in vast quantities of history, architecture, amusements, and literature. Portsmouth has variety, contrasts, and veneration. Here are a few choices.

If the sea is "your thing," Portsmouth is flanked by natural harbors, east and west. It is the home of one of the world's greatest naval bases, and its resort area, Southsea, offers the largest amusement complex on England's south coast plus four miles of beaches, promenades, and gardens.

Old Portsmouth is for those who relish fine buildings. Lombard Street boasts a host of splendid seventeenth- and eighteenth-century houses, many with distinctive Dutch gables. On adjoining High Street, the motif is primarily eighteenth century, but this gives way as you approach the ultramodern, "new" Portsmouth with its traffic-free shopping precinct, "Cascades," on Commercial Road.

The literary greats of Portsmouth—Charles Dickens, H. G. Wells, Conan Doyle, Rudyard Kipling, and Neville Shute, to name a few—have left their mark on the city in birthplaces, residences, and museums. Resting in the world's oldest dry dock in Portsmouth's naval yard is Lord Horatio Nelson's flagship, HMS *Victory*. Alongside the ship stands the Royal Naval Museum with relics of England's naval hero, ship models, and an outstanding collection of marine paintings. For priority, our first selection is HMS *Victory*. It has been described as "the proudest sight in Britain," and well it is! Meticulously preserved, it stirs the imagination as you relive the events of the Battle of Trafalgar that "made all England weep."

Portsmouth has a total of four **tourist information centers**. The one you should contact first is located on the main street, The Hard, right next to the Portsmouth Naval Base and the Harbor Rail Station (telephone 01705–826722). Trains call first at the Portsmouth and Southsea Station, so stay aboard to the end of the line. Then, instead of moving straight ahead to the ferry dock, exit the station on the right-hand side of the platform to The Hard, from where you will be able to see the gate of the naval base to your left. The tourist information center on The Hard is open daily throughout the year (except December 25 and 26) from 0930 to 1745 during the summer and 0930 to 1715 during winter (telephone 826722). The other centers are located outside the Sea Life Centre, the Continental Ferryport, the Civic Offices, and Commercial Road. The Hard Centre can direct you should you need their services.

167

PORTSMOUTH—*BRITAIN'S NAVAL PORT*

A Day Excursion from London

DEPART FROM WATERLOO STATION	ARRIVE IN PORTSMOUTH HARBOR STATION*	NOTES
0800	0935	(1)
0800	0929	(3)
0745	0941	(4)
0800	0929	(3)
0815	0953	(4)
0900	1029	(2)

DEPART FROM PORTSMOUTH HARBOR STATION	ARRIVE IN WATERLOO STATION	NOTES
1620	1810 (1753 SUN)	(2)(4)
1720	1911 (1853 SUN)	(2)(4)
1820	2006 (1955 SUN)	(2)(4)
1920 (1914 SAT)	2106 (2053 SUN)	(2)(4)
2050	2247	(1)
2121	2317	(3)
2120	2302	(4)

Distance: 74 miles/119 km
References: Table 156
Thomas Cook Table 504

* Portsmouth has two railway stations—Portsmouth Harbor and Portsmouth & Southsea. Portsmouth Harbor should be used for departures to the Isle of Wight as well as visits to Portsmouth Royal Navy Base. Consult British Rail Table 156 or make inquiries with train information personnel for Portsmouth & Southsea train service.

(1) MON–FRI   (3) SAT
(2) MON–SAT   (4) SUN

Train Information: 01703–229393
InterCity Services: 0171–928–5100

Portsmouth Tourist Information Centre
01705–826722

In addition to visiting the HMS *Victory* in the Portsmouth naval yard, you may also inspect the hull of Henry VIII's *Mary Rose*, which is undergoing restoration in a special dry-dock workshop. Launched in 1510, *Mary Rose* went down while sailing against a French invasion fleet in 1545; the remains were raised in 1982. The story of the *Mary Rose*—her loss and her dramatic recovery—is related in an audiovisual presentation, and the objects salvaged from the ship are on exhibit.

Some vital statistics in history regarding HMS *Victory* may be beneficial while you are waiting to go aboard. The ship was launched on 7 May 1765. (Lord Nelson was a mere child of six on that date.) She is a vessel of 3,500 tons with an overall length of 226.5 feet. All totaled, *Victory* carried 104 guns and a complement of 850 officers and men. In 1801, the ship was rebuilt extensively and given the appearance she has today. Recommissioned in April 1803, she became Nelson's flagship. On 21 October 1805, the English fleet under Nelson's command vanquished the combined fleets of France and Spain off Cape Trafalgar. Lord Nelson was killed aboard *Victory* in the final moments of what has been termed "the most decisive battle ever fought at sea."

Newcomer to the scene at the Portsmouth Naval Base is the Victorian iron-clad, HMS *Warrior 1860*. Launched in 1860, she was the largest, fastest, and best-armored warship of her time. She has been restored throughout to her appearance during her first commission of 1861–64; when you step aboard you can catch a unique glimpse of life as it was experienced on a nineteenth-century British warship.

The Royal Naval Museum supports these famous ships with displays that set them in their historic context and continues the story of the British Navy into the twentieth century, up to the Falklands Campaign of 1982.

In the resort department, Portsmouth offers the Pyramids Centre, a giant leisure attraction built by the sea next to King Henry VIII's Southsea Castle. A true tropical paradise, where the temperature never drops below 84 degrees Fahrenheit, the center features four areas of entertainment, ranging from swimming pools, top-name entertainment, and a patio bar to a supervised "Fun Factory" where Mom and Dad can park the kids.

Close by the Southsea Castle and the Pyramids Centre, Portsmouth's D-Day Museum and Overlord Embroidery tells the story of that historic event through pictures, plans, and the re-creation of wartime scenes, along with exhibits of various weapons and vehicles. A special audiovisual presentation relates the events leading to the recapture of Normandy. More history unfolds in the castle where an audio-visual show reconstructs scenes of "Life in the Castle."

Portsmouth bears the title "The South's Historic Maritime Resort City." We are certain that you will agree with this entitlement.

Foy Boat Inn stands behind cannon on the site where a watch house stood in eighteenth-century Ramsgate. In the days of sails, foy boats took provisions to ships anchored off Ramsgate. The original inn was destroyed in World War II.

From London . . .

A DAY EXCURSION TO RAMSGATE
DISTANCE BY TRAIN: 79 miles (127 km)
AVERAGE TRAIN TIME: 1 hour, 50 minutes

This day excursion to Ramsgate encompasses the northeast tip of England's Kent County, which is called Thanet. Although the sea inlets have almost been drained, it still bears the semblance of an island with clusters of seaside towns—Margate, Broadstairs, and Ramsgate and Villages, each with its own character. Londoners were attracted to Thanet early in the nineteenth century, and it has been a thriving resort area ever since. The attraction of sandy beaches, safe bathing, and entertainment are the assets the area has to offer.

Ramsgate has been selected as the primary point for the day excursion, for it is the terminal stop for trains departing London's Victoria Station on the North Kent line. En route stops at other Thanet towns are made on this rail line at Margate and Broadstairs. More comments about them follow. It should be noted that it is possible to return to Victoria Station via another rail route from Ramsgate through Ashford, or yet another route calling at Dover and Folkestone. With so many possibilities, you should consult the timetables posted in all three of the previously mentioned Thanet towns for possible variations of your own itinerary. The train schedule shown on the following page gives details for the London Victoria Station-Faversham-Margate-Ramsgate-North-Kent rail line only.

This frequent train service departs from the first bay (platforms 1–8) of London's Victoria Station. *A word of caution:* The first cars (usually four) closest to the ticket barrier will go to Dover. The balance of the cars (usually eight) at the head of the train will terminate in Ramsgate. The train "splits" at Faversham. You will be reminded of this again by a train announcement when the train stops briefly in the Bromley South Station after leaving Victoria Station and crossing the Thames. Stay alert and board one of the proper cars.

There are tourist information centers in all three Thanet towns touched by rail service—Margate, Broadstairs, and Ramsgate. The **Margate Tourist Information Centre** is north-east of the railway station near the harbor at 22 High Street. The **Broadstairs Tourist Information Centre** is near the railway station at the foot of the hill at 6B High Street. **Ramsgate Tourist Information Centre** is some distance from the railway station in the town center at 19-21 Harbour Street. Buses from the station will take you near there, or you can hail a taxi.

All three centers operate on similar schedules: Monday through Thursday, 0900–1730; Friday, 0900–1700. During summer periods, they also are open on Saturday and Sunday, 1000–1600.

RAMSGATE—*SEASIDE RESORT*

A Day Excursion from London

DEPART FROM VICTORIA STATION	ARRIVE IN RAMSGATE STATION	NOTES
0805	0950 (0954 SUN)	(1)(2)
0905	1050 (1054 SUN)	(1)(2)
1005	1150 (1154 SUN)	(1)(2)
1105	1250 (1254 SUN)	(1)(2)

(Plus other frequent service)

DEPART FROM RAMSGATE STATION	ARRIVE IN VICTORIA STATION	NOTES
1625	1817	(1)
1630	1820	(2)
1725	1917	(1)
1752 (1830 SUN)	2015 (2020 SUN)	(1)(2)
1852 (1855 SAT)	2047	(1)
1952 (2025 SUN)	2147 (2220 SUN)	(1)(2)

(Plus other frequent service)

Distance: 79 miles/127 km
References: Table 212
                   Thomas Cook Table 500

(1) MON-SAT
(2) SUN

Train Information: 01227–454411
InterCity Services: 0171–928–5100

Ramsgate Tourist Information Centre
01843–583333

Margate is the Thanet town that has been conjuring up visions of holidays for years. Its biggest drawing card is the famous amusement park, Dreamland Fun Park, set on a twenty-acre complex. The municipality of Margate owns nine miles of seafront with sandy beaches and promenades running practically its full distance. The atmosphere of the area differs somewhat from that of England's south coast in that it is more sedate in mood and tempo. Perhaps the presence of the North Sea is one of the contributing factors.

Arriving at Margate Station, the first sight to greet you is the golden sand of the beach. The promenade paralleling the beach is a length of souvenir shops, restaurants, confectioneries, and amusement halls. Beyond the Dreamland Fun Park lies Margate's main shopping center, where courteous Kentish clerks are most eager to assist you in your shopping. Extending from the promenade, Margate's Old Town of narrow streets and houses clusters around the town's harbor.

Broadstairs has a Victorian atmosphere about it and became a fashionable "watering hole" during the regency of King George IV. Victorians, one of the most eminent being Charles Dickens, favored holidays in Broadstairs. A leaflet from the information center will permit you to follow in his footsteps and see many interesting points within the town. Every June, townspeople remember Dickens by appearing in costume while attending a series of plays, readings, parades, and parties set against the backdrop of Victorian Broadstairs.

Ramsgate, being strong on regency flavor, centers its activities around its royal harbor and marina. Annual events include the May Spring Festival, August Harbor Heritage celebrations, and September Model Ship Ralley. The harbor is a source of constant interest, as is the model village at West Cliff, a charming miniature of England's Tudor countryside. Permanently moored on the clifftops at Pegwell Bay in Ramsgate is a Viking ship commemorating the original Viking landing in 449. Ramsgate harbor has seen Wellington's troops embark for the Continent, where they continued on to defeat Napoleon at Waterloo. The harbor also received thousands of battered British troops during the evacuation from Dunkerque in 1940.

Many recall memories of their travels through their senses of sight and sound. In the case of Ramsgate, we recall our visits there by our sense of taste. Most memorable was our dining experience at Harvey's Crab & Oyster House located on Harbour Parade. Walk down to the harbor area—you can't miss it. As the name indicates, seafood is the house specialty. The restaurant's card states: "Open 12–2:30 P.M. & 8 P.M. till late. Booking advisable. Tel: (01843) 591110."

Fifteenth-century clock tower standing in St. Albans's French Row was originally a curfew tower, the bell dating back to 1335. To the left of the tower stands the Fleur-de-Lys Inn on a site where King John of France was held prisoner after the Battle of Poitiers in 1356.

From London . . .

A DAY EXCURSION TO ST. ALBANS
DISTANCE BY TRAIN: 20 miles (32 km)
AVERAGE TRAIN TIME: 25 minutes

St. Albans takes its name from Britain's first Christian martyr, a Romano-British citizen who was beheaded for his faith on a hilltop outside Verulamium, one of the most important towns at that time in the western Roman Empire. A magnificent fifteenth-century Norman cathedral now stands on the hilltop, and Verulamium has become a parkland on the western side of the city.

St. Albans has much to offer its visitors. Tucked away in various corners of the city are old coach inns, many with a fascinating history. The White Hart Inn, built in the fifteenth century, was restored in 1930. The Fleur-de-Lys Inn on French Row was erected between 1420 and 1440 on the site where King John of France was held prisoner after the Battle of Poitiers. Another inn, the Fighting Cocks, claims to be the oldest licensed house in England. It derived its name from the cock fights that were held there for many years. All three of these ancient "watering holes" are open to the public during licensed hours. St. Albans has always had an open mind concerning alcoholic beverages—Elizabeth I granted the city permission to issue wine licenses in 1560.

French Row in St. Albans, a narrow street of medieval appearance, is fronted by a clock tower built between 1402 and 1411 from the flint and rubble of Verulamium. Its original curfew bell was cast in 1335. Across from the bell tower stands the Wax House Gate, where once candles and tapers were made and sold to pilgrims visiting the shrine of St. Albans. The path through the gate is still the shortest route for pedestrians en route to the cathedral, proving that the ancients had a sharp eye for customer traffic flow. The St. Albans Cathedral contains traces of an eighth-century Saxon church. It has one of the largest Gothic naves in Europe. The cathedral tower was built largely of stone from Verulamium.

Arriving in St. Albans, leave the train station by walking uphill towards the city center on Victoria Street. At the junction of St. Peters and Chequer streets, the **tourist information center** can be seen opposite, in the town hall. Office hours are 0930–1730 Monday through Saturday from Easter to October. From mid-July to mid-September it is also open Sundays from 1030-1630. Between November and Easter hours are 1000–1600 Monday through Saturday (telephone 01727–864511). The uphill walk takes about fifteen minutes. The alternative is city bus transportation, which departs from a bus shelter in the station area. The bus stop for returning to the station is at the top of Victoria Street.

Many of the points of interest in St. Albans must be reached on foot. The

175

ST. ALBANS—*FROM ROMANS TO ROSES*

A Day Excursion from London

DEPART FROM KING'S CROSS THAMESLINK	ARRIVE IN ST. ALBANS STATION	NOTES
0807 (0800 SUN)	0827 (0835 SUN)	(1)(4)
0844 (0830 SUN)	0904 (0905 SUN)	(1)(4)
0914 (0900 SUN)	0944 (0935 SUN)	(2)(4)
1000	1026 (1035 SUN)	(2)(4)
1030	1054 (1056 SUN)	(1)(4)
1100	1123 (1126 SUN)	(2)(4)
1130	1154 (1156 SUN)	(1)(4)

(Plus other frequent service)

DEPART FROM ST. ALBANS STATION	ARRIVE IN KING'S CROSS THAMESLINK	NOTES
1430 (1428 SUN)	1453 (1457 SUN)	(2)(4)
1530 (1528 SUN)	1553 (1557 SUN)	(2)(4)
1614	1636	(1)
1615	1638	(3)
1632	1657	(4)
1712	1735	(1)
1715	1738	(3)
1732	1757	(4)

(Plus other frequent service)

Distance: 20 miles/32 km
References: Table 52
Note: To reach King's Cross Thameslink, follow directions to the underground Piccadilly Line from King's Cross.

(1) MON–FRI   (3) SAT
(2) MON–SAT   (4) SUN

Train Information: 0171–387–7070

St. Albans Tourist Information Centre: 01727–864511

information center has a pamphlet describing a walking tour, *St. Albans's Town Trail*, which includes the cathedral and the abbey. The tour (two and one-half miles) may prove a bit too ambitious for the less-experienced, less-conditioned walker, but both lead past one or more of the previously described inns, where a libation will probably instill a desire to press on—or stay at the inn until "time" is called.

Helpful publications to take on the trails are *A Historical Map* of St. Albans and *Mini Guide*. The center has them available for a small fee. The information center is close to the marketplace. Markets are held in St. Albans every Wednesday and Saturday. If you are in town on these days, be sure to "go to market" and enjoy the opportunity of watching the locals barter back and forth with the tradesmen. Everything from apples to zinnias, including the weather and current prices, will become subjects of discussion.

The Roman city of Verulamium is engrossing. You can spend an entire day at the site visiting its 200-acre grounds, which include a temple, forum, museum, hypocaust, and theater. The museum houses an impressive collection of Roman antiquities. From the center of St. Albans, you can reach Verulamium in about twenty minutes on foot, or you can opt for a local bus. The tourist information office will give you the directions.

At the Verulamium Museum, artifacts taken from the ruins are displayed in an environment of natural surroundings. The small items from the houses and shops range from iron hinges, latches, and locks to personal ornaments worn by the inhabitants. A full range of pottery and glassware, both for table and kitchen use, are on exhibit.

Exploratory excavations of the site have taken place from time to time, but experts estimate that only one-third of the area within the Roman town walls has been uncovered. Modern techniques such as aerial photography continue to reveal additional features.

The gardens of the Royal National Rose Society are in St. Albans. The rose trial grounds is the place to see the future "greats" of the rose world. The society made its first award for a new rose in 1883 and subsequently established its own trial grounds. New varieties from all over the world are sent to St. Albans to undergo a comprehensive, three-year assessment. The twelve acres of gardens, a spectacle for the casual visitor, are a total fascination to rose enthusiasts. Open from June through October, the gardens are accessible to the public 1000–1800 daily.

The range of history in St. Albans extends from A.D. 43 and the first evidences of the Roman enclosure at Verulamium to the moment you arrive to enjoy the vitality of this timeless city. To step over St. Albans's threshold is to step into a land of enchantment and history.

The High Street Gate marks the boundary between the two distinct areas of Salisbury—the "close" around the cathedral and the city's marketplace. Traditionally, the gate is closed and locked every night.

From London . . .

A DAY EXCURSION TO SALISBURY
DISTANCE BY TRAIN: 84 miles (135 km)
AVERAGE TRAIN TIME: 1 hour, 25 minutes

Salisbury holds the distinction of being one of the few English cities *not* originally founded by the Romans. The old town, Old Sarum, had been in existence since the Iron Age. The Romans fortified it, and the Saxons later developed it into an industrial town. All went well in Old Sarum until arguments between the occupants of the church and the castle caused a new church to be built in the valley below the original town site. This new location proved to be more popular than the old. Consequently, although known as Salisbury, the town's official name is New Sarum.

The center of Salisbury has traditionally been divided into two distinct areas, the cathedral and the marketplace. This tradition still exists, and the gates leading to the cathedral and the buildings in the "close" surrounding it are locked every night. Beautiful houses of medieval and Georgian architecture overlook the green.

The marketplace has a history all its own. In the original Charter of 1227, the town was authorized to hold a Tuesday market. This got out of hand and grew into almost a daily market until protests from nearby towns resulted in a reduction of market days in Salisbury to Tuesdays and Saturdays only. Today, Salisbury maintains those traditional market days.

Salisbury boasts a brace of historic inns that have given rest and refreshment to travelers down through the centuries. The fireplaces in the King's Arms Inn have the same stone as that used in the construction of the cathedral. The Haunch of Venison, an old English chop house, was built about 1320. The Red Lion Hotel, dating back to the same era, was the starting point for the Salisbury Flying Machine, the nightly horse-drawn coach to London.

In Salisbury, you will find many impressive examples of architectural styles, ranging from the town's thirteenth-century cathedral to a modern pedestrian shopping district known as the Old George Mall. The most unexpected structure is the foyer of the movie theater on New Canal Street. Once the banqueting hall of the merchant John Halle, four-time Mayor of Salisbury, it is now a splendid example of fifteenth-century black-and-white timbering.

Salisbury's tourist information center is situated at the rear of the Town Guildhall where Market Square corners on Fish Row. Telephone ahead from the rail station (334956) for directions, or proceed on foot down Fisherton Street, which you will find to your far left as you exit the station. After crossing the River Avon, the street will narrow and change names several times until it becomes Fish Row.

179

SALISBURY—*MAGNA CARTA ARCHIVE*

A Day Excursion from London

DEPART FROM WATERLOO STATION	ARRIVE IN SALISBURY STATION	NOTES
0709	0837	(2)
0835	0954	(2)
0858	1027	(4)
0935	1102 (1108 SAT)	(2)
1035	1154	(2)
1058	1235	(4)
1135	1302	(1)

DEPART FROM SALISBURY STATION	ARRIVE IN WATERLOO STATION	NOTES
1429	1627	(4)
1523	1646	(1)
1636	1810	(3)
1650	1838	(4)
1725	1851	(2)
1815	1946	(2)
1953	2118	(1)

Distance: 84 miles/135 km
References: Table 160
                  Thomas Cook Table 511

(1) MON–FRI   (3) SAT
(2) MON–SAT   (4) SUN

Train Information: 01722–327591
InterCity Services: 0171–928–5100

Salisbury Tourist Information Centre
01722–334956

The tourist center's hours are Monday to Saturday 0930–1700 year round, with extended opening hours and Sundays during the summer. The center operates a booking service for local hotel accommodations as well as the popular "Book-A-Bed-Ahead" program.

From May through September, you can join a daily guided walking tour of Salisbury at 1100 and 1800 from in front of the tourist information center on Fish Row. The tour lasts approximately one and a half hours.

The cathedral has a unity of design that no doubt is attributable to the fact that, unlike most other cathedrals, which took centuries to complete, the Salisbury Cathedral was constructed in only thirty-eight years. In other words, it wasn't affected by several different periods of architecture. Its foundation stones were laid in 1220, during the heyday of Gothic design. One of its greatest treasures is its ancient clock mechanism, which dates from 1386 and is one of the oldest pieces of operating machinery in the world. It originally stood in a detached belfry.

The cathedral contains a library founded at Old Sarum in 1078 and seventy of the books installed in the library at that time are still there. The great treasure of the Cathedral, housed in Chapter House, is the *Magna Carta,* written at Runnymede on 15 June 1215. It was brought to Salisbury by William, Earl of Salisbury, who placed it in the cathedral for safekeeping. It remained there until World War II, when it was hidden for five years in a quarry. Among its many historical achievements, Salisbury made its mark in the annals of medical care. Of the four hospitals currently in or near the city, the Trinity Hospital, on Trinity Street, has a rather interesting story concerning its founding in 1379 by Agnes Bottenham. Chronicles relate that Ms. Agnes ran a "house of ill repute" on the site, and when it prospered, she built a hospital and almshouse there as an act of penitence.

Visitors interested in seeing Old Sarum, one and a half miles north of the new town, can do so by city bus or taxi. Excavations and reconstruction have been under way for some time. Oddly enough, even after the old city was abandoned, the owner of the estate continued to send two members to the Parliament, despite the fact that the city had no inhabitants. It was a case of representation without taxation.

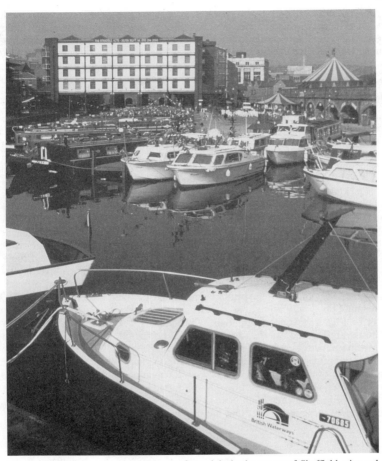

Victoria Quays, the historic canal waterfront right in the center of Sheffield, pictured during the annual Boaters' Festival. (Courtesy of Destination Sheffield Ltd.)

A DAY EXCURSION TO SHEFFIELD
DISTANCE BY TRAIN: 165 miles (265 km)
AVERAGE TRAIN TIME: 2 hours 10 minutes

Sheffield, England's fourth largest city (population 529,000) is world famous for steelmaking, toolmaking, engineering, and cutlery. Surviving records show that cutlery was being made in Sheffield in 1297 A.D., and Chaucer referred to a Sheffield *thwitel* (knife) in his *Canterbury Tales.* By the late nineteenth century Sheffield was regarded as steel capital of the world, and in 1913 Harry Brearley made one of the great discoveries of our century, stainless steel, at Sheffield's Brown Firth Laboratories.

But forget images of smoke-belching chimneys. Present-day Sheffield is England's greenest city. Built on seven hills and five river valleys (fast-flowing streams drove the waterwheels that powered the cutlery industry before the steam age), Sheffield has more than fifty parks and green spaces—and four trees to every person! It is surrounded by open countryside, and more than a third of the city lies within the beautiful Peak National Park.

Sheffield has won a reputation for sporting excellence and in 1995 was the first city to be awarded the official title *National City of Sport.* The country's top teams in ice-hockey (Sheffield Steelers) and basketball (Sheffield Sharks) are based here as is the national diving squad. The city has hosted more than 200 national and international sports events in the past five years.

With the Peak National Park nearby, outdoor sports are particularly popular. A completely unexpected attraction, set in the heart of the city, is Europe's largest artificial ski slope complex, Sheffield Ski Village. Just bring your gloves; you can rent everything else.

Another well-known export is music. Joe Cocker, Def Leppard, Pulp, and many other bands started here. In spring 1998 this heritage will be recognized when the National Centre for Popular Music, an exciting interactive "museum" with no static exhibits at all, opens in the city center.

Two traditional museums, commemorating Sheffield's industrial heritage, are Kelham Island and Abbeydale Industrial Hamlet. At the former the largest working steam engine in Europe can be seen in action. The latter museum displays a water driven machinery, parts of which date back to the seventeenth century, that produced scythes. The City Museum, Weston Park, has excellent collections of Sheffield cutlery and Sheffield Plates. The Cutler's Hall, on Church Street, is the headquarters of the Cutlers' Company, which was formed in 1642. The present Cutlers' Hall dates from 1832 and houses the Company's silver and cutlery collections, which can be viewed by appointment only

SHEFFIELD—*TRADEMARK OF QUALITY*

A Day Excursion from London

DEPART FROM ST. PANCRAS STATION	ARRIVE IN SHEFFIELD STATION	NOTES
0830	1053	(1)
0830	1058	(3)
0915	1230	(4)
1000	1226	(3)
1030	1251	(1)

DEPART FROM SHEFFIELD STATION	ARRIVE IN ST. PANCRAS STATION	NOTES
1524	1750	(1)
1554	1825	(3)
1625	1858	(4)
1624	1855	(1)
1724	1951 (1957 SAT)	(2)
1924	2205 (2210 SAT)	(2)

Distance: 165 miles/265 km
References: Table 53
              Thomas Cook Table 560

(1) MON–FRI	(3) SAT
(2) MON–SAT	(4) SUN

Train Information: 01742–726411
InterCity Services: 0171–278–2477

Sheffield Tourist Information Centre
01742–734671/2

(inquire at the Tourist Information Center).

A heritage site is Victoria Quays, Sheffield's canal basin. The canal was built to ship in iron ore from Sweden and ship out steel products to England's east coast ports; now Victoria Quays is a waterside oasis in the heart of the city center, with its beautiful warehouse buildings, a cobbled waterfront and the Sheaf cutlery works, now a family pub and restaurant.

Another historic building in the city center is the Lyceum (in Tudor Square), a magnificently-restored Victorian theater which, together with the modern Crucible Theatre, forms the country's largest theatrical complex outside London. Nearby is the Ruskin Gallery, which displays the collection of the Guild of St. George—left to the city by Victorian safe, artist, and critic John Ruskin. Next door, the Ruskin Craft Gallery displays contemporary craft products, many of them for sale.

A fifteen-minute journey from city center on the new supertram, Britain's largest and most advanced urban light rail transport system, will take you to Britain's most successful shopping mall, Meadowhall, with 270 shops, food court, and cinemas. On the way you pass Britain's newest airport, Sheffield's business and short-haul airport, scheduled to open in March 1997.

The Tourist Information Centre, Peace Gardens, (0114)2734671/2, is about a ten-minute walk from the rail station. Cross the road by the traffic light controlled pedestrian crossing. Pass to the left of the Sheffield Hallam University Nelson Mandela Building and walk straight up the steep Howard Street, passing the University's main entrance on your right. Take the pedestrian underpass straight ahead; at the other side turn right then go up the steps on your left, on to Surrey Street. When you see Hibberts art shop on your right (just past the end of Tudor Square, where the Crucible and Lyceum Theatres can be seen), turn left, and walk past the front of the modern Town Hall extension (the Peace Gardens is to your right). The Tourist Information Centre is at the far end. A taxi service is also available from the station.

The Tourist Information Centre is open 0930 to 1715, Monday to Friday and 0930 to 1630 on Saturday. An excellent city map is available. Helpful brochures, including *A City in my Pocket,* the *Sheffield Venue,* and a number of other visitor publications, are available at no cost. The center also offers accommodation information and advance booking services.

Sheffield visitor information on the Internet is at **http://www.shu.ac.uk/city**. More information, including a calendar of events, can be found at **http://www.shef.ac.uk/city.**

Southampton's Bargate, one of four medieval gates in the wall surrounding the original city, has not lost its character despite numerous alterations since its construction in the twelfth century.

From London . . .

A DAY EXCURSION TO SOUTHAMPTON
DISTANCE BY TRAIN: 79 miles (127 km)
AVERAGE TRAIN TIME: 1 hour, 10 minutes

In the minds of many, Southampton conjures visions of the great transatlantic ocean liners, for it is Britain's prime ocean-passenger port and home of many of the world's greatest passenger ships, including Britain's flagship, the *Queen Elizabeth II* (*QE2*). Many visitors, however, know little about Southampton's span of centuries, which has given it a rich heritage in the history of England and of Europe. Southampton's museums, classic buildings, and ancient ruins help reveal this rich and interesting heritage.

Southampton is best seen on foot, with the possible assistance of a city bus now and then. From the railway station, you can board any "City Centre" bound bus and ask the driver to "deposit" you at the Civic Centre, next to which you will find the city **tourist information center**. The center is open for business Monday through Saturday, 0900 (1000 on Thursday)–1700 throughout the year. It is closed on Sunday.

The center can make hotel and bed-and-breakfast reservations in Southampton and its surroundings. Written and telephone requests for reservations may also be made. Write to the Southampton Tourism Unit, Civic Centre, Southampton SO147LP, England, telephone (01703) 221106, or fax (01703) 832082.

There is a map outside the Southampton railway station showing the route to the center. Pick up the free *Southampton's Visitors Guide.* It contains suggestions for sightseeing. Visitors from the United States will take special interest in the sailing of the *Mayflower* from Southampton in 1620. Persons proving descent from original *Mayflower* passengers can have their names entered on the memorial.

As mentioned in the official handbook, there are many places of interest within easy walking distance of the city information center. A visit to them will gradually unfold a picture of Southampton's past. To catch Southampton's seagoing flavor, a visit to the Ocean Village or the Town Quay Marina would be in order. Similar to the harbor renovation of Baltimore, Maryland, Southampton's Ocean Village has transformed some of its old docks into a cosmopolitan playground with a bevy of specialty shops and eateries overlooking a yacht basin. The Town Quay Marina plays host to the cream of the yacht-racing world. Both areas are close to the terminal used by the *Queen Elizabeth II*. Check with the information center concerning walking directions and the possibility of the *QE2* being in the harbor.

Next in line is the Tudor House Museum, where the costumes, paintings,

SOUTHAMPTON—*AN IMPOSING HERITAGE*

A Day Excursion from London

DEPART FROM WATERLOO STATION	ARRIVE IN SOUTHAMPTON STATION	NOTES
0730	0843	(1)
0750	0914	(2)
0845	1028	(3)
0850	1014	(2)
0930	1039 (1057 SUN)	(2)(3)
1030	1157	(3)
1030	1139	(2)

DEPART FROM SOUTHAMPTON STATION	ARRIVE IN WATERLOO STATION	NOTES
1615	1736	(3)
1615	1728	(2)
1715	1829	(2)
1815	1936	(3)
1815	1929	(2)
1915	2028 (2036 SUN)	(2)(3)
2015	2136	(3)

Distance: 79 miles/127 km
References: Table 158
            Thomas Cook Table 505

(1) MON–FRI   (3) SUN
(2) MON–SAT

Train Information: 01703–229393

Southampton Tourist Information Centre
01703–221106
01703–221106 for accommodations

and furniture of centuries past are displayed against the oak beams and stone carvings of Tudor House itself. The Tudor House is one of the few surviving examples in Southampton of a large town house from the early Tudor period. It contains a banquet hall and is surrounded by an authentic Elizabethan herb garden. Don't miss the tunnel entrance to the remains of a twelfth-century merchant's home. The kids will love it.

Next on the agenda is Wool House, once a medieval warehouse and now a showplace for the city's involvement with the sea. Since early times, Southampton has been an important port of call. Its docks have been piled high with luxuries from the Mediterranean and the East, brought there by Genoan and Venetian fleets. If you are not fortunate enough to see the *QE2* during your Southampton visit, Wool House will make up for it with its history of the "Queens," highlighted by a scale model of the *Queen Mary* from the board-room of the Cunard Shipping Company.

If you never expected to see a marine museum in a wool house, you'll be equally surprised to find an archaeological collection in a museum bearing the name God's House Tower. It started out as a gunnery store, changed its use many times, and finally opened as a museum in 1950. It currently houses the most extensive collection of post-Roman European pottery to be found in Europe.

Also in Southampton's repertoire is the Hall of Aviation on Albert Road. The museum is a memorial to R. J. Mitchell, Southampton's famous aircraft designer of the Spitfire, the fighter that valiantly defended the country during the Battle of Britain. The exhibits include a Spitfire Mark 24, possibly one of the last of 24,500 Spitfires produced by the Supermarine Aircraft Company in nearby Woolston, a quarter mile from the museum. The museum's collection also includes a Sandringham Flying Boat as well as hundreds of photographs, plans, and models connected with inventor R. J. Mitchell and the Supermarine factory.

The route between the museums, by the way, is dotted with historic buildings, such as the Duke of Wellington Pub and the Red Lion Pub. Pausing for a pint may provide a pleasant period for pondering Southampton's past and present.

Free guided walks through medieval Southampton depart from the Bargate at varying times throughout the year. Ask for complete details at the tourist information center.

Quay side at Southampton's port, you stand in history. Four-hundred years before the pilgrim fathers departed on their journey to the new world, Richard the Lion-Hearted embarked on the Third Crusade.

A unique wonder of the world, Stonehenge is viewed annually by more than a million visitors. The monument stands on a bed of solid chalk. Because it has been constantly robbed of stone and defaced throughout the centuries, visitors are no longer permitted to enter the stone circle.

From London . . .

A DAY EXCURSION TO STONEHENGE
DISTANCE BY TRAIN: 84 miles (135 km)
AVERAGE TRAIN TIME: 1 hour, 45 minutes

"Observatory, altar, temple, tomb, erected none knows when by none knows whom, to serve strange gods or watch familiar stars . . ." wrote the poet Sir John Squire about Stonehenge. Stonehenge is unmatched—truly one of the wonders of the world. There are many opinions regarding the use and purpose of the monument. Whatever the reason for its existence, however, Stonehenge remains an awe-inspiring reminder of the past.

The landscape for a few miles around the Stonehenge monument reportedly contains more prehistoric remains than any other area of the same size in Britain. There are earthworks, burial sites, erected stones, and hill carvings. Because they belong to the prehistoric period, long before any written records were made, there are many questions about them all that we shall never be able to answer. Through technology, modern man has been able to tell *how* they were made and, in some cases, *when* and *by whom.* The unanswered question is *why.*

Stonehenge sits on the Salisbury plain, an almost treeless, windswept plateau. With its origins dating from 2950 B.C. to about 1600 B.C., Stonehenge comprises a circular group of stones roughly 110 feet in diameter that stand in an area surrounded by a low earthen rampart and ditch approximately 330 feet in diameter. The largest stones, some weighing as much as fifty tons, were brought to the site from quarries some twenty miles distant. The stones are placed in such a manner as to reflect the position of the sun on the four main dates of the seasons, possibly for an agricultural or a religious purpose.

The monument stands on approximately 300 feet of solid chalk. Unfortunately, Stonehenge has been robbed constantly of its stone throughout the centuries. In Victorian times, it was common practice for visitors to bring hammers and chisels to carve their names and other graffiti and to chip off souvenir sections of the temple stones.

Deodorus Ciculus, historian to Julius Caesar, described Stonehenge as a temple to the sun god Apollo. Modern Britons have marked the area with small clumps of trees to commemorate the Battle of Trafalgar in 1805.

There are several means by which you can proceed to Stonehenge from the Salisbury railway station. If time is of the essence, a taxi can get you there in about twenty minutes. Buses, operated by Wilts & Dorset, depart from the station for Stonehenge via Salisbury and Amesbury on a daily basis, Sundays and public holidays included. The adult round-trip fare is £3.85; admission to the Stonehenge site (£3.70) is not included. The Wilts & Dorset bus schedule is

STONEHENGE—*MYSTERIOUS PAGAN SHRINE*

A Day Excursion from London

DEPART FROM WATERLOO STATION	ARRIVE IN SALISBURY STATION	NOTES
0709	0837	(2)
0835	0954	(2)
0858	1027	(3)
0935	1102 (1108 SAT)	(2)
1035	1154	(2)
1058	1235	(3)
1235	1354	(1)

DEPART FROM SALISBURY STATION	ARRIVE IN WATERLOO STATION	NOTES
1429	1627	(3)
1523	1646	(1)
1650	1838	(3)
1725	1851	(2)
1815	1946	(2)
1953	2118	(1)

Distance: 84 miles/135 km
References: Table 160
          Thomas Cook 511

(1) MON–FRI   (3) SUN
(2) MON–SAT

Train Information: 01722–327591
InterCity Services: 0171–928–5100

Salisbury Tourist Information Centre
01722–334956

arranged so as to connect with all express trains to and from the Waterloo Station in London. If you plan to linger at the site, this will provide you with ample time to do so.

In conjunction with Wilts & Dorset, Guide Friday, one of Britain's leading operators of town and city tours, offers a combined tour of both Stonehenge and Old Sarum, the ancient site of Salisbury, for an adult fare of £11.00 (senior citizens £9.50; children under the age of twelve, £5.50). Fares include entrance to Stonehenge, and you are accompanied by a guide throughout the tour. Tour time is just under two hours. For complete details and bus schedules, we suggest that you call ahead to the Wilts & Dorset travel office in Salisbury (0722) 336855.

Time permitting, upon arriving back in Salisbury, you may want to explore the city prior to boarding your London-bound train. If so, stay aboard the bus returning from Stonehenge until it arrives at the Salisbury bus terminal approximately five minutes after its arrival at the rail station. You will note on both the Stonehenge and Salisbury rail schedules that three later train departures to London will still be available to you.

We recommend that you use one of the special excursion buses. If you use the regular public bus system between Salisbury and Amesbury, you will be obliged to walk or take a taxi for the two miles between Amesbury and the Stonehenge site.

Stonehenge is open daily from 0930–1800 from March 16 to October 15 with extended hours 0900–1900 from June 1 to August 31. The remainder of the year, hours are daily 0930–1600. A gift shop, refreshments, and public toilets are available. All facilities at the site provide access for the disabled.

A sad note: Because of damage to the monument, visitors are no longer permitted to enter the stone circle but can view it only from a distance. Now, visitors are required to remain behind a fence built around the Stonehenge temple to protect it. "Time," as the announcement observes, "is taking its toll."

The Royal Shakespeare Theatre, built in 1932 to replace the original theater destroyed by fire in 1926, employs both decorative and structural brickwork.

Anne Hathaway's Cottage, two miles from the center of Stratford, attracts tens of thousands of visitors annually during visits to Shakespeare country.

From London . . .

A DAY EXCURSION TO STRATFORD-UPON-AVON
DISTANCE BY TRAIN: 121 miles (195 km)
AVERAGE TRAIN TIME: 2 hours, 30 minutes

William Shakespeare, the superb English poet and playwright recognized universally as the greatest of all dramatists, was born in Stratford-upon-Avon in 1564. His mother was the daughter of a local farmer; his father was a glove maker and a wool merchant who entered politics to become mayor of Stratford. Although Shakespeare lived throughout his professional career in London, he kept his home ties with Stratford. In 1597 he purchased New Place, one of Stratford's largest houses. He died there in 1616 and was buried in Stratford's parish church.

Rail travelers can travel from London's Paddington Station to Stratford-upon-Avon via the Thames Trains, Ltd., Turbo Express trains. Trains depart from Paddington beginning at 0918 and at regular intervals throughout the day, Monday through Friday. There are four direct return services from Stratford-upon-Avon to London, including a late train especially for theatergoers. For more detailed information on these services, telephone 0171 262 6767 or 01295 262256 or 01865 722333. Saturday and Sunday departures on this route, however, are limited. InterCity services also are available to Leamington Spa or Birmingham, with connecting services to Stratford (telephone 01788 560116 or 0121 643 2711).

Stratford's tourist information center is located at Bridgefoot and it's open Monday-Saturday -0900-1800 and 1100-1700 on Sunday. Telephone 01789 293127; fax 01789 295262.

Our advice is to take a guided tour of Stratford-upon-Avon. The popular "Stratford and Shakespeare Story Tour" is operated by the Guide Friday Tourism Centre, Civic Hall, 14 Rother Street (tel: 01789 294466; fax: 01789 414681). The open-top bus tours stop at each of the Shakespearean properties: Shakespeare's Birthplace on Henley Street; Anne Hathaway's Cottage; Mary Arden's House where Shakespeare's mother grew up; New Place,/Nash's House in which Shakespeare spend his retirement years before his death in 1616; and Hall's Croft, home of Shakespeare's daughter Susanna. Visitors have the freedom to get on and off the bus as frequently as they wish since the ticket is valid all day.

From May-September, tours depart every fifteen minutes; March to mid-May and October-November, every half hour; December and January, every hour. You can join the tours at any of the Shakespearean Properties, the Pen & Parchment Inn on Bridgefoot Street, Evesham Place, the Swan Theatre, or on Windsor or Meer streets. Holders of the Guide Friday Bus Tour tickets receive

STRATFORD-UPON-AVON—*SHAKESPEARE COUNTRY*

A Day Excursion from London

DEPART FROM PADDINGTON	ARRIVE IN STRATFORD-UPON-AVON	NOTES
0918	1131	Mon-Sat
0940	1203	Sun
1340	1603	Sun
1345	1600	Mon-Sat
1645	1904	Mon-Sat
1848	2113	Mon-Thu
1903	2125	Fri

DEPART STRATFORD-UPON-AVON	ARRIVE IN PADDINGTON	NOTES
0650	0913	Sat
0655	0923	Mon-Fri
1155	1414	Mon-Sat
1225	1449	Sun
1650	1910	Sun
1731	1951	Mon-Sat
2005	2241	Mon-Fri
2315	0129	Mon-Fri

Distance: 121 miles/195 km
References: Table 73,Thomas Cook, Table 526

Train Information in Stratford-upon-Avon: 0121–6432711
Stratford-upon-Avon Tourist Information Centre: 01789–293127
Guide Friday Tourism Centre: 01789–294466

a £1.00 discount on the fully inclusive Birthplace Properties Admission ticket (regularly £9.00 for adults and £4.00 for children) to all five Shakespearean properties. Just show the Guide Friday bus tour ticket at the first property you visit.

Other tour highlights include the Royal Shakespeare Theatre, The Swan and Other Place Theatres, the Holy Trinity Church where Shakespeare is buried and protected by a purportedly cursed tombstone, the Old Fifteenth-Century Century Grammar School, which Shakespeare attended, and Harvard House, home of Katherine Rogers, whose son founded the library in the U.S. that became Harvard University.

A visit to the Royal Shakespeare Theatre is a must. It is advisable to reserve theater seats as far in advance as possible. Telephone 01789 269191 for 24-hour information on program and seat availability. To book seats, telephone the theater box office direct at 01789 295623 or fax 01789 261974. The theater has several restaurant/bar facilities. Telephone 01789 414999 for more information and reservations for special restaurant/theater packages. The Box Tree is a luxuriously appointed restaurant overlooking the Avon River and serves classical cuisine (closed on Sunday). The River Terrace is a modern restaurant/coffee shop/wine bar serving light international dishes. You can even "Pick-up-a-Picnic" by placing your order with the cashier at the River Terrace Restaurant two hours in advance.

Royal Guard stands at castle-hill entrance to Windsor Castle grounds. Changing of the guard ceremony takes place mid-morning daily.

Royal Oak Restaurant, on Datchet Road immediately opposite the Windsor Riverside train station, is a delightful rally point following a castle tour.

From London . . .

A DAY EXCURSION TO WINDSOR
  DISTANCE BY TRAIN: 25 miles (41 km)
  AVERAGE TRAIN TIME: 50 minutes

Historic Windsor Castle is the official home of English royalty. William the Conqueror built the first structure on this site, a wooden fort that doubled as a royal hunting lodge. Other English kings added to the castle during their reigns, but despite the multiplicity of royalty and architects, the castle has managed to retain a unity of style all its own. It's the largest inhabited castle in the world.

The present queen, Elizabeth II, uses the castle far more than any of her predecessors. For this reason, it is wise to inquire if the queen is in official residence before going to Windsor. When she is, which is usually during the months of April, June, and December, the state apartments will be closed to the public. There will still be many areas of Windsor Castle open to the public; however, you will miss seeing the splendor of the various rooms contained within the state apartments. Chances of seeing Her Majesty, should she be in residence, will be rather slim. Nevertheless, during that time you may find Prince Philip watching his son Charles, the Prince of Wales, and his polo team bashing about in the Great Windsor Park. Again, it may be difficult to find the princes, for although the castle itself occupies a mere thirteen acres, the park stretches over 4,000 acres below the battlements of the castle.

You have a choice of two rail routes from London to Windsor. For the schedule given here, we have selected the route from Waterloo Station in London to Windsor Riverside Station. This line does not require changing trains en route. The alternate route, which departs Paddington Station in London, requires a change at Slough to a shuttle train before arriving at Windsor Central Station. If you take the Paddington-Slough route, the shuttle train arrives and departs in Slough from track 1. Either route gives you a magnificent view approaching Windsor Castle. On either train, sit on the left-hand side (outbound) to take full advantage of the scenery.

The **tourist information center** is at No. 24 High Street. Signs with the traditional "i" will lead the way from either arrival point. The grounds of Windsor Castle are immediately across the street from the tourist information center. The center operates 0930–1800 in summer and 0930–1600 in winter (telephone 01753–852010). Be sure to purchase an illustrated guidebook on Windsor Castle. It will become a fond reminder of your visit.

Rare state occasions such as the investiture of the Garter, when the queen proceeds down the walks of Windsor Castle accompanied by a full entourage of castle guards and Knights of the Garter, are difficult for the general public

WINDSOR—*THE ROYAL CASTLE*

A Day Excursion from London

DEPART FROM WATERLOO STATION	ARRIVE IN WINDSOR RIVERSIDE STATION	NOTES
0812	0902	(1)
0842	0934	(1)
0850	0945	(2)
0912	1003	(1)
0942	1034	(1)
0950	1045	(2)

(Plus other frequent service)

DEPART FROM WINDSOR RIVERSIDE STATION	ARRIVE IN WATERLOO STATION	NOTES
1443	1534	(1)
1543	1634	(1)
1605	1700	(2)
1643	1734	(1)
1743	1835	(1)
1805	1900	(2)
1905	2000	(2)
1943	2034	(1)
2005	2057	(2)

(Plus other frequent service)

Distance: 25 miles/41 km
References: Tables 119 and 150

(1) MON–SAT   (2) SUN

Train Information: 0171–928–5100

Windsor Tourist Information Centre
01753–852010

to view. The changing of the castle guard, however, is an event conducted in a manner in which the general public can participate. The new guard leaves the Victoria Barracks precisely at 1055, then marches along High Street to the castle. The guard changing takes place at 1100 and the old guard returns by the same route at 1130. By positioning yourself along High Street or Castle Hill, you will have a good view of the pageantry as it unfolds.

From the battlements of Windsor Castle, you may look down and across the stately River Thames onto the playing fields of Eton College, where "how the game is played" has always been more important than the final score. The importance of Eton lies less in what it is than in what it stands for. The school yard and cloisters are open 1400–1630 except during school holidays, when they are open 1030–1630 April to September.

Your initial entry into the town of Eton may be a bit frightening at first, for you will probably find yourself surrounded by a group of young gentlemen uniformed in pin-striped trousers, white bow ties, and formal black coats with tails. You have not been thrust among a flock of penguins. What you are surrounded by are the students of Eton College, one of Britain's most exclusive educational institutions and a strong reminder that the British on occasion can cling fiercely to their traditions.

A respite from pageantry and tradition during your visit to Windsor may be taken by cruising on the River Thames. At the bottom of High Street, at its intersection with Barry Avenue, the Windsor Boat Pier offers two cruises. The first is a thirty-five-minute trip upstream and the other is a full two-hour trip with light refreshments and a licensed bar aboard.

If you have not yet been introduced to the British public house, there is no better time than now. The Royal Oak, directly across the street from Windsor Riverside Station, is highly recommended. No more prim a pub can you find in all of England. Its impeccable oaken interior matches the high quality of its food and service. The inn was constructed as an ale house in 1736 and restored in 1937. Should we meet you there, we'll buy the first round!

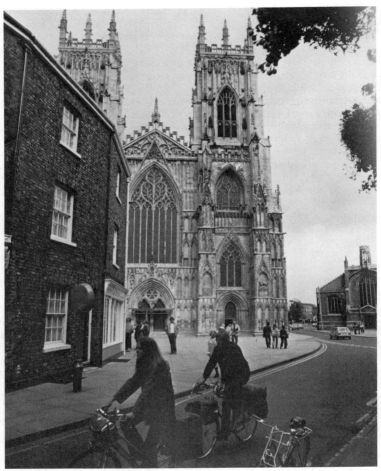

York Minster, largest Gothic church in Britain, stands on a site previously occupied by a Roman military headquarters and a former Norman cathedral. The earlier remains are still visible. Construction of the Minster, begun in 1220, required approximately 250 years.

From London . . .

A DAY EXCURSION TO YORK
DISTANCE BY TRAIN: 188 miles (302 km)
AVERAGE TRAIN TIME: 1 hour, 57 minutes

"The history of York," according to King George VI, "is the history of England." The Romans took it from a Celtic tribe, the Brigantes, in A.D. 71. According to legend, King Arthur captured the city sometime after the Roman legions retreated in A.D. 406. The Saxons took charge in the seventh century, and the Danes ran the Saxons off in 867, only to get their comeuppance from the Anglo-Saxons in 944. In 1066, York saw the fastest turnaround ever when King Harold of England defeated the King of Norway at Stamford Bridge, six miles from York. Nineteen days later, York (and all of England, as a matter of fact) passed to the Normans when Harold was killed in the Battle of Hastings.

William the Conqueror, following his victory at Hastings, came north to quell a rebellion, which he accomplished through his version of urban renewal—the "scorched-earth" policy. The ruins and rubble of the Romans, the Saxons, the Vikings, and the Anglo-Saxons, however, remain today.

Charles I, fleeing the fermenting civil war, left London in 1639 to take residence in York. Cromwell's troops finally took York in July 1644. A condition of surrender was that there would be no pillaging; thus, the fine medieval stained glass of York Minster was saved. It is estimated that the Minster contains more than one-half of all the medieval stained glass in England.

York, similar to Chester, has retained most of its fourteenth-century city walls. You will see part of them as you exit from York's railway station. The city of York is best explored on foot. Check in with the **York tourist information center** in the rail station. Once you are armed with a map, proceed on foot into the city. Although it's a ten-to-fifteen-minute walk, you'll see a lot of history en route.

Turn left leaving the station and proceed along the city wall toward the tower of the York Minster. After crossing the River Ouse, at the intersection of Duncombe Place and St. Leonard's Place, you will see the Minster straight ahead. York's main tourist office is nearby in Exhibition Square. This center is open September through June, Monday-Saturday 0900-1800: July and August., Monday-Saturday 0900-1900: year round on Sunday from 0930-1800.

The York Association of Voluntary Guides provides excellent free tours which depart from Exhibition Square daily at 1015 throughout the year, with an additional tour at 1415 from April to the end of October, and an evening tour at 1900 in June, July, and August. The tour lasts about two hours. To

203

YORK—*FINE MEDIEVAL CITY*

A Day Excursion from London

DEPART FROM KING'S CROSS STATION	ARRIVE IN YORK STATION	NOTES
0730	0927	(1)
0800	0952 (1003 SAT)	(2)
0830	1029	(3)
0900	1136	(4)
0930	1134 (1133 SAT)	(2)
1000	1153 (1203 SAT)	(2)
1000	1233	(4)
1030	1226 (1306 SUN)	(2)(4)

DEPART FROM YORK STATION	ARRIVE IN KING'S CROSS STATION	NOTES
1437	1645	(2)
1532	1738	(3)
1532	1740	(1)
1557	1827	(4)
1721	1910	(1) Pullman Service
1720	1945	(4)
1847	2118	(4)
1942	2158	(2)
2004 (2003 SAT)	2219	(2)

Distance: 188 miles/302 km
References: Table 26
              Thomas Cook Table 570

(1) MON–FRI   (3) SAT
(2) MON–SAT   (4) SUN

Train Information: 01904–642155
InterCity Services: 0171–278–2477

York Tourist Information Centre
01904–628666

request special theme tours or private tours, write to the Hon. Secretary, Tourist Information Centre, De Grey Rooms, Exhibition Square, York, Y01 2HB, or telephone (01904) 640780 between 0930 and 1130 Monday to Friday.

Another tour, The Complete York Tour, offers a reduction for holders of BritRail Passes and railway tickets to York. The tour covers the York Minster and direct admission (no queuing) to the Jorvik Viking Centre. The price is £10.00 for adults, £9.00 for seniors and students, and £5.00 for children. It starts daily at 1000 (1030 Sunday) by the tree in front of the West End of the Minster and finishes at 1400. By previous arrangements, visitors arriving on a train before 0930 may be met at the railway station for no extra charge. For information call (01904) 706643. For those who are too tired or unable to walk, a horse-and-carriage service operates outside the York Minster during good weather. Hour-long bus tours depart from the railway station and travel different routes.

Among its points of interest, York Minster draws first choice. Built between 1220 and 1472, the Minster is England's largest Gothic cathedral. As the mother church of the Church of England's northern province, it is outranked in religious importance only by Canterbury Cathedral.

Also be certain to visit the National Railway Museum on Leeman Road, a ten-minute walk from the York railway station. The Great Railway Show at the museum commemorates the Railway Age from the 1820s to the present day. Visitors walk down station platforms and, in imagination, become passengers on an Edwardian Express or on a boat train to Paris. The museum's National Railway Collection ranges from a lock of Robert Stephenson's hair to the splendor of the Royal Train.

York has one of the most interesting folk museums in the world–the Castle Museum. Famous streets of York have been reconstructed to depict the daily life and occupations of various periods from Tudor to Edwardian times. The museum also contains an eighteenth-century water mill that operates throughout the summer. Other sections are devoted to Yorkshire crafts, costumes, and military history.

While walking, you'll find the narrow, winding streets of York the most fascinating of all the city's attractions. The streets developed from the original Roman street plans. In turn, each century added a bit more color—and perhaps confusion. The Vikings left their mark in the use of street names ending in "gate," such as *Stonegate* and *Petergate*. The medieval citizens following the Vikings gave York its winding streets. One of these streets, The Shambles, is reputed to be one of the best preserved medieval streets in Europe. Originally the street was crammed with butcher shops in half-timbered, over-hanging buildings. The east-west line of the street kept the meat in cool shade for most of the day. It now houses an interesting assortment of stores and bookshops, where the meat hooks still hang.

City Chambers, headquarters of the Glasgow City Council, occupies the entire east side of George Square, the city's picturesque "breathing place." Designed by William Young, the building is an impressive treatment of Italian Renaissance architecture. The loggia balcony, marble staircase, and banqueting hall of the building are particularly impressive. (Photo courtesy of the Greater Glasgow & Clyde Valley Tourist Board, copyright © C. William Long Photography)

11 GLASGOW

In succession to Athens, Florence, Amsterdam, Berlin, and Paris, Glasgow was selected as the Cultural Capital of Europe 1990. Over the past decade, the city has undergone a sweeping renaissance, shaking off the grim, depressed industrial image of the Industrial Revolution to emerge as one of Europe's foremost cities of culture and ambiance.

Now, out from under a century or so of accumulated grime, the cleaning-up process has highlighted, in gleaming gold and red sandstone, some of Europe's finest Victorian architecture. Bustling city streets lined with imposing hand-carved facades pay homage to the optimism of the Victorian city fathers, as do the stunning marble staircases of the opulent City Chambers in central George Square. Glaswegians have reason to be proud of their city and cordially invite you to enjoy it with them.

Direct transatlantic flights into the Glasgow Airport, only fifteen minutes from the city center, as well as regular train services from London and the south, make Glasgow an ideal "base city" site for Scotland. It is conveniently located, as is Edinburgh, for access to our Scottish day excursions. For this reason we are introducing the "Glasgow Connection," wherein the choice of base cities—Edinburgh or Glasgow—becomes a matter of individual selection. The excellent train service between the two cities permits visitors to move with ease between them.

Glasgow is Scotland's largest metropolis, with a population approaching one million. It is the gateway to Loch Lomond and the western Highlands. Glasgow's River Clyde flows into the Firth of Clyde, thus opening its western waterways to a myriad of islands and the Irish Sea. At the height of its shipbuilding boom, Glasgow was launching more than one-third of the world's shipping tonnage. The *Queen Mary,* the *Queen Elizabeth I,* and the *Queen Elizabeth II* (*QE2*) were built there. With the industry now only a shadow of its former self, the River Clyde has become a scenic waterway where you can cruise aboard luxury riverboats or the paddle-wheel steamer *Waverley.*

Glasgow abounds with sights to see and things to do, ranging from its great twelfth-century cathedral to a variety of museums and universities. It is said that Glasgow has more parks than any other European city of its size. George Square, opposite the Queen Street railway station, projects a panorama of Scottish and British history in its statuary of those individuals who forged the British Commonwealth through their science, leadership, and literature.

Among the many superb galleries and museums throughout Glasgow, you shouldn't miss the renowned Burrell Collection in the Pollok Country Park, a unique collection of more than 8,000 objets d'art donated to the city by one man, Sir William Burrell.

Glasgow's Railway Stations—Central Station & Queen Street Station

Glasgow has two main railway stations. Trains arriving from southwestern Scotland and England terminate in the Glasgow Central Station. For train travel north and east out of Glasgow to Edinburgh, Perth, and Inverness or west to Oban and Fort William, the Glasgow Queen Street Station becomes the departure point. A convenient city bus service links the two rail stations. The ten-minute walk between them, however, runs through some of the city's finer shopping areas, thereby offering the opportunity to walk off a few British "pounds."

If you choose to walk from the Queen Street Station to the Central Station, walk past George Square and the tourist information center to St. Vincent Street. At this point, turn right and walk one block farther to Buchanan Street, a pedestrian shopping precinct. Turn left onto Buchanan Street and walk until your path intersects with Gordon Street. The intersection is easy to locate because this section of Gordon Street is reserved for pedestrians (and shops). Turning right at this point and continuing along Gordon Street for two blocks will bring you to the Glasgow Central Station, on your left.

From the Central Station to the Queen Street Station, merely reverse your line of march. Those who wish to avoid running the shopper's gauntlet on Buchanan Street may proceed between the two stations by traversing Queen and Argyle streets. We suggest that you consult a map of central Glasgow, which is available at the tourist information center in St. Vincent Place.

The Interstation Bus Link provides passenger transfer service between the Central and Queen Street Stations with no stops en route. Departures are approximately every fifteen minutes.

Don't look for a kiosk or a newsstand where you can purchase tickets—you pay your fare when you get on the bus. BritRail Passes are *not* accepted for the bus transfer between rail stations. The time en route varies between five and ten minutes, depending upon traffic conditions. For those in a hurry or those who are heavily ladened with luggage, taxis are standing by in queues at both stations.

If you are arriving in one of Glasgow's rail stations to transfer to the Glasgow Airport at Abbotsinch, a frequent bus service is operated for this purpose out of Buchanan Bus Station.

Glasgow Central Station, transformed radically in the past few years, caters to those needs of the train traveler ranging from rest rooms with bathing facilities to a grand Victorian hostelry—the Central Hotel. What is more, the station's old ticket office has been transformed into a delightful array of quality shops, bars, and restaurants.

The Glasgow Central Station provides InterCity electric services for English destinations, including Liverpool, Manchester, Birmingham, and London (Euston Station). Also provided are connections for Wales, the west of England, and destinations in south and west Scotland, which include Ayr and Stranraer (for connections to Northern Ireland via Larne). Commuter-train service to Gourock and Wemyss Bay for connections with steamer services on the River Clyde also operate from the Central Station.

Money exchange is available only within the station during times when the banks are closed. An office of the Royal Bank of Scotland is directly across from the main entrance of the station. After banking hours, ticket window No. 9 in the Central Station will exchange foreign currency and cash traveler's checks up to a $50 limit. The American Express office is to the left of the station entrance at 115 Hope Street. The Thomas Cook office is just one block to the right of the station entrance at 15-17 Gordon Street.

Hotel reservations may be arranged at the tourist information center located at 35 St. Vincent Place.

Tourist information is available in Glasgow's information center at 11, George Square, telephone (0141) 204–4400.

Train information is displayed in the Central Station by means of a huge, digital departures-and-arrivals board located between tracks 2 and 5. For expanded train information, visit the Inquiries and Reservations Office (travel center) on the right side of the main hall at the end of platforms 1, 2, and 3.

Train reservations may be arranged in the travel center. For sleeping-car reservations, you will be directed to the InterCity Sleeper Centre at the entrance to platform 1.

Queen Street Station is the terminal for trains operating on the scenic West Highland Line to Oban, Fort William, and Mallaig, where steamer connections can be made to the Scottish islands. From the Queen Street Station, InterCity express trains depart for Edinburgh and connect with destinations in England including York, Doncaster, and London (King's Cross Station).

Services for north and east Scotland, including Stirling, Perth, Dundee, Aberdeen, Inverness, and the Kyle of Lochalsh, depart from the Queen Street Station. Electric trains to Dumbarton and Balloch (for Loch Lomond cruises) also operate from this station.

Money-exchange services are not available within the Queen Street Station. There are several banks in the general area, including an office of the Royal Bank of Scotland adjacent to the main entrance of the Central Station. After banking hours, however, the only money-exchange facility available in the area is ticket window No. 9 in the Central Station.

Hotel reservations for Glasgow and for all of Scotland may be arranged through the "Book-A-Bed-Ahead" service with the Greater Glasgow & Clyde Valley Tourist Board located at 11 George Square, telephone (0141) 204–4400.

Tourist information in Glasgow is available at the Greater Glasgow Clyde Valley Tourist Board at 11 George Square, telephone (0141) 204–4400. Hours

Tolbooth steeple, erected in 1626, is all that remains at the intersection of High Street and Trongate in Glasgow of a once sprawling complex including the town hall and jail. Other interesting landmarks in this vicinity include the Tron Steeple (1637) and the Mercat Cross (replica–1979).

of operation June through September are 0900–1900 (2000 in July and August) Monday through Saturday and 1000–1800 Sunday. From October through May, the center is open Monday through Saturday from 0900 to 1800, closed Sunday until Easter, then open on Sunday through May between 1000 and 1800.

The center has a wealth of Glasgow tourist information on hand. Call there to request a copy of the "Greater Glasgow Quick Guide" booklet. In addition to a listing of city attractions, the booklet contains information on restaurants, pubs, events, and shopping that will be very helpful for getting to know Glasgow. There is a Bureau de Change in operation in the center as well as an office for theater and sporting events tickets.

Train information is available in the British Rail Travel Centre located on the left-hand side of the station as you face the train platforms.

Train reservations can be made in the travel center. For sleeper reservations, however, use the "InterCity Sleeper Centre" in the Central Station.

Glasgow Gazette

Glasgow's modern subway system is a circular line with trains running in both directions beneath the center of the city. It provides a three-minute service from each of its fifteen stations, achieving a circular journey in about twenty-two minutes. A separate subway, the Argyle Line, links the British Rail suburban networks. The main link with British rail services, however, is the subway station at Buchanan Street, connecting with the Queen Street Station by a moving pedestrian platform similar to those found in airports.

For readers going on the day excursion to Loch Lomond, the rail route departing Glasgow is an electric-train service that departs from subterranean platform 8 in the Queen Street Station. To reach it, after entering the main hall of the station, turn left and exit the station by the side entrance, where you turn right to follow the well-marked PLATFORM 8 signs.

In the Queen Street Station's British Rail Travel Centre, you may obtain full information and tickets for cruising on the Clyde River aboard the *Waverley*. Connecting rail services to the ship's pier originate in the Queen Street Station. The vessel offers a number of interesting cruises on the Clyde River and the Firth of Clyde. On Saturdays during the summer, a special upriver cruise is conducted. Advance bookings for the cruise are recommended.

Throughout the summer, a two-hour bus tour of Glasgow aboard specially converted double-deck buses will take you around some of the best known places—and some of the more out-of-the-way places—in the city. For bus tour schedules and rates, check with the Greater Glasgow Tourist Information Centre.

Every visitor to Glasgow, and model railroad buffs in particular, will not want to miss Glasgow's Museum of Transport in Kelvin Hall on Argyle

Street. The museum is located in the west end of Glasgow only ten minutes from the city center by bus or subway. It's open Monday through Saturday from 1000 to 1700 and Sunday between 1100 and 1700. Displays include ship models, Glasgow trams and buses, locomotives of Scottish origins, Scottish-built motorcars, fire engines, and a reconstructed subway station. There is also a section in the museum known as "The Clyde Room," where meticulously detailed models illustrate the story of shipbuilding and shipping on the River Clyde. An operating model railroad is one of the museum's highlights.

St. Mungo Museum of Religious Life and Art, at 2 Castle Street (in front of Glasgow Cathedral), provides an exploration of the different faiths of the world through paintings and religious artifacts. Included in the collection is Salvador Dali's "Christ of St. John of the Cross." The museum is open Monday through Saturday 1000–1700 and Sunday 1100–1700.

Glasgow's Art Gallery and Museum is immediately opposite Kelvin Hall. Home of Britain's finest civic collection of British and European paintings, the museum also features displays of natural history, archaeology, and collections of silver, pottery, arms, and armor. In the performing arts sector, Glasgow's Mayfest (which, of course, occurs in the merry month of May) is a key international festival for theater, dance, music, and related performing arts in Europe.

Previously, we identified that area of the city between the two rail stations as an ideal place to "walk off a few British 'pounds.'" It is. Glasgow is a shoppers' paradise, with more than ample opportunity to find that special souvenir or gift for friends back home—and pick up something for yourself, too. Department stores line the great pedestrianized shopping districts of Argyle and Buchanan streets. Adjacent to them, Princes Square provides some of Europe's top specialty shops blended into an exciting array of restaurants and bars. Slightly farther than a stone's throw from the square, St. Enochs indoor shopping mall offers a wide variety of stores beneath the same roof, and Argyll Victorian Arcade is the place to look for jewelry and fine gifts.

Farther out, but well worth it if you are visiting Glasgow over a weekend, is the city's famous "Barras Street Market." It's a bargain collector's delight with goods ranging from Victorian bric-a-brac to high fashion—all flavored by the antics of the stall holders.

The "Glasgow Connection"

All day excursions described in chapter 12 that depart from Edinburgh also may be taken from Glasgow. In fact, two of the day excursions—Ayr and Stranraer—require passing through Glasgow. For these excursions readers residing in Glasgow need only refer to the appropriate day-excursion schedule in chapter 12 for the "Glasgow Connection."

Two of the day excursions—Dunbar and Dunfermline—can be reached conveniently only through Edinburgh. Consequently, readers need only refer to the Glasgow-Edinburgh shuttle-service schedule to determine the "Glasgow Connection" for these day excursions.

Five day excursions—Aberdeen, Dundee, Montrose, St. Andrews, and Stirling—are so situated on Scotland's rail lines that they may be reached either by direct connection from the Queen Street Station in Glasgow or through Edinburgh. A condensation of the "Glasgow Connections" for direct service appears on page 214.

Three other day excursions—Inverness, Kyle of Lochalsh, and Perth —are reached more conveniently from Glasgow by direct train service from the Queen Street Station rather than through Edinburgh. For a condensation of the "Glasgow Connections," you are referred again to page 214 for details.

The "Glasgow Connection" for express trains to London is given on page 215 of this chapter. All services shown are subject to alteration. Readers are advised to consult with the schedules posted in the train stations or with a British Rail Travel Centre for train information before commencing each journey. The publishers cannot be held responsible for changes or inaccuracies in the schedules.

Regardless of which city you select as your "base," don't forget that the frequent train service between Glasgow and Edinburgh enables you to make a "day excursion" to the one you didn't select as your base. For what to see and do in Edinburgh, consult the following chapter on Scotland's capital for details.

There are times throughout the year when one of the two cities, either Glasgow or Edinburgh, may be "fully booked." This can take place in Glasgow during May when the city hosts a Mayfest—a festival focusing attention on Glasgow's many activities within its cultural sphere. On the other hand, Edinburgh can be filled to overflowing when visitors attend its world famous "Edinburgh Tattoo." When this happens, and your reservationist gives up on the city of your choice—try the other. Your chances of finding accommodations there are very good, and the ease of rail travel between Glasgow and Edinburgh will make it an "easy commute," far better than anything that the Long Island Railroad could come up with!

"GLASGOW CONNECTIONS"

Excursion Destination	Depart Glasgow	Destination Arrive	Destination Depart	Return Glasgow	Notes
Aberdeen	0725	1009	1525	1814	Mon–Sat
	0825	1100	1630	1912	Mon–Sat
	0915	1212	1932	2220	Sundays
	0925	1205	1826	2110	Mon–Sat
Dundee	0725	0852	1545	1710	Mon–Sat
	0825	0945	1745	1912	Mon–Sat
	0915	1057	1645	1824	Sundays
	0925	1050	1907	2035	Mon–Sat
Inverness	0710	1032	1650	2012	Mon–Sat
	1155	1515	2005	2332	Mon–Sat
Montrose	0725	0924	1710	1912	Mon–Sat
	0915	1129	2013	2212	Sundays
	0925	1122	1906	2110	Mon–Sat
Perth	0725	0829	1608	1710	Mon–Sat
	0825	0927	1808	1912	Mon–Sat
	0915	1034	1708	1824	Sundays
	0925	1027	1930	2035	Mon–Sat
Stirling	0825	0853	1740	1814	Mon–Sat
	0915	0956	1744	1824	Sundays
	0925	0953	2040	2110	Mon–Sat
	1025	1053	2140	2212	Mon–Sat

St. Andrews Train from Glasgow Queen Street Station to Dundee. Transfer to St. Andrews bus, departing every hour on the half-hour.

Reference: Thomas Cook Table 600

Glasgow-Edinburgh Shuttle Service

Weekday Service: Departs Glasgow Queen Street Station for Edinburgh at 0622, 0655, 0730, and every half-hour thereafter until 2300. Departs Edinburgh at 0700 and every half-hour thereafter until 2330. Journey fifty to seventy minutes.

Sunday Service: Departs Glasgow Queen Street Station for Edinburgh at 0800 and on the hour thereafter until 2100; also at 2030, 2130, and 2230. Departs Edinburgh at 0830 and on the half-hour thereafter until 2330; also at 1805 and 1905. Journey takes fifty-five minutes.

Reference: Thomas Cook Table 590

GLASGOW-LONDON TRAIN SERVICE

(First- and second-class accommodations for all services listed)

DEPART FROM GLASGOW CENTRAL	ARRIVE IN LONDON			STATION
	MON–FRI	SAT	SUN	
0610	1215	1230	—	ES
0720(R)	1255	1305	—	ES
0800	1338	1349	—	KC
0950(R)	1450	1500	—	ES
1000	1540	1538	—	KC
1050	—	—	1730	KC
1140	1655	1705	—	ES
1200	1740	1738	—	KC
1220(R)	—	—	1749	ES
1250	—	—	1926	KC
1340(R)	1850	—	1911	ES
1400	1910	1935	—	KC
1450	—	—	2118	KC
1430(R)	—	—	2034	ES
1540	2110	2120	—	ES
1600	2158	2150	—	KC
1600(R)	—	—	2149	ES
1650	—	—	2332	KC
1700(R)	2215	2235	—	ES
1800	0006+1	—	—	KC
2335(R)(2340 SAT)	—	0748+1	0656+1	ES
2355(R)*	0700+1	0710+1	—	ES

Distance: 402 miles/647 km
References: Table 26, 26A
              Thomas Cook Table 550

High-speed trains, food service available; reservations recommended for all above-listed trains
(R) Reservations required
KC = King's Cross Station
ES = Euston Station
*Sleeping cars only. Passengers may remain aboard until 0730.

Train Information: 0141–204–2844
InterCity Services: 0171–387–7070

Glasgow Tourist Information Centre
0141–204–4400

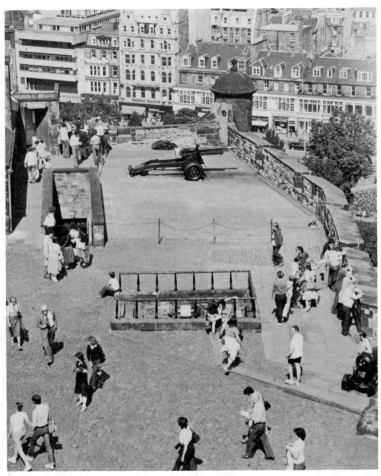

The one o'clock gun at Edinburgh Castle is fired every day except Sunday to provide an unusual time check for the city. Visiting shoppers on Princes Street (visible at the lower level in the background), unaware of the firing, may be seen doing their own version of the "One O'clock Jump" at precisely the same moment.

12   EDINBURGH

"This profusion of eccentricities, this dream in masonry and living rock," wrote Robert Louis Stevenson of Edinburgh, "is not a drop-scene in a theater, but a city in a world of everyday reality!" There is an understandable feeling of rocklike perpetuity enveloping Edinburgh. Formed by volcanic heat, scoured and shaped by ice-age glaciers in a valley punctuating its skyline with upward-thrusting crags, Scotland's capital city of Edinburgh is nothing short of dramatic in its setting.

Edinburgh's exact origins are lost in antiquity. Although dissenting opinions exist, it appears that the historical jigsaw of Edinburgh was pieced together in the following pattern. A primitive fortress was established around A.D. 452 by the Picts on the sloping ground leading from the great Castle Rock on which Edinburgh Castle stands today. There have been fortresses on Castle Rock since that time, each in turn razed by a challenger, rebuilt by the challenger, only to be razed again by another challenger. By the time of the eleventh century, however, Edinburgh began to calm down and get on with the task of becoming a civilized and prosperous town.

From its earliest days, Edinburgh's stern, almost aloof countenance has retained and fostered those enduring qualities that have inspired great men to great achievements. Edinburgh is actually two cities. The Old Town, built on a rocky ledge running from Edinburgh Castle to the Royal Palace of Holyroodhouse, is steeped in ancient history. It huddled on high ground in typical medieval fear of attack.

The New Town, which took form on the lower side of Nor' Loch, a lake created from a swamp and eventually drained in 1816, spread serenely in a succession of streets and avenues reflecting the optimism of the latter centuries. The New Town was conceived in 1767 when the Scottish Parliament approved an extension of the city and the Town Council lost no time in proceeding with the work. The city planning that followed made possible Edinburgh's present wide streets and spacious squares.

Its contrasts of two cities within a city are further reflected, on the one hand, by Edinburgh's reserved exterior and, on the other, by its ability to express great warmth and, upon occasion, a high degree of gaiety. Edinburgh has been termed one of the most attractive capital cities in the world. As Oliver Wendell Holmes aptly put it, "Edinburgh is a city of incomparable loveliness."

From the beauty of its setting, enhanced by its architecture, to the turbulence of its history and the quality of its citizens, Edinburgh is a city of inexhaustible delight. Edinburgh Castle, the Palace of Holyroodhouse, the Royal Mile, and Princes Street await you. Welcome to Scotland's capital!

Day Excursions

A "baker's dozen," thirteen exciting day excursions, have been selected for our readers. All were chosen so that those who prefer staying in Glasgow rather than in Edinburgh can enjoy them as well. (See "Glasgow Connections" in chapter 11.)

Scotland is known as "the land that likes to be visited." To ensure that your opportunity to visit this marvelous country by rail includes seeing as many of its features as possible, we have divided the selected day excursions into Scotland's four geographic areas: the east coast, central region, west coast, and Highlands.

East Coast. Along the east coast of Scotland, starting at the harbor of Dunbar near the English border, we then swing north from Edinburgh through Dundee, Montrose, and Aberdeen—not overlooking a stop en route at the golf capital of the world, St. Andrews.

Central Region. In the central part of the country, we have selected excursions to two of Scotland's most historic cities—Perth and Stirling—plus a visit to Andrew Carnegie's birthplace, Dunfermline, and a visit to Linlithgow to view the palace where Mary Queen of Scots was born.

West Coast. For our forays to the western coast, we delve deep into the heart of Robert Burns's country by a visit to Ayr, the poet's favorite town. Further south, we call at Stranraer, the gateway to the Irish Sea and the "Emerald Isle" of Ireland.

Highlands. North in the Highlands, Inverness serves as a gateway to explorations of Loch Ness, with its legendary monster, "Nessie," and as a "base city" for a dash to the west to Kyle of Lochalsh and the Isle of Skye.

Scotland has often been compared to an iceberg—in that there is much more than first meets the eye. Come to Scotland with an open mind, a keen eye, and a sense of adventure.

Arriving and Departing

By Air. Though Edinburgh has its own international airport, direct service to or from North America is not provided. Travelers arriving in Britain via London (Gatwick or Heathrow) or Manchester airports have the option of a connecting flight to Edinburgh or via rail. International air service is provided to Edinburgh from most European cities.

Glasgow, Scotland's international airport, located ten miles west of the city from which it takes its name, is a convenient port of entry for visitors arriving in Britain from overseas. The airport is situated in an area that is relatively fog free throughout the majority of the year, for the wind moving across the Irish Sea has few natural obstructions to interrupt its flow. Prestwick airport (twenty-nine miles southwest of Glasgow), which for years served as the international airport for the area, is the most fog-free airport on the British Isles.

Along with its excellent weather, the Glasgow airport offers travelers the opportunity of "open jaw" airline ticketing—arriving or departing on one leg of their transatlantic flight in Scotland rather than flying both in and out of the London complex of Gatwick, Stansted, or Heathrow. Currently, transatlantic service is provided by the following air carriers: Air Canada, American Airlines, British Airways, Icelandair, and Northwest Airlines.

The airport information desk also provides information to incoming passengers. The office is open from 0715 to 2230 daily. Currency exchange services are operated by Thomas Cook. The office is open daily in the summer between 0700 and 2300; in the winter (November to April), it is open from 0800 to 2000 Monday–Saturday, and Sunday, 0800–1800.

Airport coach service is available between the airport and Glasgow every thirty minutes from 0550 to 2250 weekdays; Sunday service is every thirty minutes from 0720 to 2220. Journey time is approximately twenty-five minutes and the fare is £2.00. Bus service direct to Edinburgh departs the airport at twenty and fifty minutes past the hour from 0550 to 2250 weekdays; Sunday, service is every thirty minutes. Journey time is one hour and forty-five minutes; the fare is £6.50.

In Glasgow, buses terminate at the Glasgow Airport Terminal Building. In Edinburgh, buses terminate at the St. Andrew Square bus station.

By Train. Waverley Station is the main train station in Edinburgh. Some InterCity trains from London go on to Aberdeen after a brief station stop in Edinburgh. If you are aboard one of these trains, be prepared to "set down" in the Waverley Station as quickly as possible following your arrival. Edinburgh does have another station, Haymarket, where all trains halt en route to Glasgow or Aberdeen. Trains arriving from England via Newcastle and York, however, bypass Haymarket Station.

Edinburgh's Railway Station—Waverley

The train terminal in Edinburgh appears to be completely immersed in an open ravine. The area was once a swamp that was converted into a lake as a northern defense for Edinburgh Castle during the reign of King James II (1437–1460). The lake was drained in 1816 to become the site of the Princes Street Gardens separating the Old Town and New Town in Edinburgh.

In 1847, rail lines were laid through the middle of the Princes Street Gardens to the east end, where Waverley Station was constructed. The tracks are now all but concealed by landscaping. Today's Waverley Station complex is the second largest in Britain.

Waverley Station is equipped with twenty-one tracks strewn about in a labyrinth of steps and passageways that could easily drive a laboratory white rat berserk. But a plenitude of signs and the helpful presence of Edinburghers (who appear to be specially trained to assist visitors) will help you put it all together.

Floral clock attracts Edinburgh's citizens and visitors alike. Built in 1903 in the city's West Princes Gardens, it is the oldest floral clock in the world. A cuckoo pops out to herald every quarter hour, and the flowers are changed frequently for important events.

Basically, there are three accesses to Waverley Station. The first is a set of rather steep steps, the Waverly Steps connecting the north side of the station (the trackage runs east and west) with Princes Street, the city's main artery. The second and third approaches are ramps leading from the main floor of the station to the Waverley Bridge, which runs between the Old Town and the New Town. Both ramps have pedestrian walkways. The northern ramp serves incoming vehicles; the one to the south is for outgoing vehicles.

Many of the facilities sought by incoming passengers, such as banking, city information, and hotel accommodations, are located nearby in the Edinburgh and Scotland Information Centre beyond the north end of Waverley Bridge at the corner of Waverley Bridge and Princes streets. To reach the center, use the pedestrian ramp on the north side of the station, turning right as you reach the Waverley Bridge level. There are several TOURIST INFORMATION signs to help guide the way. The Edinburgh and Scotland Information Centre is located at 3 Princes Street.

Tracks 12 to 18 form the backbone, or center, of the Waverley Station. At the entrance to these tracks is a digital-display bulletin board for train arrivals, departures, and special announcements. If your train is departing from tracks other than 12 to 18, ask the railroad personnel at the ticket barriers for directions; otherwise, you may end up in some dark corner like a berserk white rat.

Pay special attention to multiple train departures from the same track. In other words, a line of coaches on a single train track can actually be two trains departing for two separate destinations. They are announced with red-bannered FRONT TRAIN or REAR TRAIN signs. It pays to ask questions however—one advantage you have over the rat!

The British Rail Travel Centre (train information center) is located in the waiting-room area of the station. Covered by a huge glass dome, the waiting area also contains digital arrival/departure information and a series of facilities, including rest rooms, a magazine kiosk, and the Talisman Bar and the Talisman Buffet. The principal entrance to this area is located across the main-station concourse from the stub ends of tracks 16 and 17.

Since 1902, a landmark for Edinburgh as well as the Waverley Station is the Balmoral Hotel (formerly known as the North British Hotel), situated between the station and Princes Street. Topped by a mammoth 200-foot Gothic clock tower, the hotel served as a transition between the hustle of commerce on Princes Street and the bustle of the passengers arriving and departing the station. Erected during the Age of Steam, the hotel's spacious foyer and well-appointed lounges provided a brief but necessary respite for weary travelers.

Victorian throughout, the hotel underwent a £23 million restoration. It has emerged new in face but old in grace as the Balmoral Hotel. Undoubtedly, the hotel is still one of Edinburgh's most familiar and most elegant landmarks, commanding an important position at the east end of Princes Street.

Two bus departure points serve the area surrounding the Waverley Street rail station. The first, at Waverley Bridge, is located immediately up the ramps leading out of the rail station. This departure point serves the city bus system and the sightseeing buses. Coach service for the Glasgow Airport and other main destinations utilizes the bus terminal on St. Andrew Square. To reach it, cross Princes Street where it intersects with Waverley Bridge at the city's tourist information center. Then, walk north one block to St. Andrew Square.

Money exchange (Bureau de Change) is available from the Edinburgh & Scotland Information Centre. Hours of operation are (July and August) 0900–2000 Monday through Saturday and 1000–2000 on Sunday. During May, June, and September, the hours are 0900–1900 Monday through Saturday and 1100–1900 on Sunday. April and October, it is open 0900–1800 Monday through Saturday and 1100–1800 Sunday; November through March, the hours are 0900–1800 Monday through Saturday (closed Sunday).

Hotel accommodations are provided by the Edinburgh & Scotland Information Centre. Hours are: (July and August) Monday through Saturday, 0900–2000, and Sunday, 1000–2000; (May, June and September) Monday through Saturday, 0900–1900, and Sunday, 1100–1900; (April and October) Monday through Saturday, 0900–1800, and Sunday, 1100–1800; (November–March) Monday–Sunday, 0900–1800. The hotel-accommodations reservation fee is £3.00 per booking.

Tourist information is available at two locations within Edinburgh's information center, both operating at the same hours as the "Hotel Accommodations" section mentioned above. The first section has information on Edinburgh and all of Scotland; go straight ahead as you enter for self service. Go to the right for counter service. For entertainment information, proceed through the shopping section, where Scottish books, maps, and posters are available at the ticket desk (telephone (0131)558–1072).

For bus tours of Edinburgh, we refer you to the tourist information office and its selection of bus tour brochures. Among those available, we have found that the Guide Friday bus tour of the city is complete and the commentary of their guides accurate and amusing. Guided walking tours (Robin's Walking Tours) depart daily from outside the tourist information center. There are several to choose from: The "Grand Tour of the City" departs at 1000, the "Royal Mile" tour at 1100, and 1900 for "Ghosts and Witches." Telephone (0131) 661–0125.

Train information is available at the British Rail Travel Centre in the waiting-room area of Waverley Station. City information is *not* available in this office. Operating hours are 0700–2300 daily.

Train reservations may be made in the travel center at any one of the counters in operation during the time of your visit.

Shopping in Edinburgh

The city of Edinburgh is well known for its fine boutiques, shops, and department stores. You can still find bargains in the famous Harris tweeds, Fair Isle sweaters, and Tartan plaids. Princes Street is lined with shops displaying a variety of Scottish wares from argyles and bagpipes to whiskey. And when you run out of stores and shops to visit on Princes Street, turn north two blocks to George Street and continue your shopping there. (You may need to stop by the bank on the way.)

Shoppers' havens on Princes Street include large department stores such as Jenners and C. & A., opposite the Scott Monument in the Waverley Street Station area. If you've not been in a store 180 years old, try Romanes & Paterson, Ltd. at 62 Princes Street. You will find traditional Scottish tweed, exquisite Edinburgh crystal, Caithness glass, knitwear from the borders, and, of course, tartans.

Still not tired of shopping? The Scotch House nearby contains more than 300 tartans available by the meter, along with Shetland knitwear and original gifts. If you know a wee person, check out Hop Scotch, The Scotch House's special department for children.

With all that shopping, you may be ready for a libation and a snack. You don't have far to go—between, and parallel to, Princes Street and George Street is Rose Street, which probably has more convivial pubs to the meter than any other street in the world.

Greyfriars Bobby

On Candlemaker Row, a short distance from Edinburgh's Royal Mile, stands a statue in tribute to a small dog's affection and fidelity to his master. In 1858, a wee Skye terrier followed the remains of his master, Auld Jock, to Greyfriars churchyard, where the dog lingered and slept on his master's grave for fourteen years until his death in 1872.

People tried to take Bobby away. They even found a home for him in the country. Still, Bobby returned to the churchyard, where friends began bringing food to sustain him during his vigil. The story of Greyfriars Bobby spread throughout Edinburgh, and soon Bobby's tale of devotion reached Queen Victoria in London. She sent a special envoy, Lady Burdett-Coutts, to investigate this unusual story.

Bobby, in the meantime, had made friends with a number of children in a nearby orphanage. The terrier brought joy and love to the children, particularly to Tammy, a crippled boy with whom Bobby would play by the hour. Bobby lived his own life, however, and returned nightly to his master's grave—at first secretly, for the presence of a dog in a churchyard was unthinkable in those times. But as Bobby won hearts, he gained privileges, too. He even won

223

Greyfriars Bobby, a small Skye terrier whose devotion to his master in both life and death captured hearts throughout Edinburgh, is commemorated there by a fountain with his statue on it. A film by Walt Disney has made Bobby world-famous. The Greyfriars Bobby Bar may be seen in the background.

the heart of the Lord Provost of Edinburgh, who had a collar made for the dog in 1867 and paid Bobby's licensing fee. (The collar can be seen today in the Canongate on the Royal Mile.)

Bobby never went to London to see the Queen, but royal annals reflect that the Queen actually was planning to pay *him* a visit at Greyfriars. Bobby died, however, before that honor became a reality.

The dog's body was buried alongside that of his master. Although Bobby is no longer visible, his presence is felt so strongly by the residents of the area that they frankly admit to opening their doors briefly before retiring at night— just in case. Perhaps, when the door to heaven is opened for them, they will see Bobby again, running on the green pastures at the heels of his master, beside the still waters. Bobby is there. If there wasn't room enough in God's heaven for the love of this dog for his master, Bobby would not have kept the vigil at his master's grave—he would just have gone away.

Bobby's statue stands close to the iron gates of Greyfriars churchyard, where Auld Jock and his faithful dog are interred. The story of Greyfriars Bobby was filmed by Walt Disney. We think it's worth your while to visit Greyfriars, just as we do each time we return to Edinburgh.

Enticing Edinburgh

Amid the contrasting charms of its Old Town and New Town, Edinburgh takes its place among an elite group of European cities conspicuous for their romance and physical attributes. As more and more enclosures were built during the post-medieval period, the term *close* came into existence in old Edinburgh to describe the narrow passageways giving access or right of way to the buildings in the rear of others. There are well over one hundred closes in Old Town, many of which have brass tablets at their entrances to explain their historical significance.

There are many aspects of Edinburgh to see on conducted tours, but the city's real beauty is best seen by exploring it on foot at your own pace. Walk the Royal Mile in Old Town from Edinburgh Castle to the Palace of Holyroodhouse. En route, you'll pass a fantastic assembly of picturesque old buildings, such as Brodie's Close, the John Knox House, the Cannonball House, Anchor Close, and the Canongate Tolbooth.

Brodie's Close housed Deacon Brodie, a respectable town councilor by day and a burglar by night. Brodie's life-style supposedly provided the basis for Robert Louis Stevenson's *Dr. Jekyll and Mr. Hyde.* The John Knox House dates from the sixteenth century. It's traditionally connected with both John Mossman, Keeper of the Royal Mint to Mary Queen of Scots, and John Knox, Scotland's religious reformer. A brief video presentation amid original timber-framed galleries and oak paneling will take you back to the sixteenth century.

The John Knox House is located at the halfway mark of The Royal Mile in The Netherbow. Admission is £1.75.

The Cannonball House, dating from 1630, got its name from a cannonball lodged in its gable, ostensibly fired from the castle by an errant cannoneer during the blockade of 1745. Anchor Close is the site where the first edition of the *Encyclopedia Britannica* was printed. The Edinburgh edition of Robert Burns's poems was also printed there. Reportedly, Burns himself read the proofs on the premises. Last renovated in 1591, the Canongate Tolbooth has been used as the Town Council House and a prison for the ancient village of Canongate, now incorporated into the city of Edinburgh. The Canongate Tolbooth now houses the People's Story Museum, which relates the life and work of ordinary people in Edinburgh from the late eighteenth century to the present.

Although the Palace of Holyroodhouse originated as a guest house for the Abbey of Holyrood, most of the palace we see today was built for Charles II in 1671. The most famous figure associated with the palace, however, was Mary Queen of Scots, who spent six years of her tragic reign there. On the palace grounds, you can view Queen Mary's Bath House where, according to today's Scottish tour guides, Mary Queen of Scots bathed daily. The guides also explain that her cousin, Queen Elizabeth I, bathed once a month—whether she needed it or not.

The Royal Mile was for many centuries the center of Edinburgh life. Its citizens lived and conducted their affairs on this busy, crowded street. At the entrance to the Palace or Holyroodhouse, you will find a line of the letter "S" embedded in the pavement. Until 1880, it marked the limits of sanctuary extended by Holyrood Abbey. It is said that debtors were often seen running toward the line with creditors in hot pursuit and bystanders wagering on the outcome.

EDINBURGH-LONDON TRAIN SERVICE
(First- and standard-class accommodations for all services listed)

DEPART WAVERLEY STATION	ARRIVE LONDON KING'S CROSS STATION		
	MON–FRI	SAT	SUN
0610	1058	—	—
0700	1137	1145	—
0800	1237	1239	—
0835	—	1314	—
0900	1338	1349	1438
0930	1403	1403	—
0945	—	1411	—
1000	1440	1450	1532
1030	1455	1455	—
1100	1540	1538	1625
1130	1557	1558	—
1200	1645	1644	1730
1230	1651	1652	1748
1300	1740	1738	1827
1330	—	1757	1837
1400	1839	1842	1926
1500	—	1935	—
1500*	1910	—	—
1530	—	—	2033
1600	2038	2035	2118
1630	—	—	2141
1700	2158	2150	2205
1730	2219	2215	—
1800	—	—	2332
1900	0006+1	—	—
2355(R)**	0700+1	—	—

Distance: 393 miles/632 km
References: Table 26A
Thomas Cook Table 570
High-speed trains, food service available; reservations recommended
(R) Reservations required
(1) Sleeper service Monday–Friday and Sunday. No sleeper service on Saturday.
*Pullman service, supplement payable
** Sleeping cars only, arrives in Euston Station

Tourist Information
British Tourist Authority: 0171–499–9325
Edinburgh: 0131–557–1700

Train Information
Edinburgh: 0131–556–2451
InterCity Services: 0171–278–2477

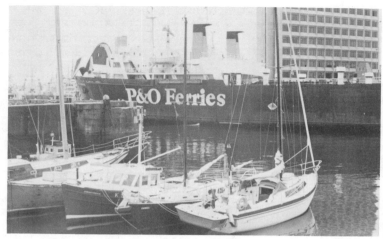

Aberdeen's many faces (above) are depicted in its harbor and academic countenances. Its harbor bustles with commercial fishing craft, outlying-island ferries, and vessels resupplying offshore oil rigs. King's College (below) provides tranquillity with its seventeenth-century crown tower.

From Edinburgh . . .

A DAY EXCURSION TO ABERDEEN
DISTANCE BY TRAIN: 131 miles (211 km)
AVERAGE TRAIN TIME: 2 hours, 30 minutes

Since the discovery of oil in the North Sea, Aberdeen has earned the title of "Europe's offshore oil capital." The city, however, has not been spoiled by this new industry. Oil does not come ashore in Aberdeen; moreover, only occasionally can an oil rig be seen on the horizon—under tow to a new location or at anchor awaiting a new contract.

The development of North Sea oil plus the gathering strength of northeast Scotland's agriculture, fishing, and manufacturing industries have combined to give Aberdeen the highest growth rate of any city in Great Britain. Therefore, you will find Aberdeen a city of many moods. It is steeped in history. It is an ancient university town and a thriving seaport as well. It has grown very cosmopolitan, yet it remains old in grace. Above all else, the Aberdonians always have time—time to help, time to be interested, and time to talk.

Aberdeen lies between the rivers Dee and Don with two miles of golden sand connecting them. But don't think of Aberdeen merely as a large city with a beach. Union Street bisects the city and provides a mile-long shopping center lined with excellent shops.

Aberdeen University comprises King's College and Marischal College. Both are architecturally attractive yet totally different. Marischal College is one of the largest granite buildings in the world. It was founded in 1593 and united with King's College in 1860 to form the University of Aberdeen. King's College, in Old Aberdeen, was founded in 1495. The ivy-covered building with its distinctive crown tower has stood for centuries as a symbol of Aberdeen.

Standing like a sentinel, the gleaming white Girdleness Lighthouse guarding Aberdeen's harbor will be the first welcoming sign you'll see in Scotland's third largest city. It becomes visible on the right as the train curves away to the left from Nigg Bay to cross the River Dee, then glides to a halt in Aberdeen's rail station.

The port of Aberdeen is the jumping-off place for adventurers bound for the Orkney Islands and Shetland Islands to the north. Don't be surprised if you see a cruise ship or two in Aberdeen's harbor. Aberdeen has attracted the cruise ships by constructing a passenger landing stage in its Victoria Dock area. It appears that everyone wants to visit Europe's offshore capital, Aberdeen.

Aberdeen maintains tourist information in the form of a well-stocked literature stand alongside the Travel Centre information counter in the rail station.

ABERDEEN—*THE GRANITE CITY*

A Day Excursion from Edinburgh

DEPART FROM WAVERLEY STATION	ARRIVE IN ABERDEEN STATION	NOTES
0705	0942	(1)
0810	1045	(1)
0855	1125	(2)
0910	1138	(1)
1025	1300	(1)
1055	1326	(2)

DEPART FROM ABERDEEN STATION	ARRIVE IN WAVERLEY STATION	NOTES
1455 (1510 SUN)	1720 (1741 SUN)	(1)(2)
1615	1848	(1)
1712	1952	(1)
1815	2044	(1)
1900	2127	(2)
2000	2223	(1)
2050	2320	(2)

Distance: 131 miles/211 km
References: Table 229
                   Thomas Cook Table 600

(1) MON–SAT   (2) SUN

Train Information: 01224–594222
InterCity Services: 0171–278–2477

Aberdeen Tourist Information Centre: 01224–632727
Aberdeen Whats on Line—24-Hour Service
01224–636363

There's also a twenty-four-hour "View Data" service—a very user-friendly computerized inquiry unit.

The main **tourist information center** is in St. Nicholas House on Broad Street (telephone 01224–632727). When leaving the station, turn right onto Guild Street and walk until you arrive at Market Street, where the docks come into view. A left turn onto Market Street followed by a right turn onto Union Street will keep you on course (mind the shops!) until you spy Aberdeen's Town House at the head of Broad Street leading to your left. The center is a short distance up Broad Street on the left-hand side, opposite Marischal College and its award-winning Museum of Human History.

This information center is open daily throughout the year except on Sundays from November through March. From November through March it is open Monday through Friday 0900–1700 and Saturday 1000–1400; in April, May, and October, Monday through Friday 0900–1700 and Saturday and Sunday 1000–1600; in June and September; Monday through Saturday 0900–1800 and Sunday 1000–1600; and in July and August Monday through Friday 0900–2000, Saturday 0900–1800 and Sunday 1000–1800. On public and local holidays, with the exception of Christmas and New Year's Day, the center is normally open 0900–1700.

The Aberdeen information center has a wide variety of booklets, leaflets, and posters of Aberdeen and the surrounding area. Also available are the publications of the Scottish Tourist Board covering the entire country. The center is divided into three operating sections: inquiries, accommodations, and tickets. Walking-tour and bus-tour information is also available here.

Clustered around the tourist information center on Broad Street, many of Aberdeen's places of interest are only a short walk away. In the restored Provost Skene's House on Broad Street, the oldest domestic dwelling in Aberdeen, dating from 1545, you will find rooms furnished in styles covering different periods in Aberdeen's history.

The Aberdeen Maritime Museum is housed in Provost Ross's House overlooking the city's harbor. Here, attractive displays not only depict Aberdeen's maritime heritage of fishing, shipbuilding, and trade, but also its offshore oil industry (with scale-model oil rigs). Provost Ross's House, a restored sixteenth-century dwelling, also houses a visitor's center featuring audiovisual displays of National Trust for Scotland properties, a fascinating collection of more than 100 properties representing a rich variety of castles, gardens, scenic areas, islands, and historic sights.

The new Tolbooth Museum, housed in the seventeenth-century tolbooth at Castlegate, explores the history of crime, punishment, and incarceration as well as the evolution of local government, from the sixteenth-century to the present day.

Tam o'Shanter Inn on High Street is a part of the lore of Scotland's bard, Robert Burns. The town of Ayr is a principal point for starting out on the Burns Heritage Trail, developed by the Scottish Tourist Board. The trail tours places linked to the history of Scotland's greatest poet. (Courtesy of Ayrshire and Arran Tourist Board)

From Edinburgh . . .

A DAY EXCURSION TO AYR
DISTANCE BY TRAIN: 88 miles (142 km)
AVERAGE TRAIN TIME: 1 hour, 30 minutes

What William Shakespeare is to England, Robert Burns is to Scotland. Ayr is the acknowledged center of the celebrated "Burns Country." The town is rich in the history of Scotland's bard. Many famous landmarks remain in Ayr today to tell the Burnsian stories.

The Tam o'Shanter Inn on High Street is where Tam began his celebrated ride. The Auld Brig (old bridge) that for 500 years was the only bridge in town still offers a delightful passage across the River Ayr. In a conspicuous location outside the Ayr train station, a statue of Robert Burns waits to greet travelers.

In Alloway, a pleasant southern suburb of Ayr, you will find the Burns National Heritage Park, where visual displays introduce you to the life of Robert Burns and acquaint you with locations in and around Ayr that you may later want to visit. A brief walk from the exhibit will bring you to Burns's Cottage, where the poet was born on 25 January 1759. More than 100,000 visitors pass through the park annually. The ruins of the Alloway Auld Kirk (old church), also close to the center, were the inspiration for Burns's narrative poem "Tam o'Shanter."

It was from the ruins of the Auld Kirk that witches pursued Tam, but he escaped over the Auld Brig O'Doon—the bridge over the River Doon—and eluded his pursuers, because according to legend witches were unable to cross running water. Maggie, the mare that Tam rode, was less fortunate: "Ae spring brought off her master hale,/But left behind her ain gray tail:/The carlin claught her by the rump,/And left poor Maggie scarce a stump."

Ayr was a seaside resort long before the term was invented. Well-heeled Glasgow merchants came to Ayr for short vacations, liked what they saw, and built houses there. In addition to providing Scottish gentry with suburban abodes, Ayr is also an industrial town, a market center, and a fishing port—for good measure. With all these assets, Ayr is assured of retaining its prosperous, bustling atmosphere even after the summer visitors have gone.

After arriving in Ayr, head for the town's **tourist information center** which is directly across from the rail station. Depart the train station through the main exit and walk directly across the street for Burns Statue Square. The tourist information office is in Burns House. The office is open from mid-October to Easter, Monday through Saturday 0915–1700 (and Easter weekend, Saturday 0915–1800, Sunday 1000–1800). In April the hours are Monday through Saturday 0915–1700 and Sundays 1000–1700; in May, June, September, and the beginning and middle of October, Monday through

A Day Excursion from Edinburgh

DEPART FROM EDINBURGH WAVERLEY STATION	ARRIVE IN GLASGOW QUEEN STREET STATION	NOTES
0700 or 0900	0750 or 0950	(1)
0830	0935	(2)

Transfer to Glasgow Central Station (See chapter 11)

DEPART FROM GLASGOW CENTRAL STATION	ARRIVE IN AYR STATION	NOTES
0830 or 1030	0928 or 1122	(1)(2)

(Plus other frequent service)

DEPART FROM AYR STATION	ARRIVE IN GLASGOW CENTRAL STATION	NOTES
1543	1634	(1)(2)
1613 or 1813	1709 or 1909	(1)

Transfer to Glasgow Queen Street Station (See chapter 11)
(Plus other frequent service)

DEPART FROM GLASGOW QUEEN STREET STATION	ARRIVE IN EDINBURGH WAVERLEY STATION	NOTES
1700 or 1930	1750 or 2020	(1)
1700	1802	(2)

Distance: 88 miles/142 km
References: Table 221, 228
              Thomas Cook Tables 596, 591

(1) MON–SAT   (2) SUN

Train Information: 1345–212282
InterCity Services: 0171–387–7070

Ayr Tourist Information Centre: 01292–284196

Saturday 0915–1800 and Sundays 1000–1800; in July and August, Monday through Saturday, 0915–1900 and Sundays 1000–1900.

Literature on Ayr, the district surrounding it, and Scotland's famous poet, Robert Burns, abounds by the pound in the information center. You will want to collect such informative booklets as the one published by the district that's crammed with facts and photos. In addition, ask for a copy of the city map. It is the best authority for a tour of Ayr on foot that we have found.

You will hear mention of the Burns Heritage Trail during your visit in Ayr. If you are interested in taking it or a bus to "Burns Country," you should gather all the details from the information center. The Burns Heritage Trail has been developed by the Scottish Tourist Board. It is a tour of the places linked with Scotland's poet. On the trail, you can see many places that have been developed to tell the story of Burns and his lifetime. The trail tour includes a visit to Tarbolton and the Lochlea Farm, where the Burns family lived from 1777 to 1784, and a stop at Mauchline, where it is said that Robert Burns met his wife to be, Jean Armour.

With more than two miles of golden, sandy beach, Ayr gets more than its fair share of the summer Scottish sun. Golf, bowling, and tennis are among the many sports activities that can be enjoyed there. The town has three golf courses, forming part of the famous fifteen-mile stretch of "golfing coast" you'll see from the train approaching Ayr. All the traditional seaside amusements can be enjoyed in Ayr, as well as horse racing, held at the Ayr Racecourse throughout the year.

Away from the beaches, there are many beautiful parks and gardens, notably Belleisle, Craigie, and Rozelle. Rozelle is also the home of Ayr's Maclaurin Art Gallery and displays one of the very few Henry Moore sculptures to be seen in Scotland. Ayr's beauty has frequently brought it the coveted titles, "Britain's Floral Town" and "Scotland's Floral Town." If you delight in old houses, Ayr has many, including one that was built in 1470—twenty-two years before Columbus discovered America!

Following your visit to Ayr, you probably will be in accord with "Robbie" Burns when he wrote, "Auld Ayr, wham ne'er a town surpasses/For honest men and bonie lasses."

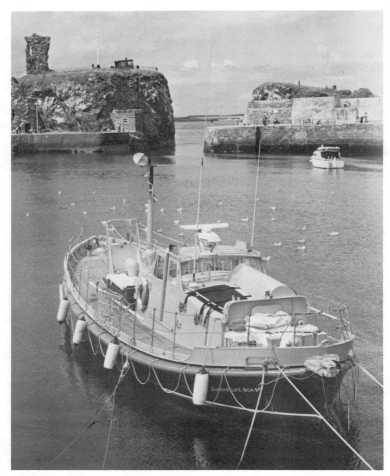

RNLB *Margaret,* a Royal National Life Boat, stands ready for rescue duty in Dunbar's Victoria Harbor. The ruins of Dunbar Castle mark the narrow passageway leading from the harbor into the North Sea. The old lifeboat house on the harbor's quay is now a museum.

From Edinburgh . . .

A DAY EXCURSION TO DUNBAR
DISTANCE BY TRAIN: 29 miles (46 km)
AVERAGE TRAIN TIME: 30 minutes

Put on your walking shoes—we're going to Dunbar. The town offers two wonderful walking opportunities: one through the historic center of old Dunbar to appreciate the great and varied wealth of its traditional Scottish buildings, the other along the cliffs brooding over the North Sea in the John Muir Country Park. Those unaccustomed to walking or slower of pace can take solace in Dunbar's harbor area by watching fishermen and their customers on the quay buying and selling freshly caught fish as their colorful fishing boats bob about on the tide. Further assurance of a pleasant outing for all is the presence of several public houses in the harbor area. Among them is the Volunteer Arms, which houses the Volunteer Bar and the Haven Lounge, where one can either seek haven or volunteer.

Dunbar is situated amid some of the most beautiful countryside and coastline in Scotland. There are few other places where it is possible to witness the full range of history of a Scottish east-coast fishing port and market center. Dunbar has always played an important part in Scotland's history. Due to its strategic location, the town has been a stronghold down through the centuries. Dunbar, Gaelic for "the fort on the point," had a castle fortress at least as early as 856. The remains of the castle stand on the promontory overlooking Dunbar's Victoria Harbor.

The Dunbar Castle was the place where Bothwell brought Mary Queen of Scots when he abducted her in 1567. That same year, the Scottish Parliament ordered that Dunbar Castle should be demolished. When the Victoria Harbor was constructed in the nineteenth century, the channel leading into the harbor was cut through the rocky palisade where the ruins of the castle lay. The remains that you may inspect during your visit to Dunbar are only a fragment of the original great castle.

There are two harbors: the old harbor, extended by Oliver Cromwell, and Victoria Harbor. Construction on the old harbor began in 1655, and it was improved and extended in the eighteenth century. This harbor, now nearly deserted, still retains the old paving stones as well as a fishermen's barometer that was erected in 1856. As part of the redevelopment, the harbor areas have had cottage-type houses built since 1951 to the special design of Sir Basil Spence, the architect of the new Coventry Cathedral. Perhaps the best evidence of Dunbar's beauty is the large number of visitors walking about simply admiring the scenery.

An interesting part of Victoria harbor is Dunbar's RNLB (Royal National

DUNBAR—*"FORT ON THE POINT"*

A Day Excursion from Edinburgh

DEPART FROM EDINBURGH WAVERLEY STATION	ARRIVE IN DUNBAR STATION	NOTES
0610	0631	(1)
0700	0721	(2)
0900	0923	(1)
1000	1023	(2)
1200	1221	(3)
1400	1421	(1)

DEPART FROM DUNBAR STATION	ARRIVE IN EDINBURGH WAVERLEY STATION	NOTES
1524	1556	(3)
1656	1725	(1)
1713	1739	(2)
1816	1846	(3)
2107	2133	(2)
2147	2216	(1)
2242	2312	(3)

Distance: 29 miles/46 km
References: Table 26

(1) MON–FRI   (3) SUN

(2) SAT

Train Information: 0131–556–2451
InterCity Services: 0171–278–2477

Dunbar Tourist Information Centre
01368–63353

Life Boat) *Margaret.* Opposite its mooring is the Lifeboat Museum, which is well worth a visit. Lifeboats out of Dunbar have saved more than 200 lives since beginning operation in 1808.

The **Dunbar tourist information center** is at 143 High Street, near the Town House (telephone 01368–863353). Part of the Town House, incidentally, is a tolbooth (toll gate) dating back to the seventeenth century, when a toll road between Edinburgh and Newcastle ran through Dunbar. The center is a short walk from the railway station. Station Road runs from the front of the station to where it crosses Countess Road and becomes Abbey Road. When you reach the general post office on your left, the thoroughfare has another name change to High Street and remains so until you reach the information center.

The information center is open during summer 0900–2000 Monday through Saturday and 1100–1800 on Sunday. During the balance of the year, it is open Monday through Friday, 0900–1700, and closed Saturday and Sunday. Note the sundial on the tolbooth tower as you enter the information center. You can still set your watch by it—provided, of course, that the sun is shining during your visit.

For the town tour we mentioned, ask for a copy of *A Walk Around Historic Dunbar* (£2.50). A guidebook for the self-guided trail laid out along the cliffs running out of Dunbar is also available. This cliff-top trail is prominently marked on the previously mentioned street plan, as are other features of the town, including the two harbors.

If you brought your walking shoes with you, the place to try them out is the John Muir Country Park, which begins at Dunbar harbor and extends to the Ravensheugh sands to the west, on the south approaches to the Firth of Forth. The cliff-top trail has controlled public accesses to the beaches below. Throughout the summer, a ranger is normally on duty in the park and is available to answer your questions and provide directions. You may join the ranger on a ramble along the cliff-top trail, but times and routes may vary. Check with the tourist office. There are several horse riding routes within the park. If interested in equestrian pursuits, ask the tourist information center for a copy of *Horse Riding Guide.*

If you are a golf nut and have not been able to obtain a tee time for the Old Course at St. Andrews, try the par-64 Winterfield Golf Course maintained by the town of Dunbar. Call Dunbar 62280 to get a tee time.

There is a bowling green on the right-hand side of the Station Road as you proceed toward town. We asked an old Scot, "How can such a green be so smooth and flat?" "It's easy," he explained, "you just plant the best of grass seed and then roll it for a few hundred years."

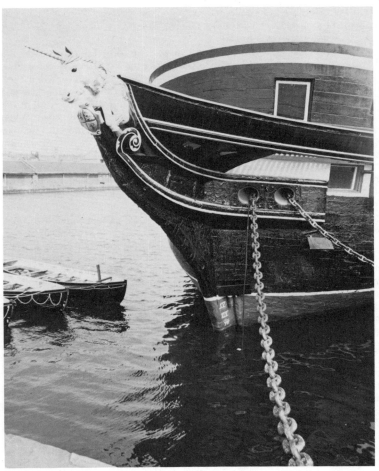

Unicorn figurehead of the frigate *Unicorn* glistens at the bow of Britain's oldest warship still afloat. Moored at the Victoria Dock in Dundee, the vessel is open to visitors year-round and features an exhibition of Royal Navy development.

A DAY EXCURSION TO DUNDEE
DISTANCE BY TRAIN: 60 miles (96 km)
AVERAGE TRAIN TIME: 1 hour, 30 minutes

As your train approaches the city of Dundee, you will be able to witness a scene of railroading history—one of disaster and yet one of triumph. Following the station stop at Leuchars, where you detrain for St. Andrews, watch as the train passes through the local station of Wormit and on to the railway bridge crossing the Firth of Tay inbound to Dundee. The bridge, a double-track structure 11,653 feet long, was opened in 1887 and was considered at that time (as it is even now) to be a triumph of railroad engineering. Look alongside the present bridge and you will see a series of old bridge piers. These once supported a single-track bridge that was swept away during a violent storm in 1879, along with a train and seventy-five of its passengers.

Turn your gaze to the east during the crossing of the great Firth (estuary) where the Tay River empties into the North Sea and you will see a two-lane vehicular bridge 7,365 feet in length that was opened by Queen Elizabeth II in 1966. The River Tay and its rail and vehicular bridges are a vital part of Dundee's existence.

Dundee, the capital of Tayside and Scotland's fourth largest city, lies in a magnificent setting between the Sidlaw Hills and the banks of Britain's finest salmon river, the Tay.

Dundee was famous for generations as the city of "jute, jam, and journalism." Its prolific writers still abound and Dundee marmalade is still made locally, but jute is slowly sinking into the shadows of time as synthetic fibers take over in the cordage industry.

Dundee lies in the heart of Scotland, where the game of golf originated. The latest count reveals forty golf courses within one hour's drive of the city. Five actually lie within the city's district. In Dundee, the name of the game is golf, and its citizens have proven to the world that they can construct courses that can confound, confuse—but always entertain. In Dundee and throughout the area, you also will note that the hospitality in the nineteenth holes throughout the region is second to none.

By the way, if your original day-excursion plans were for St. Andrews but you failed to leave the train at Leuchars Station, you can still make it back to the golf capital by bus out of Dundee in less than one hour. You also can capitalize on your error, however, and enjoy Dundee.

Dundee's tourist information center is easy to find. From within the rail station proceed across the pedestrian bridge, then exit and follow Whitehall Street to the right until you come to Crichton Street. Turn left up this street

DUNDEE—*CITY OF DISCOVERY*

A Day Excursion from Edinburgh

DEPART FROM EDINBURGH WAVERLEY STATION	ARRIVE IN DUNDEE STATION	NOTES
0705	0827	(2)
0810	0926	(2)
0855	1011	(3)
0910	1024	(2)
1025	1145	(2)
1055	1209	(3)

DEPART FROM DUNDEE STATION	ARRIVE IN EDINBURGH WAVERLEY STATION	NOTES
1427	1548	(2)
1501	1620	(3)
1606	1720	(2)
1627	1741	(3)
1727	1848	(2)(3)(4)
1827	1952	(2)
1927	2044	(2)(3)(5)
2109	2223	(2)

Distance: 60 miles/96 km
References: Table 229
Thomas Cook Table 600

(1) MON–FRI   (4) Departs 1725 and arrives 1859 on Sundays
(2) MON–SAT   (5) Departs 1925 and arrives 2059 on Sundays
(3) SUN

Train Information: 01382–28046
InterCity Services: 0171–278–2477

Dundee Tourist Information Centre
01382–434664

until you reach the top. Turn right again and you have reached the City Square. The tourist information center is at No. 4. You can phone the center from the railway station on (0382) 434664. The center is open Monday through Saturday, 0830–2000; Sunday, 1100–2000 during May, June, and September. It closes one hour later during July and August. From October through April, it is open Monday through Friday, 0900–1800, and Saturday, 1000–1600.

The cultural aspects of Dundee are enhanced by its McManus Galleries as well as the University Botanical Gardens. Camperdown Park and the Wildlife Centre are also stellar attractions for those who prefer outside activities. Among Dundee's many other attractions, one that we think will prove to be of interest to all is the frigate *Unicorn,* Britain's oldest warship still afloat. The *Unicorn* is one of the world's four remaining frigates, those fast, lightly armed sailing ships of yesteryear now replaced by the destroyer class of naval vessel. Launched in 1824, the *Unicorn* remained in naval service until 1968. Ask the information center for the *Unicorn* and RRS *Discovery* brochures and instructions to reach Victoria Dock and Discovery Quay.

Dundee's newest attraction is *Discovery* Point, a state of the art visitor's center portraying the history of Captain Scott's Royal Research Ship *Discovery* and her Antarctic voyages. Built in Dundee, Britain's first scientific research vessel set sail on her voyage to the Antarctic in 1901. You can visit *Discovery* berthed adjacent to the visitor's center.

Dundee's other points of interest include its old steeple, its four castles—Dudhope, Mains, Claypotts, and Broughty—and the Mercat Cross, which is moved about as the population center changes. The old steeple, standing at a height of 156 feet above the ground, dates from the fourteenth century. The steeple has withstood many storms, both natural and manmade. It was the site of the siege of 1651, when the town was invaded by Cromwell's army. The old steeple and all of the castle sites can be reached by public transport buses from the city bus station a three-minute walk from the British Rail terminal.

The Mercat Cross, a replica of the old structure that was demolished in 1877, is currently located at the end of High Street. The original cross was erected in the Seagate area. About the beginning of the fifteenth century, however, the city's population began to increase, and the town began to spread westward. The Seagate was abandoned as the principal center of the city in favor of a more open space to the west, which is now High Street.

Dundee has a passion for plaques and has erected a number of them on buildings having historical associations. At latest count, twelve such monuments are located throughout the city. Of particular interest to visitors is the plaque marking the Greyfriars monastery, which was granted to the city as a burial site by Mary Queen of Scots in 1564 and is now known as the Howff.

Humble weaver's cottage in Dunfermline (above), birthplace of steel millionaire Andrew Carnegie, is open to the public. Carnegie's benevolence brought amenities such as a concert hall, library, and sports center to the city. Old Pug Engine No. 11 (below) stands in Pittencrieff Park close by the Carnegie memorial statue.

From Edinburgh . . .

A DAY EXCURSION TO DUNFERMLINE
DISTANCE BY TRAIN: 17 miles (27 km)
AVERAGE TRAIN TIME: 32 minutes

Dunfermline was once the capital of Scotland and holds an important position in Scottish history. The majestic spires of the Dunfermline Abbey dominate the town's skyline. Within the abbey are the graves of seven Scottish kings, including the tomb of Robert the Bruce. The abbey was founded by Scotland's King David in the twelfth century as a Benedictine monastery. In the course of time, through royal gifts and other extensive endowments, it became one of the most magnificent establishments in Scotland. In its time, the monastery has played host to a wide range of people, from Edward I of England to Oliver Cromwell.

A second attraction in Dunfermline is Pittencrieff Park, a lovely area with its flower gardens, music pavilion, aviary, and museum. It was given to the town by Andrew Carnegie, the Scottish-American philanthropist who was born in a humble weaver's cottage in Dunfermline in 1835. His birthplace is open to the public, and it attracts thousands of visitors every year. A statue of the steel millionaire stands in the center of Pittencrieff. It was erected by the citizens of Dunfermline in grateful appreciation of his many gifts to his native city.

Arriving in Dunfermline by train, you can go to the center of the city either by bus or by taxi. The walk is not too distant to the abbey and the other attractions in town. It is a bit longer, however, than the stationmaster's advice, "Not more than a four-minute walk from here." Allow fifteen minutes to cover the ground between the train station and the center of the city. The tourist information center, the abbey, Pittencrieff, and Carnegie's birthplace lie between these two points. Taxis queue at the front of the station. About £2.00 will see you to the city center. The bus stop is close to the station at an underpass on the left.

The tourist information center is located near the historic sixteenth-century Abbot House, right next to the abbey in the Maygate. It is open from April to the end of September from 0900-1800 Monday through Saturday and 1030-1530 on Sundays. October on Saturday only. To contact the center by telephone, call 01383–720999.

Of course, Dunfermline's tourist information center specializes in the features of the abbey and Carnegie's cottage, but you'll find that the staff is very helpful in suggesting other things to do, too.

To reach the tourist information center on foot from the railway station,

DUNFERMLINE—*ANDREW CARNEGIE BIRTHPLACE*

A Day Excursion from Edinburgh

DEPART FROM EDINBURGH WAVERLEY STATION	ARRIVE IN DUNFERMLINE STATION	NOTES
0815	0845	(1)
0915	0945	(1)
0955	1027	(2)
1015	1045	(1)
1115	1145	(1)
1155	1227	(2)

DEPART FROM DUNFERMLINE STATION	ARRIVE IN EDINBURGH WAVERLEY STATION	NOTES
1503	1536	(1)
1603	1636	(1)
1703	1736	(1)
1739	1812	(2)
1808	1844	(1)
1903	1936	(1)
1939	2012	(2)
2020	2053	(1)
2120	2153	(1)
2139	2212	(2)
2220	2253	(1)

Distance: 17 miles/27 km
Reference: Table 242

(1) MON–SAT   (2) SUN

Train Information: 0131–556–2451
InterCity Services: 0171–278–2477

Dunfermline Tourist Information Centre
01383–720999

cross St. Margaret's Drive in front of the station and walk down Comely Park. After crossing New Row, Priory Lane joins St. Margaret's Street. Bear right and continue on St. Margaret's to the intersection of Abbot Street, where you'll find the center to your left round the corner, beyond the newly opened Heritage Centre, the Abbot House.

The triangle of interest is the Dunfermline Abbey, Pittencrieff Park, and the Andrew Carnegie birthplace. We suggest visiting the park first, due to its close proximity to the information center. Stop at the abbey, next, then the Carnegie cottage as you proceed back to the rail station.

The site of the Dunfermline Abbey has had continual Christian worship for about 1,500 years. In the fifth or sixth century, the first building on the site was the Culdee Church. Later, it was rebuilt on a larger scale by Malcolm III, father of King David I, and was dedicated in 1072. Traces of both buildings are visible beneath gratings in the floor of the abbey's Old Nave.

April through October, the abbey church is open 0930–1700 daily and 1400–1700 on Sunday. Between November and March, the abbey is closed, except for services. The abbey shop is open during the same hours as the church between April and October.

It was Andrew Carnegie who generously donated Pittencrieff Park to Dunfermline and gave funds for its upkeep. It has become a popular place for visitors to pause and reflect on his donations of a library, public baths, and a theater in addition to the park. During your stroll through the park, swing aboard Old Pug and marvel at the advances that have been made in railroading since its engine's fires were banked for the last time.

Andrew Carnegie's birthplace is open to the public daily from April through October from 1100 to 1700 (Sunday opening, 1400). From November through March, it's open 1400–1600 daily. From his humble beginnings, Andrew Carnegie found his fortunes in the new world. Nevertheless, with his philanthropist attitude, he never forgot his home town of Dunfermline. At age thirty-three, with an annual income of $50,000, Carnegie said, "Beyond this never earn, make no effort to increase fortune, but spend the surplus each year for benevolent purposes." This, he certainly did. His generosity in Dunfermline is administered today by a trust fund.

When you visit Dunfermline, you will be following in the footsteps of British royalty. Both Queen Victoria and Queen Mary visited there, and in 1972, Queen Elizabeth and Prince Philip were present to dedicate a Royal Pew in celebration of the abbey's 900th anniversary. You'll find, however, that Dunfermline extends a royal welcome to all of its visitors.

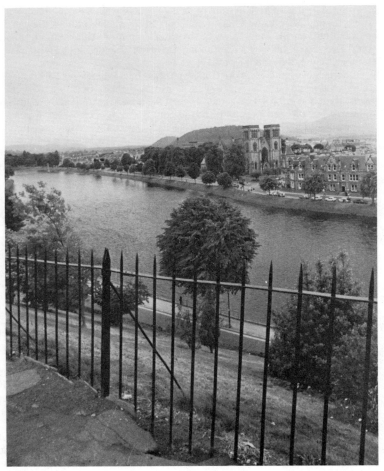

River Ness, as viewed from Inverness Castle, leads southwest to Loch Ness, mythical lair of "Nessie," the Loch Ness monster. Known as the "Capital of the Highlands," Inverness, because of its increasing popularity, has expanded its hotels and recreational facilities to meet its visitors' needs.

From Edinburgh . . .

AN "OUT-AND-BACK" EXCURSION TO INVERNESS
DISTANCE BY TRAIN: 176 miles (283 km)
AVERAGE TRAIN TIME: 3 hours, 40 minutes

The position of Inverness at the eastern head of Loch Ness, Scotland's famous inland sea, earns the city its title, "Capital of the Highlands." From Inverness, you can get to more places in the Highlands than you can from any other location in Scotland. For this reason, we have termed the excursion to Inverness an "out-and-back" excursion, for you may want to use Inverness as your "base city" for exploring the Highlands.

Should your schedule for visiting Inverness be limited, you may want to utilize the excellent British Rail sleeper services. For example, you could board a sleeper one night in London and awaken the following morning in Inverness. You could spend an entire day sightseeing, followed by boarding another sleeper back to London.

It is an ambitious program, but going in and out of Inverness by sleeper could permit you to board the 1045 train from there to the Kyle of Lochalsh (see page 254), where you arrive at 1315, then ferry to the Isle of Skye, soak in the sights, and leave Lochalsh on the 1705 to be back in Inverness by 1938 with some time to spare before boarding the sleeper again.

But why hurry? The scenery is superb and the climate is invigorating. Take our advice and plan to spend at least several days in hospitable Inverness, exploring the Highlands at a leisurely pace.

The **tourist information center** in Inverness is at Castle Wynd. To reach it by the shortest route turn left when leaving the train station and continue until you see Marks & Spencer. Cross the street and continue up Inglis Street, then turn right onto High Street walking until you come to McDonald's. Cross the pedestrian walk, past the Town House and across Castle Wynd where the tourist information center is located at the top of a short flight of stairs.

The tourist information center is open Monday through Saturday, 0900–2030; and Sunday, 0930–1800. During the off-season, we suggest that you call the center at (0463) 234353 for information.

There is so much to do in and around the "Capital of the Highlands" that not even a series of action-packed days could absorb all the possible activities.

Here are but a few of the sightseeing possibilities in and around Inverness. Visit the castle grounds and walk along the garden paths at the River Ness. Cruise on Loch Ness, as far away as Urquhart Castle if you like, where most of the sightings of the Loch Ness "monster" (or "beastie," as the locals call it) have occurred. Journey on the renowned railway line between Inverness and

INVERNESS—*HIGHLAND GATEWAY*

An "Out-and-Back" Excursion from Edinburgh, Change in Perth

DEPART FROM EDINBURGH WAVERLEY STATION	ARRIVE IN INVERNESS STATION	NOTES
0648	1032	(1)(3)
0935	1310	(2)
0940	1312	(1)
1125	1515	(1)(3)
1540	1915	(1)
1640	2010	(1)
1754	2140	(2)
1940	2312	(1)

DEPART FROM INVERNESS STATION	ARRIVE IN EDINBURGH WAVERLEY STATION	NOTES
0638	1013	(1)
0750	1118	(1)
0940	1317	(2)
1030	1410	(1)
1435	1814	(1)
1830	2106	(1)(2)
1830	2210	(1)
2005	2357	(1)(4)

Distance: 176 miles/283 km
References: Table 231
          Thomas Cook Table 595

(1) MON–SAT   (3) Change in Perth
(2) SUN   (4) Change in Stirling

NOTE: London-Inverness sleeper service: Depart London Euston Station 2130 Monday–Friday; arrive Inverness 0840+1. No Saturday service. Sundays, depart 2110; arrive 0840+1. Returning sleeper service: Depart Inverness 2030 Monday–Friday, 2020 Sunday; arrive London Euston Station 0747+1.

Train Information: 01463–238924
InterCity Services: 0171–278–2477

Inverness Tourist Information Centre: 01463–234353

Kyle of Lochalsh along eighty-two miles of railroad right of way that involved beauty, romance, history, and endurance in its building. Forge northward to Thurso, Scotland's most northerly town, on a dramatic rail route holding 162 miles of Scotland's better scenery captive for your viewing. If you prefer the solitude that surf breaking on a shore can bring, take a train east to Nairn, fifteen miles from Inverness. Or train south a mere thirty miles to Scotland's St. Moritz—where the ski boom has transformed the town of Aviemore into a continental sports village.

Eons ago, Loch Ness was carved out along a geological fault between two land masses in northern Scotland. The earth's forces formed a long narrow lake of approximately twenty-four miles with depths of up to 750 feet, possibly 1,000 feet in some parts. To go to Inverness and not have a look at Loch Ness would be like eating one potato chip and throwing the rest of the bag away. We urge you to dip into the mystery, the history, and the beauty of Loch Ness.

Loch Ness is reportedly the home of "Nessie," the Loch Ness monster, which has often been described as one of the world's greatest mysteries. The first recorded sighting of Nessie was made by an unimpeachable witness (Saint Columba, no less) in A.D. 565. According to the report, the monster attacked one of the members of his group. Since then, there have been too many visual and photographic sightings of the monster for it to be easily explained.

Fact or fiction, there is a continuing similarity in the descriptions of Nessie given by most of those who claim to have seen the monster over the years. Photographs also support a common description, that of a small head at the end of a long thin neck with an overall body length between twenty to thirty feet. Underwater evidence gathered by every means from space-age technology to yellow submarines suggests that it may have four flippers. Zoologists recognize this description as a plesiosaur, a type of marine dinosaur that existed more than seventy million years ago and should have become extinct.

Scientific data notwithstanding, the fact that malt whiskeys have been produced in large volumes throughout the area since the beginning of recorded time may account for many or all of the sightings!

Kyle of Lochalsh, a narrow channel (Kyle) connecting Loch (Lake) Alsh with the open sea through the Sound of Raasay, offers superb views to its visitors. The Lochalsh Hotel is located conveniently beside the ferry dock for transport to the Isle of Skye, seen in the background.

From Edinburgh . . .

A DAY EXCURSION TO KYLE OF LOCHALSH
DISTANCE BY TRAIN: 82 miles (132 km)
AVERAGE TRAIN TIME: 7 hours, 35 minutes

The railway between Inverness and Kyle of Lochalsh has been accorded the distinction of being the premier scenic rail line in Britain. It offers a lovely journey through the Highland towns of Dingwall, Garve, Achnasheen, and Stromeferry before terminating on the western shores of Scotland overlooking the Isle of Skye. The rail line passes through a region of superlative natural beauty loaded with Scottish folklore. This eighty-two-mile journey, which appears rather uninspiring in the cold prosaic type of the timetable, is in reality a rare mixture of beauty, romance, history, and endurance.

When the railroad opened in 1870, the western terminal was the town of Stromeferry on the saltwater Loch Carron. Although the original intention was to build right through to Kyle of Lochalsh, construction money ran out and Stromeferry remained the terminus for twenty-seven years. Completing the remaining twenty-six miles of right of way proved to be a formidable task of engineering. Most miles were forged through solid rock, requiring cuts up to eighty-eight feet deep. Even the area of the train terminal at Kyle required blasting and removing rock. When you reach Kyle of Lochalsh, pause to appreciate the backbreaking toil that created the train station and the right of way leading to it.

A ferry plies between Kyle of Lochalsh and Kyleakin on the Isle of Skye. The ruins of Castle Moil stand on a promontory close to the Kyleakin ferry dock. During the time of the Vikings, the castle was the home of a Norwegian princess. History relates that the princess made quite a bundle during her stay in the castle by exacting a toll from ships passing through the narrow straits. To ensure prompt payment, she had a heavy chain attached between the castle and the Kyle of Lochalsh, which was drawn taut when a ship approached. The chain was probably depreciated and charged off as a business expense, for there's no evidence of its existence today.

During the summer, the 1040 train from Inverness includes a special observation car, for which a supplement is payable. The special car returns to Inverness in the late afternoon, departing from Kyle of Lochalsh at 1705. A guide aboard the observation car offers interesting commentary en route. If you're unable to obtain a seat in that car, ask at the railway-station magazine stand for the illustrated booklet *Inverness to Kyle of Lochalsh*. It describes much of the scenery en route, along with a sprinkling of Scottish folktales.

In Kyle of Lochalsh, you'll find the **tourist information center** conve-

KYLE OF LOCHALSH AND THE ISLE OF SKYE

A Day Excursion from Edinburgh through Inverness

DEPART FROM INVERNESS STATION	ARRIVE IN KYLE OF LOCHALSH STATION	NOTES
0810	1041	(1)
1045	1315	(1)(2)
1235	1505	(1)
1800	2030	(1)(2)

DEPART FROM KYLE OF LOCHALSH STATION	ARRIVE IN INVERNESS STATION	NOTES
0720	0949	(1)
0952	1225	(2)
1145	1423	(1)
1515	1748	(1)
1705	1938	(1)

Distance: 82 miles/132 km
References: Table 239
            Thomas Cook Table 602

(1) MON–SAT   (2) SUN

Train Information: 01463–238924
InterCity Services: 0171–278–2477

Kyle of Lochalsh Tourist Information Centre
01599–4276

niently located midway between the train station and the ferry dock. It is open Monday through Saturday, 0930–2130, and Sunday, 1230–1630. To reach it, use the stairs to the overpass and then walk downhill.

Don't pass up the opportunity of visiting the Isle of Skye. You'll be treated to one of the finest land-and-seascapes in the world during the seven-minute crossing. The ferry service operates year-round and departs every fifteen minutes during peak season and every half-hour after 2100. Rest assured that you will not be left on the Isle when your train departs the Kyle. For a quick review of the village of Kyleakin and its points of interest, check the tourist-information three-sided sign just outside the Castle Moil Restaurant, a short distance from the ferry dock. It is a relatively short walk from Kyleakin to Castle Moil.

Scottish legends leap out at you as the train plies between Inverness and Kyle. The castle at Dingwall was said to have been ruled by Finlaec, the father of MacBeth. In a graveyard opposite the castle ruins, the ghost of a young girl wanders nightly in search of her faithless lover. Approaching Garve, you'll pass Loch Garve, where even in the dead of winter there is a small part that never freezes—attributed to the water-horse monsters who carry off local girls. The inn at Garve purveys Athole Brose, a libation of whiskey, oats, and honey, several drafts of which could produce a whole herd of water horses.

The right of way passes areas that stir the imagination. Departing Achnasheen en route to Stromeferry, passengers may get a fleeting glance at the Torridon range of mountains—the oldest mountains on earth. They are so old that geologists have been unable to find any trace of fossils, indicating the mountains were formed long before life of any description began. The range, consisting of peaks such as Liathach (3,456 feet), Beinn Eighe (3,300 feet), and Beinn Alligin (3,021 feet), has sparkling quartzite peaks, often mistaken for snow.

In the seventeenth century, Brahan Seer, the Highland's prophet extraordinaire, said, "The day will come when every stream will have its bridge, balls of fire will pass rapidly up and down the Strath of Peffery and carriages without horses will cross the country from sea to sea." And so it came to pass when, on 10 August 1870, the railroad steam engines began operating from sea to sea.

Linlithgow Palace (top), birthplace of Mary Queen of Scots, broods over Linlithgow Loch. The waters of the loch provide recreational opportunities for townspeople and tourists alike. **Union Canal** (below), once the main water artery for coal from nearby Falkirk, runs through the center of the town as an additional asset to the attractions offered by Linlithgow and the Forth Valley. (©Terence Hughes Photography)

From Edinburgh ...

A DAY EXCURSION TO LINLITHGOW
DISTANCE BY TRAIN: 18 miles (29 km)
AVERAGE TRAIN TIME: 20 minutes

Linlithgow lies between Edinburgh and Glasgow and stands in the midst of Scotland's history. To its visitors, the town offers a bevy of attractions, so many in fact that our advice on going there is to go early and plan to stay late, *very late.*

Linlithgow Palace, the birthplace of Mary Queen of Scots, is the town's main attraction; however, a variety of others will vie for your attention. A mere 100 yards from the Linlithgow Station, there's a canal where you may board a replica of a Victorian steam packet boat. A short walk westward from the Palace along High Street, you'll discover "The Linlithgow Story," a fascinating Museum telling of life in one of Scotland's most important Royal Burgh's. A scant distance from the town you can visit The Binns—one of the most "lived in" mansions in Scotland, and a short bus ride will take you to the town of Bo'ness with its unique set of attractions ranging in historical significance from Roman ruins to the Industrial Revolution.

Bo'ness also has a reconstructed Victorian railway station where you may board a steam train for a delightfully romantic 7-mile round-trip—including a stop in Birkhill where you can go down in a mine. Also nearby is Blackness Castle, at one time one of Scotland's most important strongholds, with a prison cell that's under water at high tide! Meanwhile, back at the palace ...

Linlithgow Palace lies in what historians would describe as a splendid ruin. Nevertheless, it tells a poignant tale of Scotland's royal history in an intriguing manner. The palace was the successor to a wooden fortress that burned down in 1424. King James V, father of Mary Queen of Scots, was born in Linlithgow Palace on 10 April, 1512. Mary's mother, Mary of Guise-Lorraine, described the palace as equal to the noblest chateaux in France. Defeated by the English at the battle of Solway Moss in November 1542, the king died on 14 December of that year, only six days after the birth of his daughter. The infant child became Mary Queen of Scots at the age of six days.

In the years to follow, Bonnie Prince Charlie and Oliver Cromwell took brief residence in the palace. At the beginning of 1746, troops belonging to the Duke of Cumberland's army were billeted in the palace. As they marched out of the palace on 1 February, fires were left burning that soon spread throughout the building. Since that time, the palace has remained unroofed and uninhabited. Through the years, there has always been talk about restoring Linlithgow Palace. In 1906 the fireplace in the great hall was restored; King George V held court there in 1914; and now you can let your imagination "restore" it.

LINLITHGOW—BIRTHPLACE OF MARY QUEEN OF SCOTS

A Day Excursion from Edinburgh or Glasgow

DEPART EDINBURGH WAVERLEY STATION	ARRIVE LINLITHGOW STATION	NOTES
0818	0837	(1)
0830	0849	(1)(2)
0848	0907	(1)
0918	0937	(1)
0930	0948	(1)(2)
0948	1007	(1)
1018	1037	(1)
1118	1037	(1)
1130	1148	(2)

(Plus other frequent service)

DEPART GLASGOW QUEEN STREET STATION	ARRIVE LINLITHGOW STATION	NOTES
0800	0828	(1)
0800	0843	(2)
0900	0928	(1)
0900	0943	(2)
1000	1028	(1)
1000	1043	(2)
1100	1128	(1)

DEPART LINLITHGOW STATION	ARRIVE EDINBURGH WAVERLEY STATION	NOTES
1628	1650	(1)
1634	1656	(1)(2)(3)
1734	1756	(1)(2)(3)
1758	1820	(1)
1804	1826	(1)(2)(3)
1834	1856	(1)(2)(4)
1928	1950	(1)(2)(4)
2028	2050	(1)(2)(4)
2128	2150	(1)(2)(4)
2332	2353	(1)

DEPART LINLITHGOW STATION	ARRIVE GLASGOW QUEEN STREET STATION	NOTES
1649	1720	(1)(2)
1749	1820	(1)(2)
1849	1920	(1)(2)
1949	2020	(1)(2)
2049	2120	(1)(2)
2149	2220	(1)(2)
2249	2325	(1)(2)

Note: Sunday trains may have later arrival times

Distance: 18 miles/29 km

References: Passenger Timetable, Tables 228 and 230

(1) MON–SAT   (2) SUN   (3) Departs 2 minutes later on Sundays   (4) Departs 8 minutes later on Sundays

The Union Canal runs through the center of Linlithgow. Some 31 miles in length, the canal was once a major thoroughfare for taking coal from the mines in Falkirk to Edinburgh. You can cruise the Union Canal on board the *Victoria* or *Janet Telford,* two diesel-powered replicas of Victorian steam packet boats, every half hour on Saturday and Sunday afternoons from Easter until the end of September. Short trips of about twenty minutes' duration depart from the Canal Basin at Manse Road, located about 100 yards from the rail station. The Canal Museum at the basin has a small restaurant and is open when the *Victoria* operates from 1400 until 1700. The last boat trip departs at 1630. Admission to the museum is free; boat trips are £1.50 for adults; children, 75 pence.

The Binns has been occupied by the Dalyell family for three and a half centuries. The house dates from the sixteenth century. General Tam Dalyell (1599–1685) had some hair-raising adventures in his lifetime, including an escape from the Tower of London and military service in Russia. The house reflects the early seventeenth-century transition from the fortified castle to a more comfortable and gracious house. You'll enjoy a visit there.

Bo'ness is a seaport on the Firth of Forth. It has been the site of many activities including coal mining, iron founding, and maritime trading. You can get the full details from the tourist center in Linlithgow or from the center in Bo'ness. The Bo'ness center is housed in Hamilton's Cottage, a re-creation of a working man's home from the 1920s.

The Bo'ness & Kinneil Railway runs to the Birkhill clay mine where fireclay was mined. Without fireclay, many say there could never have been an Industrial Revolution. While in Kinneil, you can visit the Kinneil Estate, where there is an interesting museum, an ancient mansion, and the remains of the Roman Antonine Wall.

The running dates for the Bo'ness & Kinneil Railway are on Saturdays and Sundays from April 1 through October 15; daily from July 5 through August 20. The standard fare, including the stop at Kinneil, is £3.60 for adults, £1.80 per child. If you have the whole gang with you, you can take advantage of the £9.00 family rate.

Accommodations can be booked through the Edinburgh and Lothians Tourist Board in Linlithgow. The Tourist Board can be contacted by phone at (01506) 844600, by fax at (01506) 671373, or by writing to them at Burgh Halls, The Cross, Linlithgow West Lothian EH49 7AH Scotland.

We're certain that no one will object to our suggestion to call at the Four Marys' Public House on High Street in Linlithgow. A great atmosphere, excellent libations, and superb food will reward you. Don't miss it!

Eighteenth-century Town Hall dominates the broad main street of Montrose, a city that has served as a fashionable Scottish spa for almost three centuries. Montrose profited from trade with the Low Countries, consequently bringing Flemish-style architecture into its own decor.

From Edinburgh . . .

A DAY EXCURSION TO MONTROSE
DISTANCE BY TRAIN: 90 miles (145 km)
AVERAGE TRAIN TIME: 2 hours, 10 minutes

Travelers who have visited many villages, towns, and cities throughout Continental Europe and the British Isles can "read" the history of a place in its architecture and street names. Montrose is an outstanding example of this point.

Even at first glance, Montrose does not look like a typical Scottish town. Its broad main street, High Street, has many elegant houses with the gabled ends on the street side. There was a time in the city's history when only Edinburgh surpassed it in prosperity and elegance. The Town House of Montrose—Americans would more properly term it the city hall—is fronted by a broad piazza. From its facade, Montrose looks more like a page out of a Flemish picture book rather than a Scottish one. Its great houses are surrounded by garden walls—not ordinary ones, but remarkably high garden walls. There are oddly named streets, such as "America" and "California"—another hint that the history of Montrose is different in many ways.

When Glasgow was still a village, Montrose was one of Scotland's principal ports. For centuries, the merchants of Montrose traded with the Low Countries. It was only natural that they would bring back to Montrose some of the things they admired on the Continent: for example, houses with gabled ends to the street side as they are constructed in Holland. The wide streets? From the promenades of Europe, no doubt. And what about the street names? Almost within living memory, ships sailed from Montrose to America carrying emigrants and returned ladened with lumber.

For many years, Montrose was Scotland's primary port for tobacco with its fleet sailing regularly to and from Virginia. Today, North Sea oil is virtually pumping life back into the city's harbor, where, until the recent past, an air of sleepiness prevailed as the trade with America began to subside. The first part of the civic motto of Montrose—*Mare ditat* (the sea enriches)—is again coming true.

Baffled by the high garden walls? History relates that more than 300 years ago, the streets of Montrose ran red with blood when a band of Highlanders raided the town. Its inhabitants were defenseless as they slept without the protection of a city wall and with only low garden walls about their residences. The carnage was swift and horrible. Within months, the majority of the walls within the town were built up to their present height to prevent attacks from intruders.

When you arrive in Montrose from Edinburgh, take a moment at the train station to direct your gaze to the west, away from the town. You will see a

MONTROSE—*SEASIDE RESORT*

A Day Excursion from Edinburgh

DEPART FROM EDINBURGH WAVERLEY STATION	ARRIVE IN MONTROSE STATION	NOTES
0705	0859	(1)
0810	1002	(1)
0855	1043	(2)
0910	1056	(1)
1155	1241	(2)

DEPART FROM MONTROSE STATION	ARRIVE IN EDINBURGH WAVERLEY STATION	NOTES
1534	1720	(1)
1552	1741	(2)
1605	1809	(1)
1652	1848	(1)
1754	1952	(1)
1940	2127	(2)
2037	2223	(1)

Distance: 90 miles/145 km
References: Table 229
            Thomas Cook Table 600

(1) MON–SAT   (2) SUN

Train Information: 01224–594222
InterCity Services: 0171–278–2477

Montrose Tourist Information Centre
01674–72000

tidal basin where thousands of wild fowl forage for food, including the pink-footed Arctic goose during the winter. Seasonally, there is a great gathering of swans in the basin dotting the water with their white tufts of plumage like so many bread crumbs scattered on a watery lawn.

From the station, turn right on Western Road until it reaches Hume Street, where a quick left followed by a right turn one block away onto High Street puts you in view of the town hall and its grand piazza. Stay on the right-hand side of High Street and walk a short distance south. Just before reaching the town's public library, you will come to the **tourist information center** at 212 High Street.

The office has a wealth of information available regarding both Montrose and the area surrounding it. A Heritage Trail leaflet provides information on walks through Montrose. It is available at the information office for a nominal fee. The information office also has a street map for sale that lists many points of interest.

Montrose is one of Scotland's leading seaside resorts, and it can become crowded during the peak summer season. Four miles of magnificent sandy beaches attract many an inlander to seek the sea. Beaches have a way of indicating their latitudes, however, just as places reflect their history in their names and facades. Beaches in Britain, for example, attract huge crowds in summertime, but note the distribution of the people on the beach. With exception of a hardy few, the majority of holiday makers are on the sands and not in the water.

The city's large indoor swimming pool and two eighteen-hole golf courses, plus numerous other sports facilities, make up for the other-than-tepid temperature of the North Sea waters off Montrose. The seaside also offers something rather unusual—something you'd never find at Atlantic City. On the beaches beside Elephant Rock, you can search for semiprecious stone such as agates, amethysts, carnelian, and onyx.

Cultural life is not lacking in Montrose. The name of William Lamb immediately relates to the world of art in fine sculptures and etchings. This well-known artist maintains a studio at 24 Market Street. On Panmure Place, the Montrose Museum houses an excellent collection of art relating to the natural and maritime history of the area.

If you've been waiting for us to drop the other shoe, the second part of the Montrose civic motto is *rosa decorat* (the rose adorns). If you walk in the Mid Links Park on a summer day, the air is scented with the perfume of roses. Although the city's name has nothing to do with roses—it was originally called "Monros" (the mossy promontory)—there are few towns in Scotland where roses grow more abundantly.

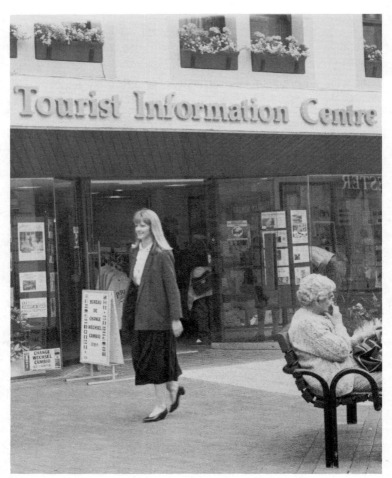

Pretty pedestrian passes Perth's tourist information center, situated in the pedestrian section of the city's old town. To reach it from the railway station, follow King's Place just outside the station to where it intersects with Scott Street. Four blocks up Scott Street lies High Street and the information center—or go for the taxi queue at the station.

From Edinburgh . . .

A DAY EXCURSION TO PERTH
DISTANCE BY TRAIN: 58 miles (93 km)
AVERAGE TRAIN TIME: 1 hour, 30 minutes

"Behold a river more mighty than the Tiber!" History relates that these words were uttered by a Roman commander as, approaching what is now the city of Perth, he caught his first glimpse of the River Tay. Beginning as a mountain stream at Ben Laoigh, the Tay trickles down the hillsides, gaining tributaries as it flows on its 120-mile journey to the sea. Perth stands astride the Tay, her history inexorably linked with the "river more mighty than the Tiber."

Two vehicular bridges, plus a rail bridge (all with pedestrian footpaths), cross the River Tay today, but "Old Man River" Tay kept the locals quite busy in earlier years, when floods swept away the first bridge in 1210 and its successor in 1621, leaving travelers no alternative but ferries for the 150 years to follow.

Perth is often referred to as "the gateway to the Highlands," but this is far from being its only attraction. Its prominent position in the history of Scotland has left a legacy of distinctive buildings in an area that is compact enough so that they can easily be examined on foot. Perth's architecture mixes the modern with the ancient. City fathers are justly proud of Perth's sports centers with an ice rink, swimming pools, tennis courts, and indoor bowling stadium.

Tay Street fronts the river on the city side. Without straying too far from the river, it is possible to enjoy the riverside and visit places of interest such as St. John's Kirk, the Perth Art Gallery and Museum, the Fergusson Gallery, the Lower City Mills, and the Fair Maid's House, as described in Sir Walter Scott's novel *The Fair Maid of Perth*. Turn left off Tay Street at Queen's Bridge and proceed two blocks to sight St. John's to your right. One of Perth's most famous landmarks, St. John's Kirk is where the Protestant reformer John Knox, following his return from exile in Geneva, preached his famous sermon against idolatry in 1559. The congregation was so taken with his sermon that as a result, they wrecked the church and then went on to create similar outrages on the monastic houses of the friars. Originally founded in 1126, St. John's is a fine example of Gothic-style architecture from the mid-sixteenth century.

Returning to Tay Street, continue to walk to the Perth Bridge, where you will find the art gallery and museum on George Street close to the bridge approach. In quest of the Fair Maid's House, ask directions when leaving the museum. It is at North Port, a short distance away, but there are several ways to reach it.

Close by the Fair Maid's House is the North Inch, a beautifully situated park bordered by Georgian terraces and the River Tay and overlooked by

PERTH—*FIRST CAPITAL OF SCOTLAND*

A Day Excursion from Edinburgh

DEPART FROM EDINBURGH WAVERLEY STATION	ARRIVE IN PERTH STATION	NOTES
0935	1050	(2)
0940	1057	(1)

DEPART FROM PERTH STATION	ARRIVE IN EDINBURGH WAVERLEY STATION	NOTES
1449	1610	(1)
1655	1814	(1)
2050	2206 (SUN)	(1)(2)

Distance: 58 miles/93 km
References: Table 230
             Thomas Cook Table 595

(1) MON–SAT   (2) SUN

Train Information: 01738–37117
InterCity Services: 0171–278–2477

Perth Tourist Information Centre
01738–38353

Balhousie Castle, the historic home of the Black Watch Regimental Museum. Across the river lies the colorful Branklyn Garden, owned by the National Trust for Scotland and said to be "the finest two acres of private garden in the country." It sits on the wooded slopes of Kinnoull Hill and offers an excellent view over the town.

For centuries, Perth has been a prosperous market town, serving a rich agricultural hinterland and profiting from its geographical position in the heart of Scotland. The town's livestock markets flourish, with the famous Perth Bull Sales in February and October attracting buyers from all over the world. Perth's reputation as a trading center, however, rests principally with its excellent shops. Much of Perth's center is traffic-free and bedecked with floral displays thanks to the city-wide "Perth in Bloom" campaign.

In the pedestrianized High Street, call at the **Perth Tourist Information Centre**, located at the intersection of Kirkgate and Skinnergate. Operated by the Perthshire Tourist Board, the center is open from March 29 to June 27 and September 5 to October 31 from 0900 to 1800 on weekdays and 1200–1800 Sundays. From June 28 to September 4, the hours are Monday through Saturday, 0900–2000 and Sunday, 1000–1800. From November 1 to March 21, the office is open only from Monday through Saturday, 0900–1700.

An excellent addition to Perth's city center attractions is the Fergusson Gallery in the Round House (Perth's old waterworks) at Marshall Place. Here you can view the largest and most important collection of the works of the famous Scottish colorist John Duncan Fergusson. Three specially designed galleries display rotating exhibits taken from a total collection of 6,000 items.

Scone Palace, a mile north of Perth, stands close to the historic spot where Scottish kings were crowned through 1651. The Moot Hill, which stands in front of the palace, is an artificial mound that was constructed in the Dark Ages. Traditionally, Scottish chiefs and lairds came to Scone to pledge their allegiance to the king. This they did, filling their boots before they left home with the earth of their own districts. Thus, with the earth still in their boots, they were standing on their own land when they swore allegiance to their king. Afterwards they ceremoniously emptied their boots on the Moot Hill (or Boot Hill, as it is more appropriately known today).

The palace is open to the public, and there is an admission charge. You can reach the palace by taking bus No. 58 from the Leonard Street bus station or No. 8 from South Street Post Office. Check with the information center for details if you plan to go. By the way, don't plan to heist the stone of Scone— it's safely back in Westminster Abbey.

Home of golf, St. Andrews *lives* golf. The Royal and Ancient Clubhouse (above) lies almost within the city itself. Founded in 1160 and consecrated in 1318, St. Andrews Cathedral (below) was destroyed by fire in 1380, then rebuilt, only to be destroyed again during the Reformation.

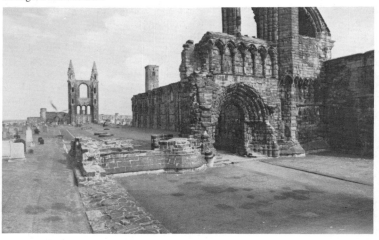

From Edinburgh . . .

A DAY EXCURSION TO ST. ANDREWS
DISTANCE BY TRAIN: 57 miles (92 km)
AVERAGE TRAIN TIME: 1 hour

No town in the world is so completely identified with one game as St. Andrews is with golf. No matter where in the world they have played the game, there is nothing as exhilarating to devoted golfers as a round on the Old Course at St. Andrews. Anyone may play the Old Course, provided they can produce a current, official handicap certificate or a letter of introduction from a bona fide golf club, together with proof of identity. This rule applies only to play on the Old Course. Play on the other six courses at St. Andrews is not affected. The links belong to the townspeople and, as such, are open to all.

In summer and autumn, most available tee times on the Old Course are reserved—in many instances, a year in advance. To be certain of obtaining a starting time for the Old Course, it is essential to make application well in advance of the date of play. Latecomers still have a chance because some starting times are retained each day for issue by a random ballot procedure. To enter your ballot, it is necessary to apply to the starter by 1400 on the previous day. (The Old Course is closed on Sunday.)

To obtain full details and reservations for golf in St. Andrews, we suggest you telephone the St. Andrews links secretary at (01334) 475757 at least one day in advance of your intended visit. In total, St. Andrews and its surrounding area list sixteen courses from which to choose.

How old is the game of golf? Apparently, no one knows. Seemingly it originated on the stretches of grassland along Scotland's east coast next to the sandy beaches—the ground known in Scotland for centuries as "links." The sand dunes interspersed throughout the grasslands became the original traps or bunkers. A round of golf consisted of whatever number of holes were possible in the terrain of a particular link. For more on the history of golf, ask the tourist information center about the British Golf Museum.

At first, the pastime of golf was indulged in predominantly by the Scottish aristocracy. With the advent of the inexpensive golf ball, however, golfing in Scotland soon became a mass sport. Aristocracy again moved to the fore by establishing clubhouses for the leisured gentlemen, where they could attend dinners to observe the end of matches between players.

Such was the case at St. Andrews in 1754 when twenty-two "noblemen and gentlemen being admirers of the ancient and healthful exercise of the golf," founded the Society of St. Andrews Golfers, which is now known throughout the world as the Royal and Ancient Golf Club.

St. Andrews and history go together hand in hand. Such stellar sights as the

ST. ANDREWS—*WORLD'S GOLF CAPITAL*

A Day Excursion from Edinburgh

DEPART FROM EDINBURGH WAVERLEY STATION	ARRIVE IN LEUCHARS STATION	NOTES
0705	0810	(1)
0810	0911	(1)
0840	0951	(2)
0910	1009	(1)
1025	1128	(1)
1110	1211	(2)

DEPART FROM LEUCHARS STATION	ARRIVE IN EDINBURGH WAVERLEY STATION	NOTES
1619	1720	(2)
1657	1809	(1)
1739	1848	(2)
1839	1952	(1)
1940 (1939 SUN)	2042 (2058 SUN)	(1)(2)
2006	2123	(1)
2122	2223	(2)

Distance: Train, 51 miles/82 km; then bus, 6 miles/10 km
References: Table 229
                  Thomas Cook Table 600

(1) MON–SAT   (2) SUN

Train Information: 01334–839206
InterCity Services: 0171–278–2477

St. Andrews Tourist Information Centre
01334–472021

St. Andrews Castle, with its bottle dungeon and secret passage, vie for your attention along with the ruins of St. Andrews Cathedral, once the largest in Scotland. Mary Queen of Scots had a house in St. Andrews that you can still see. The town is the home of Scotland's oldest university (1412). Long before Columbus discovered America or Cooke discovered Australia, students were attending classes at St. Andrews University. Another attraction is St. Mary's College and its unique quadrangle. Founded in 1537, St. Mary's is a part of the university complex. To visit St. Andrews and to roam its streets and scenes is to establish a tangible link with the past.

Leuchars is the rail station serving St. Andrews. This becomes rather obvious when you arrive, for there are signs at both ends of the station announcing LEUCHARS ALIGHT FOR ST. ANDREWS. The bus fare to St. Andrews is inexpensive, and taxis are readily available for about £7.00.

From the bus station in St. Andrews, cross City Road, and continue along Market Street. The **tourist information center** is at No. 70 Market Street, on the right-hand side after Church Street. The center is open 0930–2000 Monday–Saturday and 1100–1700 Sunday during July and August. In June and September, hours are 0930–1900 Monday–Saturday and 1100–1700 Sunday. October through April, it's open 0930–1700 Monday–Friday; Saturday, 1400–1700. The hours in May are 0930–1700 Monday–Saturday; 1400–1700 on Sunday. Telephone: (01334) 472021. Fax: (01334) 478422.

St. Andrews Castle may be reached by proceeding along North Street until reaching Castle Street, where you turn left and then proceed one block to the castle. Continuing one block farther on North Street will put you in front of the cathedral ruins.

Golfer or not, you must see the Royal and Ancient Clubhouse of St. Andrews during your stay. Though founded in 1754, the present clubhouse was built in 1854. The Royal and Ancient Golf Club is now the ruling authority of the game, and its clubhouse is recognized as the world headquarters for the game of golf. From the castle ruins, walk along The Scores until you come to Gillespie Terrace. From this point, the clubhouse and the eighteenth hole of the Old Course come into view.

Of all the places and views in St. Andrews, we give our nod to St. Andrews Castle overlooking St. Andrews Bay. Initially constructed in 1200, the castle was destroyed and rebuilt during a war between Scotland and England, only to be demolished again during the Reformation. The savagery of those times may be noted on a stone outside the castle gate where George Wishart was burned at the stake. The castle has lain in ruins since the seventeenth century, when much of its stone was removed for repairing the harbor.

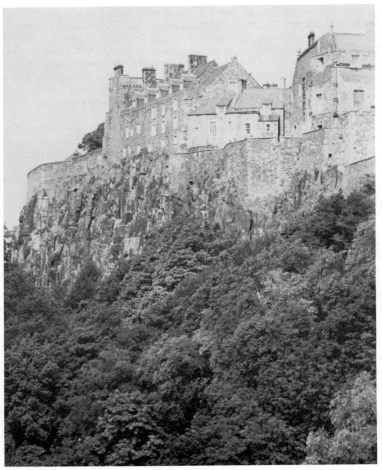

Stirling Castle, astride its great 250-foot rock promontory, has dominated much of Scotland's history. Showplace of Stirling, the castle and its surrounding buildings house a variety of exhibitions, including the Regimental Museum of the Argyll & Sutherland Highlanders.

From Edinburgh . . .

A DAY EXCURSION TO STIRLING
DISTANCE BY TRAIN: 37 miles (59 km)
AVERAGE TRAIN TIME: 50 minutes

Stirling Castle cannot be ignored. Standing on a 250-foot rock overlooking the River Forth valley, it offers one of the finest panoramic views in Scotland. The area surrounding the crag on which the castle sits has given up relics of early man's presence from the Stone Age down through the Bronze Age. There is no evidence that the Romans occupied the area, but it seems implausible that they didn't "take the high ground."

Stirling Castle has witnessed endless struggles for power. Kings and Queens have been crowned in its halls and great battles fought on the plain below it. Originally named Striveling—which may be translated as "a place of strife"—Stirling has been the scene of strife within the Scottish nation since before the time of recorded history. The town of Stirling and its castle truly stand at the crossroads of Scotland. Its position overlooking the Forth Valley and the crossing of the River Forth at its tidal limits has contributed to its past and present importance.

The castle, as seen today, began to develop around 1370 with the accession of the Stewart kings. It served as a royal residence from then until Mary Queen of Scots' son, James VI of Scotland, departed for London in 1603 to become James I of England. Scotland's tragic queen spent the first five years of her life in and around Stirling Castle. The castle is perhaps the finest example of renaissance architecture in Scotland, most of its buildings dating to the fifteenth and sixteenth centuries. It having been the royal Stewart residence, Scotland's kings and queens held court there, and parliaments met on its premises.

Between the castle and the old town of Stirling is a **tourist information center**. The summer operating hours are 0900–1830 daily. The center combines a multilanguage audiovisual presentation and photographic exhibition with a bookstore and souvenir shop. According to its innovators, it is the first building in Europe to be designed specifically to bring alive the history of a town. The theme is Stirling Castle through seven centuries. All is bustle and noise as ships from France and Holland unload their cargoes and farmers drive their cattle to market. Stirling's market, now the city's Broad Street, is lined with shops selling everything from swords to spices. Meanwhile, back at the castle, a roistering banquet is being held in the great hall, packed with honored guests.

All of the information you might need for an enjoyable day excursion in Stirling also is available in Stirling's tourist information center on Dumbarton

STIRLING—*AND STIRLING CASTLE*

A Day Excursion from Edinburgh

DEPART FROM EDINBURGH WAVERLEY STATION	ARRIVE IN STIRLING STATION	NOTES
0748	0837	(1)
0848	0937	(1)
0918	1006	(1)
0948	1037	(1)
1048	1137	(1)

DEPART FROM STIRLING STATION	ARRIVE IN EDINBURGH WAVERLEY STATION	NOTES
1603	1656	(1)
1704	1756	(1)
1803	1856	(1)
1903	1956	(1)
2003	2056	(1)

Distance: 37 miles/59 km
References: Table 230
Thomas Cook Table 595

(1) MON–SAT

Train Information: 01786–64754
InterCity Services: 0171–387–7070

Stirling Tourist Information Centre
01786–475019

Road. To get there from the train station, make a left turn onto Murray Place, a short distance in front of the station. Walk to the first traffic light and turn right onto Dumbarton Road, immediately opposite the city wall. The center's hours of operation during July and August are Monday through Saturday, 0900–1930, and Sunday, 0930–1830. The center operates on more restricted hours during winter.

Several publications describing walks around Stirling are available in the center. One of particular interest is *Stirling Heritage Trail,* published by the Stirling District Council. It covers a course starting and ending at Stirling Castle and includes photographs and drawings as well as colorful text on the history of Stirling Old Town.

Throughout Stirling during the summer months, the presence of flowers is always evident. You will notice this first in the railway station, and it continues all around town. Possibly Stirling developed its love for flowers from the King's Knot, an octagonal, stepped mound that was laid out as the royal gardens in 1627–28 beneath the walls of Stirling Castle by an Englishman, William Watts, who was brought from London to supervise the project. The raised central portion of the Knot is thought to have originated as a Bronze Age burial mound. It was probably used as an outdoor royal court for tournaments before being incorporated into the formal gardens by Mr. Watts.

There are many historic buildings in Stirling. Below the castle stands the imposing Church of the Holy Rude. It has seen great moments in history. Here, at its altar, the infant son of Mary Queen of Scots, James VI of Scotland and subsequently James I of England, was crowned at the tender age of eighteen months to succeed his exiled mother. The tower of the church still bears the marks of the 1745 rebellion, during which Bonnie Prince Charles's troops attempted to capture Stirling Castle. In the overture to the Reformation, the strident voice of John Knox boomed from the church pulpit.

Stirling is indeed a historic center that has played a vital role in the making of Scotland. It purveys an atmosphere that is hard to match in any other part of Scotland. Over the centuries of its involvement in historical events, it has preserved its heritage.

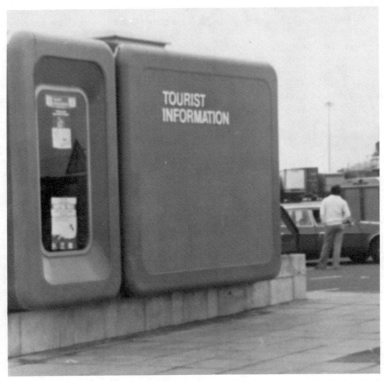

Gateway to Ireland, Stranraer's importance stems primarily from its being the terminal for ferry service to Larne in Northern Ireland.

From Edinburgh . . .

A DAY EXCURSION TO STRANRAER
DISTANCE BY TRAIN: 147 miles (237 km)
AVERAGE TRAIN TIME: 4 hours, 45 minutes

Stranraer is primarily the terminal for passenger and car ferry service to Belfast in Northern Ireland. We emphasize, however, that the BritRail Pass *is not accepted* for travel on trains operated by the Northern Ireland Railways. Travelers wanting to cross from Stranraer to Belfast are advised to purchase regular rail tickets or a BritRail Pass + Ireland option, which would include the sea crossing on Stena Line plus rail travel in England, Scotland, Wales, Northern Ireland, and the Republic of Ireland.

All arrangements for visiting Northern Ireland should be completed prior to departing on the journey rather than en route. One important requirement is a control ticket each passenger *must* have prior to boarding the Stranraer-Belfast ferry. These tickets are issued free of charge. Ticketing and reservations are available in the ferry terminal, along with a comfortable passenger lounge with rest rooms and refreshments.

The crossing between Stranraer and Belfast usually takes three hours by conventional ferry, and trains are waiting at the terminals to take travelers to their final destinations. In both ports, the train terminal is directly alongside the ferry dock. Porter service is available. Hoverspeed's SeaCat catamaran crossing from Stranraer to Belfast takes only one and one half hours. Remember that the BritRail Pass + Ireland option is good on Stena Line—not Hoverspeed.

Stranraer has direct, daytime express-train connections to London. For sleeper services to London, proceed from Stranraer to Glasgow for departures out of Glasgow Central. The last train leaves Stranraer for Glasgow at 2112. Frequent train service connecting with the ferries to and from Belfast is also available out of Glasgow. Edinburgh passengers should use the Edinburgh-Glasgow train service for the fastest connections to Stranraer.

The **Stranraer tourist information center** is located on Harbour Street between the Stena Sealink and SeaCat terminals. During July and August it is open daily, including Sunday, 0930–1800. Hours vary during the remainder of the year.

The old section of Stranraer clusters around its port area. There are interesting streets and small alleyways with a variety of sights. The Stranraer Castle, which houses a Visitor's Centre with audiovisual displays, is a relic of the sixteenth century and adds a certain attraction to the area. The information center can provide you with a map of Stranraer and suggest various sights to see on a walking tour. The area is renowned for its golf and fishing, and there are a

STRANRAER—*GATEWAY TO NORTHERN IRELAND*

A Day Excursion from Edinburgh or Glasgow

DEPART FROM EDINBURGH WAVERLEY STATION	ARRIVE IN GLASGOW QUEEN STREET STATION	NOTES
0700	0750	(1)
1000	1050	(1)(2)

Transfer to Glasgow Central Station (See chapter 11)

DEPART FROM GLASGOW CENTRAL STATION	ARRIVE IN STRANRAER STATION†	NOTES
0713	0921	(1)
0825	1111*	(1)
1123	1334 (1340 SUN)	(1)(2)

DEPART FROM STRANRAER STATION	ARRIVE IN GLASGOW CENTRAL STATION	NOTES
1430	1641	(1)(2)
1900**	2114	(1)(2)

Transfer to Glasgow Queen Street Station (See chapter 11)

DEPART FROM GLASGOW QUEEN STREET STATION	ARRIVE IN EDINBURGH WAVERLEY STATION	NOTES
1730	1820	(1)
1800	1902	(2)
2130	2220	(1)(2)

Distance: 147 miles/237 km
References: Thomas Cook Tables 596, 591; Timetable 218
* Connects with ferry service to Belfast, via Larne
** Connects with ferry service from Belfast, via Larne. Consult train information offices for train/ferry schedules for Sundays and holidays.
† Food service is available at entrance to Stranraer Pier

(1) MON–SAT   (2) SUN

Train Information: 0141–204–2844
InterCity Services: 0171–387–7070
Stranraer Tourist Information Centre: 01776–702595

number of beautiful gardens, which flourish in the mild climate.

The Stranraer Castle, with the formal title of Castle of St. John, is known locally as the "Old Castle." Built in what is now the heart of Stranraer around 1510, it was erected on a site that gave the settlement its original name, Chapel. The name was later changed to Chapel of Stranrawer and finally shortened to Stranraer. *Stranrawer* was believed to have referred to a row of original houses on the strand, or beach, now buried beneath the town's streets.

There is an interesting hotel in Stranraer, one which you might mistake as the town's castle when you first see it. Its name is the North West Castle Hotel, and it's complete with a castle tower that cleverly conceals two well-stocked bars. Again, if you are anticipating a long train trip, you may want to bolster your spirits here in the quaint tower. In the lower bar, there are some fossiliferous wooden beams (no, they are not former patrons), while topside in the Explorers Lounge you are treated to a fine view of the harbor.

The hotel was originally the home of Sir John Ross, the famous Arctic explorer. He gave it the name North West Castle as a reminder of his journeys to the northern and western reaches of the Arctic. Although the "castle" has been transformed into the largest hotel in southwest Scotland, its origins with Sir John have been carefully preserved. Here you will find an indoor ice rink to cater to curling fans, and the hotel proprietor has also added a swimming pool, sauna baths, and several restaurants. A brochure at the hotel desk gives the full history of this most interesting hostelry.

Stranraer lies at the southern end of Loch Ryan, known since Roman times as a safe harbor. At the point where Loch Ryan meets the Irish Sea, the granite bulk of Ailsa Craig stands as a sentinel guarding the enclosed waters of the loch from the ravages of the storms that sweep into the area from the Atlantic across Ireland.

At one time Stranraer was a small fishing community, but it became the main port serving Northern Ireland and a busy shipping center by the middle of the nineteenth century. Involved in the shipment of ammunition from the United States at the end of World War II, the shipping firm of Townsend-Thoresen (now P&O European Ferries) turned the port into a ferry terminal for what is now the shortest sea route to Ireland.

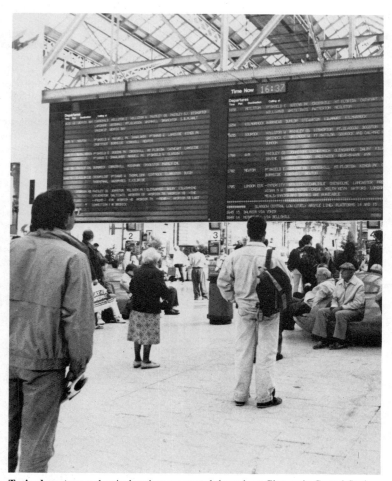

Train departure and arrival notices are posted throughout Glasgow's Central Station on digital boards. Always check at the station for departure time, destination, and loading platform prior to boarding your train.

BRITISH TOURIST INFORMATION CENTERS

Below is a listing of British tourist information centers applicable to cities appearing in this edition of *Britain by BritRail*. When telephoning or faxing from the United States, dial 011–44 (the country code for the United Kingdom) and omit the "0" prior to the city code. For example, to telephone the tourist information office in Brighton from the United States, dial 011–44–1273–23755.

Key to Listing:

* Provides summer service only
† Accommodation services available to personal callers (for same or next night)
(B) "Book-a-Bed-Ahead" accommodations service for personal callers (for same or next night) in any town with a Tourist Information Centre also offering this service

ENGLAND/WALES

Bath (B)†
Abbey Chambers
Abbey Church Yard
General: (01225) 462831
Fax: 47721

Birmingham (B)†
2 City Arcade
(0121) 643–2514
Fax: 616–1038
and 130 Colmore Row
(0121) 693–6300
Fax: 693–9600

Brighton (B)†
10 Bartholomew Square
(01273) 323755

Bury St. Edmunds (B)†
6 Angel Hill
(01284) 764667
Accommodations:
757083
Fax: 757124

Cambridge (B)†
Wheeler Street
(01223) 322640
Fax: 463385

Canterbury (B)†
34 St. Margaret's Street
(01227) 766567
Accommodations:
455567
Fax: 459840

Cardiff (B)†
Central Station
(01222) 227281
Fax: 239162

Chester (B)†
Vicars Lane
(01244) 351609
Accommodations:
(01244) 319019
Fax: 319819
and Chester Railway
 Station
Station Road
(01244) 322220
Fax: 322221

Coventry (B) †
Bayley Lane
(01203) 832304
Fax: 832370

Dover (B)†
Townwall Street
(01304) 205108
Fax: 225498

Folkestone (B)†
Harbour Street
(01303) 258594
Fax: 259754

Gloucester (B)†
St. Michael's Tower,
The Cross
(01452) 421188
Fax: 504273

Greenwich (B)†
46 Greenwich Church
Street
(0181) 858 6376
Fax: 853 4607

Hastings (B)†
4 Robertson Terrace
(01424) 781111
Fax: 781133

Ipswich (B)†
St. Stephen's Church,
St. Stephen's Lane
(01473) 258070
Fax: 258072

Isle of Wight, Shanklin
(B) †
67 High Street
(01983) 862942
Accommodations: 867979
Fax: 863047

King's Lynn †
The Old Gaol House
Saturday Market Place
(01553) 763044
Accommodations:
(01553) 767711
Fax: 777281

Lincoln (B)†
9 Castle Hill
(01522) 529828

**London British
Travel Centre** (B)†
12 Regent Street,
Piccadilly Circus

London Tourist Board
(B)†
(0171) 730–3450
26 Grosvenor Gardens
Accommodations:
(0171) 824–8844
Fax: 730–9367

Selfridges (Basement
Services);
and at Victoria Railway
Station

Margate (B)†
22 High Street
Thanet (01843) 220241
Fax: 230099

Nottingham (B)†
1–4 Smithy Row
(0115) 947–0661
Fax: 935–0883

Oxford (B)†
The Old School
Gloucester Green
(01865) 726871
Fax: 240261

Penzance (B)†
Station Road
(01736) 62207
Fax: 63600

Plymouth
Plymouth Discovery
Centre
(01752) 266030/1
Fax: 26033

Portsmouth (B)†
Terminal Building
Portsmouth Ferryport
(01705) 838635
and the Hard
(01705) 826722
Fax: 822693

City of Portsmouth
Civil Offices
(01705) 834116
Fax: 834975

Ramsgate (B)†
19 Harbour Street
Queen Street
(01843) 583333
Fax: 591086

St. Albans (B)†
Town Hall,
The Market Place
(01727) 864511
Fax: 863533

Salisbury (B)†
Fish Row
(01722) 334956
Fax: 422059

Sheffield (B)†
Peace Gardens
(0114) 273–4671/2
Fax: 272–4225

Southampton (B)†
9 Civic Centre Road
(01703) 221106
Fax: 631437

Stratford-upon-Avon (B)†
Bridgefoot
(01789) 293127
Fax: 295262

Windsor (B)†
24 High Street
(01753) 852010
Accommodations:
84176
Fax: 833450

York (B)†
De Grey Rooms,
Exhibition Square
(01904) 621756
Fax: 625618

SCOTLAND

Aberdeen (B)†
St. Nicholas House,
Broad Street
(01224) 632727

Ayr (B)†
Burns House
Burns Statue Square
(01292) 288688

Dunbar (B)†
Town House,
143 High Street
(01368) 863353

Dundee(B)†
4 City Square
(01382) 434664

Dunfermline (B)†
Maygate
(01383) 720999

Edinburgh (B)†
3 Princes Street
(0131) 557–1700
and Edinburgh Airport
(0131) 333–2167

Glasgow (B)†
35 St. Vincent Place
(0141) 204–4400
and Glasgow Airport
(0141) 848–4440

Inverness (B)†
Castle Wynd
(01463) 234353

Kyle of Lochalsh *(B)†
Car Park
(01599) 534276

Linlithgow (B)†
Burgh Halls
The Cross
(01506) 844600

Loch Lomond *(B)†
Balloch
(01389) 753533

Montrose *(B)†
Bridge Street
(01674) 672000

Perth (B)†
45 High Street
(01738) 638353

St. Andrews (B)†
70 Market Street
(01334) 472021

Stirling (B)†
Dumbarton Road
(01786) 475019
and the Esplanade
(01786) 479901

Stranraer *(B)†
1 Bridge Street
(01776) 702595

RECOMMENDED INFORMATION SOURCES

British Tourist Authority Offices in North America
http://www.bta.org.uk
New York: 551 Fifth Avenue, New York, NY 10176–0799.
  Telephone: (212) 986–2200 or (800) GO–2–BRIT. Fax: (212) 986–1188
Chicago: 625 North Michigan Avenue, Suite 1510, Chicago, IL 60611–1977.
  Telephone: (312) 787–0490. Fax: (312) 787–7746

Wales Tourist Board
http://www.tourism.wales.gov.uk

Rail Pass Express, Inc.
http://www.eurail.com
2737 Sawbury Boulevard, Columbus, Ohio 43235–4583
Telephone: (800) 722–7151. Fax: (614) 764–0711

USEFUL PHONE NUMBERS—LONDON

Calling the U.K.

To telephone or send a fax to the United Kingdom from the United States, you must first use the international dialing code 011. Then dial the United Kingdom country code 44. All of the area codes within Britain start with a "0," but you do not use it when you are dialing from the United States. For example, to call the British Hotel Reservation Centre in London from the United States, dial 011–44–171–828–1849.

Accommodations	Telephone No.
British Hotel Reservation Centre	
Victoria Station, outside Platform 8	(0171) 828–1027/828–1849
Victoria Coach Station	(0800) 716298/(171) 824–8232
Heathrow Airport Underground, Terminal 1,2,3	(0181) 564–8808
Heathrow Airport Underground, Terminal 4	(0181) 564–8211
10, Buckingham Palace Rd., London SW1W 0QP	(0171) 828–2425
	(0171) 828–6439
Expotel Hotel Reservations	
Kingsgate House, Kingsgate Place, London NW64HG	(0171) 328–1790
	Fax (0171) 328–8021
First Option Hotel Reservations	
Europoint, 5-11 Lavington Street, London SEI 0NZ	(0345) 110011
	Fax ((0171) 945–6016
Victoria Station, by Platform 9	(0171) 828–4646/828–2629
Gatwick Station	(01293) 529372
	Fax (01292) 534851
King's Cross Station, adjacent Platform 8	
Hotel Booking Service, Ltd.	
4 New Burlington Place, London WIX IFB	UK (0171) 734–4594
	worldwide (0171) 434–3434
	Fax (0171) 734–2124
Hotel Finders	(0181) 202–7000/(0181) 202–0988
20a Bell Lane, London NW4 2AD	Fax (0181) 202–3871
Hotelguide	
The Coach House, 235 Upper Richmond Road	(0181) 780–1066
London SW15 6SN	Fax (0181) 780–2352
The London Bed & Breakfast Agency	(0171) 586–2768
71 Fellows Rd., London NW3 3JY	Fax (0171) 586–6567
The London Tourist Board	(0171) 824–8844

Airlines

Aer Lingus (Irish)	(0181) 569–4646

Air Canada	(0990) 247–226
Alitalia	(0345) 222–111
American Airlines	(0181) 572–5555
British Airways	(0345) 222–111
Continental	(01293) 77 6464/(0800) 77 6464
Delta Air Lines	(01800) 414767
Icelandair	(0171) 388–5599
Trans World Airlines	(0171) 439–0707

Airport Information

Heathrow, general inquiries	(0181) 759–4321
Heathrow, Terminal 1	(0181) 745–7702/4
Terminal 2	(0181) 745–7115/6/7
Terminal 3 check-in	(0181) 745–7412
Arrivals Concourse	(0181) 745–7412/3/4
Terminal 4	(0181) 745–4540
London City Airport	(0171) 474–5555
Gatwick	(01293) 535353
Stansted	(01279) 662379/662520

American Express

6 Haymarket, Piccadilly	(0171) 930–4411

Bike Rentals

On Your Bike, 52 Tooley Street	(0171) 407–1309
22 Duke St. Hill	(0171) 357–6958

British Tourist Authority, British Travel Centre,

12 Regent Street, Piccadilly Circus SW1	(0171) 730–3404

Canadian Embassy

Canada Centre 62–65 Trafalgar Square	(0171) 258–6356

Emergency

Police or Ambulance	999

Express Bus Information

National Express	(0171) 730–0202

London Tourist Board (main office)

26 Grosvenor Gardens, SW1W 0DU	(0171) 730–3488

Medical Help

Middlesex Hospital, Mortimer Street	(0171) 636–8333
Medical Express, 117a Harley Street	(0171) 499–1991

Post Office

Paddington Main Post Office	(0171) 723–0279

Rail Information

InterCity Services to:

East Anglia, Essex, Southern England, Northeast, South, and East London	(0171) 928–5100

Avon, Cotswalds, West of England, South Wales, and West London	(0171) 262–6767
Midlands, North Wales, Northwest England and Scotland via the West Coast and Northwest London	(0171) 387–7070
Yorkshire and Northeast England, Scotland via East Coast and North London	(0171) 278–2477
Continental Europe, general inquiries	(0171) 834–2345
Continental Europe, to make credit card bookings	(0171) 828–0892
Recorded Timetable Announcements for Services to:	
Amsterdam	(0171) 828–4264
Brussels/Köln	(0171) 828–0167
Paris	(0171) 828–8747
Special Rail Offers	(0171) 828–6708
Sleeper Reservations:	
Euston Station	(0171) 388–6061
Paddington Station	(0171) 922–4372
London Regional Transport (bus/underground)	(0171) 222–1234
Hoverspeed Reservations	(01304) 240241

River Trips and Canal Cruises

River Boat Information Service	(0171) 730–4812
London Waterbus Co., Camden Lock Place	(0171) 482–2660
RiverBus	(0171) 512–0555
Catamaran Cruisers	(0171) 839–3572
Jenny Wren Canal Cruises	(0171) 485–6210

U.S. Embassy

24 Grosvenor Square	(0171) 499–9000

USA TTA (Travel and Tourism Administration)

P.O. Box 1EN, London W1A 1EN	(0171) 495–4466
	Fax: (0171) 495–4377

Victoria Student Travel Service

Need student I.D. to book accommodations	(0171) 730–8111

USEFUL PHONE NUMBERS — EDINBURGH

Tourist Information

City of Edinburgh Tourist Information and Accommodations, Waverley Market, Princes Street.	(0131) 557–1700
The Tattoo Office	(0131) 225–1188

British Rail

Waverley Station	(0131) 556–2451
Sleeper reservations	556–5633
Edinburgh Airport, information	(0131) 333–2167
Scheduled Airlines	
Aer Lingus (Irish)	(0131) 225–7392
British Airways	(0131) 225–2525
British Caledonian Airways	(0131) 225–5162
City Transport Information	(0131) 556–5656
Student Travel Centre	(0131) 668–2221
American Express	
139 Princes Street	(0131) 225–7881
Emergency	
Fire, Police, Ambulance	999
Guide Friday—city tours by open-top	
double-decker bus	(0131) 556–2244

USEFUL PHONE NUMBERS — GLASGOW

Tourist Information	
Tourist Information, 35 St. Vincent Place	(0141) 204–4400
Glasgow Travel Centre	(0141) 226–4826
British Rail	
Passengers inquiries	(0141) 204–2844
Sleeper reservations	(0141) 221–2305
Airport Information	(0141) 887–1111, Ext. 4552
	or (0141) 848–4440
Scheduled Airlines	
Aer Lingus (Irish)	(0171) 734–1212
Air Canada	(01800) 181313
Air France	(01345) 581393
British Airways	(0141) 332–9666
British Midland	(01332) 810552
Northwest Airlines	(0141) 226–4175
American Express	
115 Hope Street	(0141) 221–4366
Emergency	
Fire, Police, Ambulance	999

The Eurotunnel, or "Chunnel," opened officially on May 6, 1994. (Photo courtesy of Eurostar Passenger Services)

LONDON

London Underground: see plan on page 34

2 km

Heathrow
24 km

PADDINGTON

Marylebone

EUSTON

St Pancras

VICTORIA

Gatwick
44 km

CHARING
CROSS

WATERLOO

Kings Cross
Thameslink

KINGS CROSS

City
Thameslink

Waterloo
East

Blackfriars

Moorgate

LIVERPOOL
STREET

Fenchurch Street

Cannon Street

London
Bridge

Stansted
55 km

City
10 km

FOR CROSS CHANNEL SHIPPING SERVICES SEE MAP ON PAGE 401

For all London Transport travel enquiries
ring 01-222 1234 at any time or call at the
London Transport Travel Information Centres
at Charing Cross, Euston, Heathrow Central,
King's Cross, Oxford Circus, Piccadilly Circus,
St. James's Park, Victoria and at Waterloo
British Rail Travel Centre

▲ Piccadilly Line trains stop here early morning and late
evening Mondays to Saturdays and all day Sundays

Designed by Paul E. Garbutt
Copyright London Transport Executive

THE LONDON UNDERGROUND

Lines.... VICTORIA   CENTRAL   CIRCLE   DISTRICT   METROPOLITAN   NORTHERN   BAKERLOO   PICCADILLY   JUBILEE

East London
Section

Peak journeys only
Main service - B.R

⭕ Interchange with other Underground Lines

⭒ Interchange with British Rail   ◼ Exhibition Service only   † Open during Monday to Friday rush hours only

Certain Stations are closed at Weekends and during Public Holidays

Inter-terminal links
by London Underground

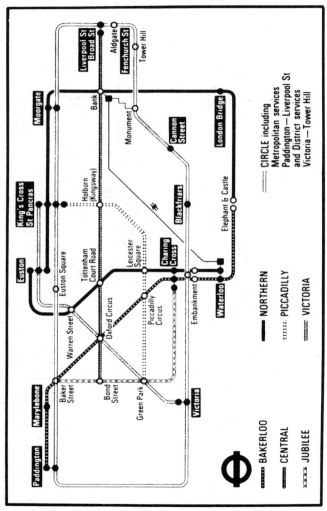

CIRCLE including
Metropolitan services
Paddington — Liverpool St
and District services
Victoria — Tower Hill

——— NORTHERN
:::::::::: PICCADILLY
///////// VICTORIA

:::::::::: BAKERLOO
████████ CENTRAL
------ JUBILEE

Courtesy London Transport

24-HOUR TIME CONVERTER

AN EASY GRAPHIC MEANS OF
CONVERTING STANDARD 12-HOUR
TIME TO 24-HOUR TIME AND
VICE VERSA

A SELECTION OF BRITISH RAIL ONE-WAY FARES

Deciding whether or not you should purchase a BritRail Pass becomes a matter of simple arithmetic. Plan your trip to Great Britain, decide what places you want to visit, and use the fares listed below to determine if the cost of the individual rail segments has exceeded the cost of a BritRail Pass. Round-trip fares are slightly less than double the one-way charge. Children five to fifteen years of age, inclusive, pay half fare. All fares are applicable as of press time and subject to change without prior notice. Fares are given in U.S. dollars. To convert to pounds sterling, apply current rate of exchange. For example, at press time, the rate was approximately $1.00 = £.65.

	One-Way Fares			**One-Way Fares**	
	First Class ($)	Standard Class ($)		First Class ($)	Standard Class ($)
From London to:			**From London to:**		
Aberdeen	175.00	123.00	Oxford	30.00	20.00
Aviemore	175.00	123.00	Penzance	123.00	90.00
Ayr	155.00	105.00	Perth	165.00	113.00
Bath Spa	66.00	44.00	Plymouth	108.00	80.00
Birmingham	64.00	48.00	Portsmouth	40.00	28.00
Brighton	35.00	25.00	Salisbury	40.00	28.00
Cambridge	36.00	24.00	Sheffield	88.00	60.00
Canterbury	35.00	25.00	Southampton	40.00	28.00
Cardiff	86.00	58.00	Stratford-upon-Avon	61.00	40.00
Chester	96.00	70.00	Windermere	120.00	86.00
Coventry	61.00	40.00	Windsor	13.00	19.00
Dover	44.00	30.00	York	116.00	80.00
Dundee	165.00	113.00			
Edinburgh	155.00	105.00	**From Glasgow to:**		
Folkestone	44.00	30.00	Aberdeen	56.00	41.00
Glasgow	155.00	105.00	Birmingham	127.00	84.00
Gloucester	61.00	40.00	Dundee (Tay Bridge)	31.00	21.00
Hastings	44.00	30.00	Inverness	56.00	41.00
Inverness	175.00	123.00	Manchester	108.00	73.00
King's Lynn	66.00	48.00	Oxford	137.00	90.00
Leamington Spa	61.00	40.00	Perth	31.00	21.00
Lincoln	71.00	49.00	Sheffield	115.00	75.00
Manchester	96.00	70.00	Stirling	24.00	16.00
Nottingham	88.00	60.00	York	99.00	67.00

To order rail tickets prior to your departure for Britain call the information department at Rail Pass Express at (614) 793–7650.

TIPS AND TRIVIA

Do not be surprised to see a 17.5 percent value–added tax (VAT) added to your bill for items purchased or services rendered. The VAT appears on just about everything, excluding bus/rail transportation.

Tipping: For luggage, generally tip £1 per bag; taxis, 10–15 percent, with a 50-pence minimum; for service staff in hotels, 10–15 percent if service charge not included in bill.

Imports: You can import into Britain 200 cigarettes, two liters of table wine along with either two liters of sparkling wine or one liter of liquor, two ounces of perfume and nine ounces of cologne, and photographic film for your own use.

Shops: Most shops are open from 0900 to 1730. Shops in smaller towns may close for one hour at lunchtime. In London, shops in the Knightsbridge area (Harrods, for example) remain open until 1900 on Wednesday, while those in the West End (Oxford Street, Regent Street, and Piccadilly areas) stay open until 1900 on Thursday.

Banks: Banks are usually open Monday through Friday from 0930 to 1530. Some are open on Saturday mornings. Most banks in Scotland are closed for one hour at lunchtime. The banks at London's Heathrow and Gatwick airports are open twenty-four hours a day.

Holidays: Most banks, shops, and some museums, historic houses, and other places of interest are closed on Sundays and public holidays. Public transport services generally are reduced, especially during Christmas time.

Voltage: The standard voltage is 240v AC, 50 Hz.

1997 Holidays

January 1	New Year's Day	May 26	Spring Bank Holiday
January 2	Bank Holiday (Scotland)	July 14	Orangeman's Day
March 17	St. Patrick's Day		(Northern Ireland only)
	(Northern Ireland only)	August 4	Bank Holiday (Scotland only)
March 28	Good Friday	August 25	Summer Bank Holiday
March 31	Easter Bank Holiday		(England and Wales only)
	(not Scotland)	December 25	Christmas Day
May 5	May Day	December 26	Boxing Day

CLIMATE

	Jan	Feb	Mar	Apr	May	June	July	Aug	Sept	Oct	Nov	Dec
Average Low (F)	35°	35°	37°	40°	45°	51°	55°	54°	51°	44°	39°	36°
Average High (F)	44°	45°	51°	56°	63°	69°	73°	72°	67°	58°	49°	45°
Average Rainfall (in inches)	2	2	1	2	2	2	2	2	2	2	3	2

TOLL-FREE AIRLINE NUMBERS
(Dialing from U.S.)

Air Canada (AC) 800-766-3000
Air France(AF) 800-237-2747
American Airlines, Inc. (AA) 800-433-7300
Austrian Airlines (OS) 800-AIRWAYS
Continental Airlines (CO) 800-525-0280
Delta Air Lines, Inc. (DL) 800-221-1212
Finnair(AY) 800-950-5000
Icelandair 800-223-5500
KLM Royal Dutch Airlines 800-374-7747
Lufthansa German
  Airlines (LH) 800-645-3880
Northwest Airlines,
  Inc. (NW) 800-225-2525

Sabena Belgan World
  Airlines (SN) 800-955-2000
Scandinavian Airlines
  System (SK) 800-221-2350
Swissair (SR) 800-221-4750
TAP Air Portugal (TO) 800-221-7370
Trans World Airlines, Inc.
  (TWA) 800-221-2000
United Air Lines, Inc. (UA) 800-538-2929
USAir (US) 800-943-5436
Virgin Atlantic Airways
  Ltd. (US) 800-862-8621

TOLL-FREE HOTEL RESERVATIONS NUMBERS
(Dialing from U.S.)

B&B My Guest 800-906-4232
Best Western International 800-528-1234
Choice Hotels International,
  Inc 800-4-CHOICE
Consort Hotels Ltd 800-55-CONSORT
Forte & Meridian Hotels 800-225-5843
Golden Tulip International 800-344-1212
Hilton Reservations
  Worldwide 800-HILTONS
Hyatt Worldwide Reservation
  Centres 800-233-1234
Inter-Continental Hotels
  Corp 800-327-0200
Inter-Europe Hotels 800-221-6509
ITT Sheraton Corporation 800-325-3535
International B&B 800-722-3679

Kempinski International 800-426-3135
Leading Hotels of the World 800-223-6800
Loews Representation Int'l 800-223-0888
Marriott Corporation 800-228-9290
MinOtels Int'l 800-336-4668
Movenpick Hotels Int'l 800-34-HOTEL
Nikko Hotels International 800-645-5687
Preferred Hotels & Resorts
  Worldwide 800-323-7500
Radisson Hotels, Int'l 800-333-3333
Ramada International Hotels
  & Resorts 800-854-7854
SRS Steinberger Reservation
  Service 800-223-5652
Swissotel 800-63-SWISS
Thistle Mount Charlotte 800-847-4358

FERRY INFORMATION
(Dialing from U.S.)

Designated Ferry Line for CalMac, P&O,
IOMan, North Sea Ferries,
Cal Princess........................ (201)768-1187

Bergen Line 800-323-7436
Scandinavian Seaways.......... 800-323-3755

TOLL-FREE THEATRE/EVENTS
(Dialing from U.S.)

Edwards & Edwards (Tattoo,
Festival, Evans Day
Tours) 800-328-2150
Keith Prowse
(Apartments)........................ 800-669-8687

London Showline (Air,
Rock ' n' Pop Concerts)...... 800-962-9246
London Theatre & More
TX (Frames Day Tours,
Hotelink, Soccer Tkts.......... 800-683-0799

PASSPORT OFFICES THROUGHOUT AMERICA

You may apply for a passport at any passport agency and at many Clerks of Court Offices or Post Offices designated to accept passport applications. The regional offices are as follows:

Boston: Thomas P. O'Neill Federal Building, 10 Causeway Street, Suite 247, Boston, Massachusetts 02222-1094; (617) 565–6990.

Chicago: Kluczynski Office Building, 230 South Dearborn Street, Room 380, Chicago, Illinois 60604–1564; (312) 353–7155.

Honolulu: First Hawaii Tower, 1132 Bishop Street, Suite 500, Honolulu, HI 96813–2309; (808) 522–8283 or (808) 522–8286.

Houston: Mickey Leland Federal Building, 1919 Smith Street, Suite 1100, Houston, Texas 77002-8049; (713) 209–3153.

Los Angeles: Federal Building, 11000 Wilshire Boulevard, Los Angeles, Room 13100, California 90024–3615; (310) 235–7070.

Miami: Claude Pepper Federal Office Building, 51 Southwest First Avenue, Third Floor, Miami, Florida 33130-1680; (305) 536–4681.

New Orleans: 701 Loyal Avenue, Postal Services Building, T-12005, New Orleans, Louisiana 70113–1931; (504) 589–6728 or (504) 589–6161.

New York: Rockefeller Center, International Building, 630 Fifth Avenue, Room 270, New York, New York 10111–0031; (212) 399–5290.

Philadelphia: U.S. Customs House, 200 Chestnut Street, Room 103, Philadelphia, Pennsylvania 19106–2970; (215) 597–7480.

San Francisco: Tishman Speyer Building, 525 Market Street, Room 200, San Francisco, California 94105–2773; (415) 744–4010 or (415) 744–4444.

Seattle: Federal Building, 915 Second Avenue, Room 992, Seattle, Washington 98174–1091; (206) 220–7788.

Stamford: One Landmark Square, Broad and Atlantic streets, Stamford, Connecticut 06901–2687; (203) 325–3530.

Washington, D.C.: 1111 19th Street NW, Washington, D.C. 20522-1705; (202) 647–0518.

PASSPORT INFORMATION

The phone numbers of the passport offices listed above provide a recorded message that describes the documents you need and the application process for obtaining a passport as well as reporting the loss or theft of your passport. It also explains how you can obtain a copy of the report of a birth or death or a U.S. citizen abroad. The message will direct you to the proper agencies for information regarding naturalization, travel advisories, customs regulations, and shots required by various countries. The National Passport Information Center at 1–900–CALLNPIC provides telephone operators that will give you a prompt and accurate response to any questions you may have. You can access more passport and travel information via the internet at: http://travel.state.gov.

GEOGRAPHIC INDEX

All places that have a main entry appear in bold–face type.

W

Y

ACKNOWLEDGMENTS

We take this opportunity to thank the British Tourist Authority, BritRail Travel International, Eurostar Passenger Services, and the British tourist information offices for their cooperation. Thanks also to our British and European researchers who are invaluable aids to us in our annual revisions: Major Robert S. Bean, Benoit and Simone Drillon, Margaret Keith, Matthew Palma, and Meredith Vinokur.

Our staff of European rail experts at Rail Pass Express, Inc., deserves profuse praise as well. Mary Kish, general manager at Rail Pass Express, runs a tight ship—must be her Navy background. Mary's managerial and organizational skills coupled with her business and computer experience are incomparable. Like a talented orchestra leader, Mary keeps the music playing. Emma-Jane McComis, assistant manager, is a graduate of the Hospitality and Tourism program. She, too, is well traveled, with her specialty in British Rail.

Contributing editor and researcher Christina DiLorenzo also serves as marketing director for Rail Pass Express. Christina achieved her Master in Business Administration from Boston University School of Management in Boston, Massachusetts, specializing in international marketing, and a Master in International Economics and Management from SDA Bocconi University in Milan, Italy. Multilingual and multi-talented, Christina's attention to detail and her research capabilities make her an invaluable asset.

Special thanks to our other European rail experts and researchers—Mary DiThomas, head of Rail Pass Express' Rail Information and Reservations Service in our Dallas, Texas, office, and Pamela Britton, Ellen Byrnes, Sheila Clowes, Faith Schneider, Staci Schroeder, German Theodoropoulos, and Tonya Young, rail information and reservations specialists in our Columbus, Ohio, office. Novice rail travelers can become confused and frustrated when trying to decipher rail schedules, plan itineraries, or make train reservations, but for our team of experts, it's elementary.

Kevin Siegmann, systems designer, webmaster, and chief of our computer and graphics department, keeps us on the right track (pun intended) by utilizing his award-winning computer and graphics design capabilities. Thanks, Kevin!

While handing out laudatory comments, we cannot forget to thank our most capable editor, Mace Lewis, at The Globe Pequot Press, Inc.

We thank you, our readers and rail pass customers. We enjoy hearing from you and welcome your suggestions. Please contact LaVerne Ferguson, Rail Pass Express, Inc., 2737 Sawbury Blvd., Columbus OH 43235-4583; (800) 722-7151; e-mail: ferguson@eurail.com; world wide web: http://www.eurail.com.

Stena Line, the world's leading ferry company, operates between Britain, France, Holland, as well as across the Irish Sea.

INTERNATIONAL TRAVEL

Here are some other guides on various international destinations. All Globe Pequot travel titles are published with the highest standards of accuracy and timeliness. Please check your local bookstore for other fine Globe Pequot titles, which include:

Europe by Eurail, $14.95

Exploring Europe by Car, $12.95

Exploring Europe by Boat, $12.95

Exploring Europe by RV, $14.95

Guide to Eastern Canada, $17.95

Guide to Western Canada, $16.95

The Best Bed & Breakfast in England, Scotland, and Wales, $19.95

The Best Hotels of Great Britain, $17.95

The Best Restaurants of Great Britain, $17.95

Hotels and Restaurants of Britain, $18.95

Ireland: The Complete Guide and Road Atlas, $19.95

The Traveler's Handbook, $19.95

Travel Smarts, $12.95

Berlitz Travel Guides

Bradt Travel Guides

Cadogan Travel Guides

Karen Brown's Travel Guides

Off the Beaten Track Travel Guides

To order any of these titles with MASTERCARD or VISA call toll-free, 24 hours a day, (800) 243–0495. Free shipping for orders of three or more books. Connecticut residents add sales tax. Ask for your free catalogue of Globe Pequot's quality books on recreation, travel, nature, personal finance, gardening, cooking, crafts, and more. Prices and availability subject to change.

British & European Rail Passes

BRITRAIL PASSES

(Prices valid until December 31, 1997. All prices are in U.S. Dollars and
are subject to change. Please call for current prices.)

BRITRAIL CLASSIC PASS* Unlimited consecutive-day rail travel in
England, Scotland, and Wales.

	Adult		Senior (60 & over)		Youth (16-25)
	First Class	Standard Class	First Class	Standard Class	Standard Class
8 consecutive days	$355	$249	$305	NA	$199
15 consecutive days	$549	$379	$469	NA	$305
22 consecutive days	$700	$485	$595	NA	$389
30 consecutive days	$815	$565	$696	NA	$405

BRITRAIL FLEXIPASS* Unlimited rail travel with the same privileges as
the consecutive day BritRail Classic pass. Days can be used at one's leisure
within the specified time period.

	Adult		Senior (60 & over)		Youth (16-25)
	First Class	Standard Class	First Class	Standard Class	Standard Class
Any 4 days within 1 month	$305	$209	$259	NA	$169
Any 8 days within 1 month	$439	$305	$375	NA	$245
Any 15 days within 1 month	$659	$459	$560	NA	——
Any 15 days within 2 months	——	——	——	——	$365

BRITRAIL PASS + IRELAND* Unlimited rail travel in England, Scotland,
Wales, Northern Ireland, and the Republic of Ireland. Days can be used at one's
leisure within one month.

	First Class	Standard Class
Any 5 days within 1 month	$440	$335
Any 10 days within 1 month	$645	$475

* Family Pass Option: Purchase one adult or senior pass and one accompanying child (ages 5
through 15) gets a pass of the same type and duration, FREE. Passes for additional children can
be purchased at half the price of a regular adult pass. Children under 5 travel free. Please note
that many local trains in England, Wales, and Scotland have second-class accommodations only.

BRITRAIL SOUTHEAST PASS Unlimited rail travel within a large section of Southern England. Days can be used at one's leisure within the specified time period.

	First Class		Standard Class	
	Adult	Child (5-15)	Adult	Child (5-15)
Any 3 days within 8	$90	$32	$69	$24
Any 4 days within 8	$121	$32	$90	$24
Any 7 days within 15	$169	$32	$121	$24

BRITRAIL + EUROSTAR Unlimited rail travel in Britain plus Eurostar ticket. No discounts for children.

	One-way Eurostar		Round-trip Eurostar	
	First Class	Standard Class	First Class	Standard Class
Eurostar trip + any 4 days of rail travel (within a 3-month period)	$430	$289	$574	$373
Eurostar trip + any 8 days of rail travel (within 3-month period)	$561	$381	$710	$466

FREEDOM OF SCOTLAND TRAVELPASS Unlimited standard-class rail travel in Scotland (on the Britrail Network). *No discounts for children.*

	Standard Class
8 consecutive days	$165
15 consecutive days	$235
22 consecutive days	$280
any 8 days out of a 15-day period	$189

THE GREAT BRITISH HERITAGE PASS Entry to over 500 public and private historic properties. No discounts for children.

	Adult
7 consecutive days	$42
15 consecutive days	$64
1 month	$90

LONDON VISITOR TRAVEL CARD Unlimited travel within the six zones of the London Underground and the red-double-decker buses in central London.

	Adult	Child (5-15)
3 consecutive days	$25	$11
4 consecutive days	$33	$13
7 consecutive days	$53	$21

LONDON DAY TOUR A 1-day guided tour of London and its main touristic sights.

Adult: $80   Child (3-15): $75

AIRPORT TRANSFERS
Gatwick Express Travel from Gatwick Airport to London Victoria Station.

First Class: $23
Standard Class:$17
Children 5-15 half price

1997 Heathrow Airbus Transfer from Heathrow Airport to one of many Central London hotels: $12

EUROSTAR The Eurostar train travels through the Channel Tunnel connecting London and Paris and London and Brussels. The following prices are for a one-way ticket (double for round trip). Special discount only on the adult fare for holders of an adult Eurail pass, Europass, or BritRail Pass.

London to/from Paris or Brussels

	First Class	Standard Class
Adult fare	$199	$139
Senior fare (60+)	$155	$109
Youth fare (12-25)	NA	$75
Child fare (4-11)	$99	$70
Adult fare with railpass	$139	$85

BRITRAIL PASS + CAR package A combination of first- or standard-class rail travel and vouchers for car rental within a one-month period. The package price applies when one person travels. Each additional person pays the additional supplement; children (5-15) pay half the adult supplement.

Auto type	3 Days Flexipass + 3 days car		6 Days Flexipass + 7 days car	
	Adult	Senior	Adult	Senior
B Economy				
First Class	$377	$342	$675	$627
Standard Class		$305	——	$575
C Compact				
First Class	$397	$362	$722	$674
Standard Class	$325	——	$622	——
D Intermediate				
First Class	$431	$396	$801	$753
Standard Class	$359	——	$701	——

E Intermediate				
Automatic				
First Class	$465	$430	$879	$831
Standard Class	$393	———	$779	———
F Fullsize				
Automatic				
First Class	$492	$457	$942	$894
Standard Class	$420	———	$842	———
Additional Adult Rail Supplement				
First Class	$229	$194	$329	$281
Standard Class	$157	———	$229	———

Includes unlimited mileage and government taxes (VAT is 17.5 percent) as well as free drop-off. Minimum rental age is 25. First, purchase the package, and then at least seven days before your departure to Britain, telephone Hertz at (800) 654–3001, mentioning that you have purchased the BritRail Pass + Car package. Be sure to make reservations for an automatic cars as early as possible.

BRITAINSHRINKERS

Fully escorted tours that depart London in the morning and return in the evening, with the exception of the 2-, 3-, and 4- night tours.

	Reg. Adult	Discounted* Adult	Reg. Child	Child	Disounted* Single Supplement
A. Salisbury/Stonehenge, etc.	$141	$99	$112	$89	——
B. Leeds Castle/					
Windsor Castle, etc.	$125	$115	$110	$105	—
C. Warwick/ Stratford, etc.	$141	$112	$112	$99	—
D. Leeds/York, etc.	$141	$84	$112	$79	—
E. Edinburgh	$185	$99	$123	$90	—
P. Paris via Eurostar					
Standard Class	$199	——	$189	—	—
PF. Paris via Eurostar					
First Class	$345	——	$300	—	——
PL. Paris/Louevre via Eurostar					
Standard Class	$230	——	$220	—	——
PFL. Paris/Louevre via Eurostar					
First Class	$376	——	$332	—	——
R. Brussels via Eurostar					
Standard Class	$199	——	$189	—	——
RF. Brussels via Eurostar					
First Class	$345	——	$300	—	——
RP. Brussels/Paris via Eurostar					
Standard Class	$367	——	$356	—	——

RPF. Brussels/Paris via Eurostar					
First Class	$570	——	$484	—	——
YH. York/Scotland					
3 nights	$843	$649	$723	$631	$89
YHX. York/Scotland					
4 nights	$1093	$900	$926	$834	$118
ZRH. Scotland					
2 nights	$664	$489	$559	$476	$59
ZRHX. Scotland					
3 nights	$915	$740	$762	$678	$89

*Discounted prices apply to holders of BritRail Passes. For more tour information, please call (800) 722–7151.

EURAIL PASSES

(Prices valid until December 31, 1997. All prices are in U.S. Dollars and are subject to change. Please call for current prices.)

EURAIL PASS Unlimited first-class rail travel throughout 17 countries of Europe: Austria, Belgium, Denmark, Finland, France, Germany, Greece, Hungary, Italy, Luxembourg, the Netherlands, Norway, Portugal, Republic of Ireland, Spain, Sweden, and Switzerland. No second-class passes available for adults.

	First Class
15 consecutive days	$522
21 consecutive days	$678
1 month	$838
2 months	$1188
3 months	$1468

EURAIL SAVERPASS. Unlimited first-class rail travel for two, three, four, or five people traveling together. Same privileges as the regular Eurailpass but the group must always travel together. Prices are per person.

	First Class
15 consecutive days	$444
21 consecutive days	$576
1 month	$712
2 months	$1010
3 months	$1248

EURAIL FLEXIPASS Unlimited first-class travel for any 10 or 15 days within a 2-month period, with the same privileges as the consecutive-day Eurailpass. Days can be used at one's leisure within the specified period.

	First Class
Any 10 days within 2 months	$616
Any 15 days within 2 months	$812

EURAIL SAVER FLEXIPASS Unlimited first-class rail travel for two, three, four, or five people traveling together. Same privileges as the Eurail Flexipass but requires that the group always travel together. Prices are per person.

	First Class
Any 10 days within 2 months Flexipass	$524
Any 15 days within 2 months Flexipass	$690

EURAIL YOUTHPASS Unlimited second-class rail travel through 17 countries of Europe for persons under 26 years of age.

	Second Class
15 consecutive days	$365
21 consecutive days	$475
1 month	$587
2 months	$832
3 months	$1028

EURAIL YOUTH FLEXIPASS Unlimited second-class rail travel for persons under 26 years of age. Days can be used at one's leisure within a two-month period.

	Second Class
Any 10 days within 2 months	$431
Any 15 days within 2 months	$568

EUROPASS Designed for travel in five of the most frequently visited countries of Europe: France, Germany, Italy , Spain, and Switzerland. Unlimited first- or second-class travel from 5-15 days within a 2-month period. Second class is only available to youths. Optional add-on zones: Benelux, Danube, Greece Plus, and Portugal. Adult Europass special: second person receives a reduction of 40 percent on the adult pass price (including zones). Children under 12 pay half price; under 4 travel free.

	Adult First Class	Youth (under 26) Second Class
Any 5 days within 2 months	$316	$210
Any 6 days within 2 months	$358	$239
Any 7 days within 2 months	$400	$268

Any 8 days within 2 months	$442	$297
Any 9 days within 2 months	$484	$326
Any 10 days within 2 months	$526	$355
Any 11 days within 2 months	$568	$384
Any 12 days within 2 months	$610	$413
Any 13 days within 2 months	$652	$442
Any 14 days within 2 months	$694	$471
Any 15 days within 2 months	$736	$500

The additional zones extend the geographic area of the pass, not your time frame in which to travel. Choose from the following zones:

Benelux—Belgium, Netherlands & Luxembourg
Danube—Austria & Hungary
Greece Plus—Greece & Ferry (Adriatica or Hellenic Lines)
Portugal

	Adult	Youth (under 26)
	First Class	Second Class
1 additional zone	$60	$45
2 additional zones	$90	$70
3 additional zones	$110	$85
4 additional zones	$120	$93

Call about **EURAIL/DRIVE** and **EUROPASS/DRIVE** programs.

COUNTRY & REGIONAL PASSES
(The following prices are valid until December 31, 1997. All prices are in U.S. Dollars and are subject to change. Please call for current prices.)

AUSTRIAN RAILPASS Unlimited rail travel throughout Austria, plus discounts on several steamers, private railways, and bicycle rentals.

	Adult		Child (4-12)	
	First Class	Second Class	First Class	Second Class
Any 3 days within 15	$145	$98	$87	$59
Additional days	$20	$14	$12	$9

Maximum number of additional days: 5

BENELUX TOURRAIL PASS Unlimited rail travel in Belgium, Luxembourg, and the Netherlands.

	Adult		Youth (4-25)	
	First	Second	First	Second

	Class	Class		Class	Class
Any 5 days in 1 month	$217	$155	.....		$104

Benelux Tourrail Pass For 2 (prices are for two people traveling together, Adult or Youth)

	First Class	Second Class
Any 5 days in 1 month	$326	$233

COPENHAGEN SIGHTSEEING PASS Rail transportation from any German/Danish border crossing to Copenhagen and return for holders of a Europass or German Railpass.

Adult		Youth		Child	
First Class	Second Class	First Class	Second Class	First Class	Second Class
$100	$70	$75	$50	$50	$35

GREEK FLEXIPASS Unlimited first-class rail travel in Greece.

	Adult First Class	Child (6-12) First Class
Any 3 days in 1 month	$86	$58
Any 5 days in 1 month	$120	$85

GERMAN RAIL PASS Unlimited rail travel in Germany. Children 4-11 pay half adult fare.

	Adult First Class	Second Class	Youth (12-25) Second Class	
Any 5 days in 1 month			$276	$188	$146
Any 10 days in 1 month			$434	$304	$200
Any 15 days in 1 month			$562	$410	$252
Twinpass for 2 adults traveling together (prices are for the 2 adults together)				
Any 5 days in 1 month			$414	$282	_____
Any 10 days in 1 month			$650	$456	_____
Any 15 days in 1 month			$842	$615	_____

HOLLAND RAILPASS Unlimited rail travel in the Netherlands.

	Adult First Class	Second Class	Youth Second Class
Any 3 days in 1 month	$88	$68	$56
Any 5 days in 1 month	$140	$104	$73
Any 10 days in 1 month	$260	$184	$130

ITALIAN RAILCARD Unlimited rail travel in Italy.

	First Class	Second Class
8 consecutive days	$254	$172
15 consecutive days	$320	$213
21 consecutive days	$371	$248
30 consecutive days	$447	$297
Any 4 days within 30	$199	$135
Any 8 days within 30	$291	$189
Any 12 days within 30	$365	$244

NORWAY RAILPASS Unlimited rail travel in Norway. Few trains in Norway offer first-class service. Children under 16 travel half price. Up to two children under 4 travel free.

		First Class	Second Class
7 consecutive days	(May-Sept.)	$250	$190
	(Oct.-Apr.)	$200	$150
14 consecutive days	(May-Sept.)	$330	$255
	(Oct.-Apr.)	$265	$205
Any 3 days in 1 month	(May-Sept.)	$190	$135
	(Oct.-Apr.)	$170	$120

PRAGUE EXCURSION Rail transportation from any Czech border crossing to Prague and return within 7 days. Must be used with a German Pass, Eurail pass, or Europass.

	First Class
Adult	$49
Youth	$39
Child	$25

SCANRAIL PASS Unlimited rail travel in Denmark, Finland, Norway, and Sweden.

	Adult First Class	Adult Second Class	Senior First Class	Senior Second Class
Any 5 days in 15	$222	$176	$198	$157
Any 10 days in 1 month	$354	$284	$315	$253
21 consecutive days	$410	$328	$365	$292
1 month	$516	$414	$459	$368

	Youth		Child	
	First Class	Second Class	First Class	Second Class
Any 5 days in 15	$167	$132	$111	$88
Any 10 days in 1 month	$266	$213	$177	$142
21 consecutive days	$308	$246	$205	$164
1 month	$387	$311	$258	$207

SPAIN FLEXIPASS Unlimited rail travel in Spain. The AVE and Talgo 200 require an additional supplement. Children (4-11) travel half price.

		Adult
Any 3 days within 2 months	$180	$144
Any 4 days within 2 months	$220	$176
Any 5 days within 2 months	$260	$208
Any 6 days within 2 months	$300	$240
Any 7 days within 2 months	$340	$272
Any 8 days within 2 months	$380	$304
Any 9 days within 2 months	$420	$336
Any 10 days within 2 months	$460	$368
Additional days	$40	$32

SWEDEN RAILPASS Unlimited rail travel in Sweden. Up to two children (under 16) travel free, together with one adult.

	Adult		Additional Children	
7 consecutive days	$250	$190	$170	$130
14 consecutive days	$330	$255	$230	$180
3 days within 7 days	$160	$120	$110	$180
5 days within 7 days	$200	$150	$140	$100

Call about **GERMAN RAIL/DRIVE** AND **SCANRAIL/DRIVE** passes.

Passes are not refundable in case of loss, theft, or after they have been validated. **OPTIONAL PASS PROTECTION** *is available for $10 per pass, which reimburses 100 percent of the **unused** portion of the pass in the event of loss or theft. Unused, unvalidated passes must be submitted to the issuing office within one year of issue date. Any refund is subject to a 15 percent cancellation charge. Please read the "Conditions of Use" on your pass. Prices applicable as of January 1, 1997.*

The following prices for hostel memberships are valid until December 31, 1996. 1997 prices not available at press time. All prices are in U.S. Dollars and are subject to change. Please call for current prices.

INTERNATIONAL HOSTEL MEMBERSHIPS

12-month membership to Hostelling International and free copy of Hostelling North America

Youth (under 18)	$10
Adult	$25
Family (parent/s or guardian/s with children under 16)	$35
Senior (over 54)	$15
Life	$250
Hostelling International: Guide to Budget Accomodation, Volume 1: Europe and the Mediterranean	$13.95

Rail Pass Express, Inc.   Ph: 800/722–7151
2737 Sawbury Blvd.   Ph: 614/889–9100
Columbus, OH 43235-4583   Fx: 614/764–0711
USA
                          http://www.
                                eurail
                                    .com

Pass you would like to purchase:_____

Days:_____ Cost:_____   *Please indicate whether the*
Estimated First Day of Travel:_____ *pass is 1st or 2nd class,*
Birthdate:_____   *Youth, Adult, Senior, or Child.*

Would you like pass protection*: Yes   No
  * Covers unused portion of pass if the pass is lost or stolen in Europe. $10 per pass.

Name as it appears on passport:
Mr. / Ms. First:_____Last:_____
Country of Permanent Residence:_____
Billing Address:_____

_____
City:_____ State/Country:_____ Zip/Postal code:_____
Phone:_____

Delivery Address (no P.O. Boxes):_____

_____
City:_____ State/Country:_____ Zip/Postal code:_____
Phone:_____

Please check one:
❑ Visa ❑ Mastercard ❑ American Express
Card Number:_____ Expiration Date:_____
Cardholder Name:_____

Signature (Required):_____

Type of shipping (signature is required for all orders):
❑ 2 Business Day FedEx - $10.00
❑ Standard Overnight FedEx (8-5 next business day) - $15.00
❑ Priority Overnight FedEx (by noon next business day) - $25.00
❑ Certified Mail (8-10 days) - $8.50
❑ International FedEx - $30.00*
* Most European countries, other countries may be more.

373

Colleen

Eurail is our rail. Eurail is *your* rail.™